Dummies 101:™ HTML

CHEAT SHEET

Basic HTML Terms

Term	Definition
Anchor	The tags used to make those hot spots (called *links*) you see in Web pages that allow you to jump to other information
Browser	Software like Netscape that you use to view HTML documents as well as those cool Web pages
Editor	Software like WebEdit that you use to create and edit an HTML document
HTML	HyperText Markup Language. A system of codes that identify parts of a document. HTML is the language used to create Web pages
Hypertext	Allows you to read a document by jumping from place to place, rather than progressing in a straight line from the beginning to the end (as you would read a novel)
Tags	Label the parts of an HTML document but don't specify what they should actually look like
Nesting	Putting one set of HTML tags inside another set of HTML tags, like this: `<B><I>text</I></B>`
URL	Uniform Resource Locator, pronounced *you-are-el*. An address on the Internet and either absolute (complete) or relative (partial).

Some Common HTML Tags

Tag	What It Does
`<H1>...</H1>` through `<H6>...</H6>`	Makes headings
`<P>...</P>`	Makes paragraphs
`<B>...</B>`	Makes text bold. Also try `<STRONG>...</STRONG>`
`<I>...</I>`	Makes text italicized. Also try `<EM>...</EM>`
`<UL>...</UL>`	Indicates beginning and end of an unordered (bulleted) list
`<OL>...</OL>`	Indicates beginning and end of an ordered (numbered) list
`<LI>`	Indicates an item within a list
`<HR>`	Makes a horizontal rule
` `	Breaks a line
`<A>...</A>`	Marks an anchor for a text or graphic link. Always used with the `HREF=` attribute and the `NAME=` attribute, for example, `<AHREF= "filename.htm"> link name </A>`
`<IMG>`	Inserts an image. Always used with the `SRC=` attribute to name the image to include. The `ALT=` attribute should also be used to provide alternate text in case the image is not viewed

D0466563

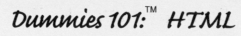

Dummies 101:™ HTML

CHEAT SHEET

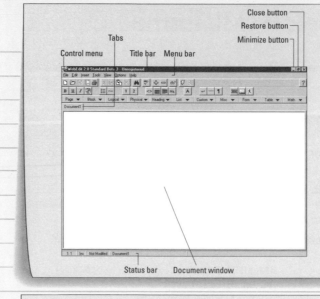

Control menu · Title bar · Menu bar · Tabs · Close button · Restore button · Minimize button

Status bar · Document window

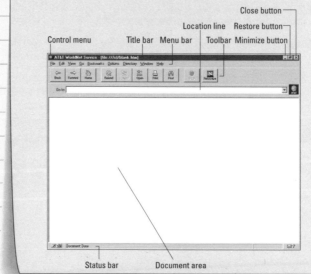

Control menu · Title bar · Menu bar · Toolbar · Location line · Close button · Restore button · Minimize button

Status bar · Document area

Accessing the CD-ROM Files

To install the files from the accompanying CD-ROM, refer to Appendix B or to the installation instructions in the Introduction. To access the files for use in the exercises in this book, use the following instructions.

To edit or create HTML documents:
1. Start WebEdit.
2. Choose File➪Open.
3. From the Open dialog box, switch to the HTML101 folder.
4. Switch to the folder numbered for the unit you want.
5. Select the file you want to open and then click Open.

To browse through HTML documents by using Netscape Navigator:
1. Start Netscape.
2. Choose File➪Open File.
3. From the Open dialog box, switch to the HTML101 folder.
4. Switch to the folder numbered for the unit you want.
5. Select the file you want to open and then click Open.

DUMMIES 101:™
HTML

by Deborah Ray and Eric Ray

IDG Books Worldwide, Inc.
An International Data Group Company

Foster City, CA ✦ Chicago, IL ✦ Indianapolis, IN ✦ Southlake, TX

Dummies 101: HTML

Published by
IDG Books Worldwide, Inc.
An International Data Group Company
919 E. Hillsdale Blvd.
Suite 400
Foster City, CA 94404
www.idgbooks.com (IDG Books Worldwide Web site)
www.dummies.com (Dummies Press Web site)

Library of Congress Catalog Card No.: 96-77272

ISBN: 0-7645-0032-5

Printed in the United States of America

10 9 8 7 6 5 4 3

1M/RV/QZ/ZX/IN

Distributed in the United States by IDG Books Worldwide, Inc.

Distributed by Macmillan Canada for Canada; by Transworld Publishers Limited in the United Kingdom; by IDG Norge Books for Norway; by IDG Sweden Books for Sweden; by Woodslane Pty. Ltd. for Australia; by Woodslane Enterprises Ltd. for New Zealand; by Longman Singapore Publishers Ltd. for Singapore, Malaysia, Thailand, and Indonesia; by Simron Pty. Ltd. for South Africa; by Toppan Company Ltd. for Japan; by Distribuidora Cuspide for Argentina; by Livraria Cultura for Brazil; by Ediciencia S.A. for Ecuador; by Addison-Wesley Publishing Company for Korea; by Ediciones ZETA S.C.R. Ltda. for Peru; by WS Computer Publishing Corporation, Inc., for the Philippines; by Unalis Corporation for Taiwan; by Contemporanea de Ediciones for Venezuela; by Computer Book & Magazine Store for Puerto Rico; by Express Computer Distributors for the Caribbean and West Indies. Authorized Sales Agent: Anthony Rudkin Associates for the Middle East and North Africa.

For general information on IDG Books Worldwide's books in the U.S., please call our Consumer Customer Service department at 800-762-2974. For reseller information, including discounts and premium sales, please call our Reseller Customer Service department at 800-434-3422.

For information on where to purchase IDG Books Worldwide's books outside the U.S., please contact our International Sales department at 415-655-3200 or fax 415-655-3295.

For information on foreign language translations, please contact our Foreign & Subsidiary Rights department at 415-655-3021 or fax 415-655-3281.

For sales inquiries and special prices for bulk quantities, please contact our Sales department at 415-655-3200 or write to the address above.

For information on using IDG Books Worldwide's books in the classroom or for ordering examination copies, please contact our Educational Sales department at 800-434-2086 or fax 817-251-8174.

For press review copies, author interviews, or other publicity information, please contact our Public Relations department at 415-655-3000 or fax 415-655-3299.

For authorization to photocopy items for corporate, personal, or educational use, please contact Copyright Clearance Center, 222 Rosewood Drive, Danvers, MA 01923, or fax 508-750-4470.

 is a trademark under exclusive license to IDG Books Worldwide, Inc., from International Data Group, Inc.

About the Authors

Deborah S. Ray and **Eric J. Ray,** coauthors of the *HTML For Dummies Quick Reference* and other computer-related books, work together out of their home as technical communications consultants. They spend a large part of their time on HTML-related development, training, and consulting.

Deborah, a technical communicator for the past three years, has been involved with the Internet for the past two. She has a variety of technical experience, including creating various computer and engineering documents as well as teaching technical writing to college students. Her areas of emphasis include writing, designing, and illustrating documents to meet various audiences' information needs. Deborah is well-accomplished in technical communication, having received awards for her achievements in the field from the Society for Technical Communication as well as from previous employers.

Eric has been involved with the Internet for over four years and has made numerous presentations and published several papers about HTML and online information. His technical experience includes creating and maintaining the TECHWR-L listserv list as well as implementing and running Web servers. As a technical communicator, Eric has received numerous awards from the Society for Technical Communication, including a Director-Sponsor Award, as well as from previous employers for his contributions to technical communcation projects.

ABOUT IDG BOOKS WORLDWIDE

Welcome to the world of IDG Books Worldwide.

IDG Books Worldwide, Inc., is a subsidiary of International Data Group, the world's largest publisher of computer-related information and the leading global provider of information services on information technology. IDG was founded more than 25 years ago and now employs more than 8,500 people worldwide. IDG publishes more than 275 computer publications in over 75 countries (see listing below). More than 60 million people read one or more IDG publications each month.

Launched in 1990, IDG Books Worldwide is today the #1 publisher of best-selling computer books in the United States. We are proud to have received eight awards from the Computer Press Association in recognition of editorial excellence and three from *Computer Currents'* First Annual Readers' Choice Awards. Our best-selling *...For Dummies®* series has more than 30 million copies in print with translations in 30 languages. IDG Books Worldwide, through a joint venture with IDG's Hi-Tech Beijing, became the first U.S. publisher to publish a computer book in the People's Republic of China. In record time, IDG Books Worldwide has become the first choice for millions of readers around the world who want to learn how to better manage their businesses.

Our mission is simple: Every one of our books is designed to bring extra value and skill-building instructions to the reader. Our books are written by experts who understand and care about our readers. The knowledge base of our editorial staff comes from years of experience in publishing, education, and journalism — experience we use to produce books for the '90s. In short, we care about books, so we attract the best people. We devote special attention to details such as audience, interior design, use of icons, and illustrations. And because we use an efficient process of authoring, editing, and desktop publishing our books electronically, we can spend more time ensuring superior content and spend less time on the technicalities of making books.

You can count on our commitment to deliver high-quality books at competitive prices on topics you want to read about. At IDG Books Worldwide, we continue in the IDG tradition of delivering quality for more than 25 years. You'll find no better book on a subject than one from IDG Books Worldwide.

John Kilcullen
CEO
IDG Books Worldwide, Inc.

Steven Berkowitz
President and Publisher
IDG Books Worldwide, Inc.

Eighth Annual Computer Press Awards ≥1992

Ninth Annual Computer Press Awards ≥1993

Tenth Annual Computer Press Awards ≥1994

Eleventh Annual Computer Press Awards ≥1995

Dedication

To Ashleigh.

Authors' Acknowledgments

We owe many people a great big thanks for helping put this book together. We would especially like to thank Colleen Rainsberger, Project Editor, for helping make this book the best it could be and for helping us become better authors. Also, a huge thanks to Gareth Hancock, Acquisitions Editor, for giving us the opportunity to write this book. You weren't kidding when you said you could keep us busy!

There are a number of other folks at IDG Books that we'd also like to thank. First, we'd like to thank the copy editors, Kelly Ewing, Tammy Castleman, Joe Jansen, and Tina Sims. We wish there were some way we could hire you *before* we submitted our stuff! Your skills and input are invaluable. Also, thanks to the indexer, Sharon Hilgenberg, for providing an outstanding information source for our readers and to the production team for bringing order to our submissions and changes.

Finally, we'd like to extend a special thanks to the technical reviewer, James Michael Stewart. Your input, comments, and suggestions brought clarity and focus to the material.

Publisher's Acknowledgments

We're proud of this book; please send us your comments about it by using the Reader Response Card at the back of the book or by e-mailing us at feedback/dummies@idgbooks.com. Some of the people who helped bring this book to market include the following:

Acquisitions, Development, & Editorial

Project Editor: Colleen Rainsberger

Assistant Acquisitions Editor: Gareth Hancock

Media Develoment Manager: Joyce Pepple

Copy Editors: Kelly Ewing, Tamara S. Castleman, Joe Jansen, Tina Sims

Technical Editor: James Michael Stewart, LANWrights, Inc.

Editorial Managers: Mary C. Corder, Seta K. Frantz

Editorial Assistant: Constance Carlisle

Production

Project Coordinator: Sherry Gomoll

Layout and Graphics: Brett Black, Linda M. Boyer, J. Tyler Connor, Maridee V. Ennis, Angela F. Hunckler, Jane E. Martin, Mark C. Owens, Theresa Sánchez-Baker, Brent Savage, Gina Scott, Kate Snell

Proofreaders: Michael Bolinger, Rachel Garvey, Nancy Price, Dwight Ramsey, Robert Springer, Carrie Voorhis, Ethel M. Winslow, Karen York

Indexer: Sharon Hilgenberg

General and Administrative

IDG Books Worldwide, Inc.: John Kilcullen, CEO; Steven Berkowitz, President and Publisher

IDG Books Technology Publishing: Brenda McLaughlin, Senior Vice President and Group Publisher

Dummies Technology Press and Dummies Editorial: Diane Graves Steele, Vice President and Associate Publisher; Kristin A. Cocks, Editorial Director; Mary Bednarek, Acquisitions and Product Development Director

Dummies Trade Press: Kathleen A. Welton, Vice President and Publisher

IDG Books Production for Dummies Press: Beth Jenkins, Production Director; Cindy L. Phipps, Manager of Project Coordination, Production Proofreading, and Indexing; Kathie S. Schutte, Supervisor of Page Layout; Shelley Lea, Supervisor of Graphics and Design; Debbie J. Gates, Production Systems Specialist; Robert Springer, Supervisor of Proofreading; Debbie Stailey, Special Projects Coordinator; Tony Augsburger, Supervisor of Reprints and Bluelines; Leslie Popplewell, Media Archive Coordinator

Dummies Packaging and Book Design: Patti Sandez, Packaging Specialist; Lance Kayser, Packaging Assistant; Kavish + Kavish, Cover Design

◆

The publisher would like to give special thanks to Patrick J. McGovern, without whom this book would not have been possible.

◆

Files at a Glance

ABC 123

Contents
at a Glance

Table of Contents

Introduction

Welcome to *Dummies 101: HTML!*

This book is designed to teach you everything you need to know (and a lot of stuff you want to know) about HTML. What's in it for you? Well, HTML is the language used to create those nifty Web pages everyone's talking about. You'll not only learn to speak the lingo with the best of 'em, but you'll also learn how to develop Web pages and Web sites yourself.

You can apply the concepts and lessons presented in this book to either personal or corporate Web sites. You can create any kind of Web site from a personal page about your family to an entire Web site that introduces your company, products and services, and employees, or even requests information for your readers to send back to you. When you're finished with this book, you'll not only be able to create HTML documents, but you'll be able to include all the cool stuff like graphics, tables, forms, background colors — and, of course, those nifty links.

This book is a tutorial that provides thorough descriptions and examples of HTML concepts as well as step-by-step instructions on how to create various effects. If you are a novice with HTML, you can start with Unit 1 and work forward. Or, if you are already somewhat familiar with HTML, you may want to skip over the units that provide basic HTML information and instructions. The important thing is that you can complete the units at your own pace, in your own time, and in the privacy of your own home or office (or home office, which is where we prefer to work).

Accompanying this book is a companion CD-ROM that contains practice files you will use to complete each lesson. Using these practice files will give you hands-on experience at creating HTML documents as well as provide you with sample documents similar to ones you might create at home or on the job.

Whom This Book Is For

This book is for beginning to intermediate users of HTML. How do you know who you are? Well, this book is for you if you fall into one of the following categories:

- You've heard rumblings in the office about HTML and are curious as to what it's all about.
- You've been checking out all the cool stuff on the Web and want to find out how you can create your own Web site.
- You've hooked yourself on HTML by doing your first basic home page, but now want to learn how to create all the fancy effects.
- Your boss wants to expand your job description to include stuff like "Web Page Author Extraordinaire" or "Chief Web Site Advisor."

◆ You have your own company and want to provide information about your company on the Internet.

◆ You want to keep up with way-cool technology.

◆ You want to put pictures of your dog, Sparky, on the Internet.

◆ You want to outdo the Joneses, at last.

We've also made some basic assumptions about the computer equipment you're using:

◆ A PC running Windows 3.1x or Windows 95

◆ At least 8MB of RAM installed

◆ At least 5MB hard disk space available

◆ Modem or an Internet connection

One final assumption we've made is that you're comfortable using either Windows 95 or 3.x. By *comfortable,* we mean that

◆ You know how to copy and paste stuff.

◆ You know how to toggle among programs.

◆ You know how to open existing documents and create new ones.

◆ You know where to find the menu bar and toolbar in Windows programs.

If you're not familiar with all these items or freak out at the thought of clicking your mouse, you can still probably get through the instructions in this book. Where possible, we've included notes and sidebars that will help you through some of the Windows functions. If you want additional help on these topics, you can check out *Dummies 101: Windows 3.1, Dummies 101: Windows 95, Windows 3.11 For Dummies,* or *Windows 95 For Dummies* all by Andy Rathbone (published by IDG Books Worldwide, Inc.).

How to Use This Book

This book is a tutorial that explains, step by step, how to develop HTML documents. Given that, we think you should go through this book a certain way to get the most out of it, and we decided on certain conventions so you'd be able to more easily complete the lessons.

We recommend that you complete the lessons in the order provided. However, you can skip to the crisis-subject-of-the-day. We've provided files and instructions so that you can begin working on any lesson.

Whenever we tell you *about* something, we use text just like this. In sections like these, we provide you with useful analogies and examples to help you understand the material. We also provide you with information about using HTML *effectively* — which is essential for creating a usable, attractive Web site.

If we're instructing you to *do* something, you'll see a numbered list of steps. Each step contains the instructions, and if necessary, you'll find a paragraph under the step telling you why you did what you did. Sometimes we also tell you specifically what to type. If so, you'll see the `stuff to type` in a funny font, or even on a line all by itself.

`This would be something to type as well.`

If the bit of information you're typing has to fit into other stuff just so (kind of the way that instructions for pouring milk come after putting the glass on the counter but before drinking), we might give you the whole sequence of steps in a funny font. The exercises build on each other, with the new information you type in bold type. When you need to do something, you'll see something like this:

1 **Type the first line.**

`Put the glass on the counter.`

2 **Type the second line.**

`Put the glass on the counter.`
`Pour the milk.`

3 **Type the next line.**

`Put the glass on the counter.`
`Pour the milk.`
`Drink up!`

Additionally, you'll see plenty of pictures of screens at the top of the pages so that you can get a quick status check and make sure that your work looks like the samples.

One last thing: Keep an eye on the margins for tips and notes that will help you, as your boss would say, "work smarter, not harder." Cliché aside, the tips really will make your work easier and let you sail through the exercises.

What's in This Book, Anyway?

Overall, this book contains a whole lot of valuable information for the budding HTML developer. Specifically, the book is divided into six parts, each with a general theme. Within each part are units that focus on one specific skill you need to produce good HTML documents. And within each unit you'll find lessons that walk you through the steps of *doing* something.

The first several units help you get started with some software and provide you with the basics of HTML. The remaining units provide you with step-by-step instructions on creating various effects using HTML. You'll find that the lessons *don't* really get any harder or more complicated as the units progress — in fact, you might find that they get easier because the principles of HTML stay the same whether you're creating a paragraph or developing a form.

The parts

This book contains six parts that contain all you need to know about your software as well as instructions, quizzes, and exercises to help you learn the material.

To make the most of this book, you need to complete each exercise using the examples, sample files, and software required for the unit. Of course, we recommend completing all sections of each part — each unit, lesson, quiz, exercise, test, and lab assignment — and completing them in the order provided. Doing so will best help you learn and retain the information.

Part I: Getting Started

Part I provides the information you need to get started with the software as well as to begin putting an HTML document together. In this part, you learn to use two software packages for creating and viewing HTML documents (these are provided on the CD), and you learn the basics of HTML.

Part II: Building Your First HTML Documents

Part II introduces you to your first HTML tags and explains how to use them. Here, you actually start creating an HTML document and using several HTML tags. At the end of this part, you learn how to link your HTML document to other documents.

Part III: Using Graphics in Your HTML Documents

Part III introduces you to the graphics software provided on the CD-ROM. In this part, you learn how to develop graphics for HTML documents and link graphics into your documents. You also learn about a special twist for graphics, called clickable images or imagemaps, that you can use to spice up your HTML documents.

Part IV: Developing Tables and Forms

Part IV explains how to create tables and forms by using HTML. Here, you learn about how and when to use tables as well as about creating effective and usable forms.

Part V: Advanced HTML Formatting

Part V shows you how to create nifty effects by using HTML. In this part, you learn things such as coloring text and backgrounds, using tables and graphics for maximum effectiveness, and including colors and backgrounds in your documents.

Part VI: Developing Your Web Site

Part VI explains how to pull all your HTML documents together into a Web site. Here, you learn how to plan and organize your Web site and establish navigation among your HTML pages.

Appendix A: Answers

Appendix A provides answers to all quizzes and tests. (We're telling you this so that you can check your answers, not so you can peek while taking the quiz or test!) Along with the test answers are references to the lesson that the question came from so that you can go back and find out, for example, why you missed a question.

Appendix B: About the CD

Appendix B provides all the information you need to know about installing the CD contents onto your computer. Not only do you get the full scoop about what's on the CD (both cool programs and a whole slew of files for you to use), but also you find out all about how to install the files, remove the files (not that you'd want to), and selectively reinstall files in case you want to redo a lesson.

About quizzes and tests

Just to make sure that you really have the information under control, we've provided a quiz at the end of every unit. If you've worked straight through the unit, you won't have any problems with the quiz. There are no trick questions, we promise. (Okay, so there are trick questions — at least you don't get a grade.) If any of the questions trip you up, you'd better set aside a few minutes for a review. Answers to the quiz questions are provided in Appendix A.

Finally, after you've cruised through a whole part, you'll find a test at the end of the part just to make sure you haven't missed anything. The test questions cover the major topics and test your knowledge of the concepts and how-tos provided in each unit. Answers to the test questions, as well as references back to specific lessons, are provided in Appendix A.

Really, though, you'll spend much more time with this book doing stuff than taking tests. The tests shouldn't be more than a quick and successful break from staring at your monitor.

About exercises and lab assignments

At the end of each unit you'll find an exercise that will let you practice the skills you learned in the unit. These exercises won't take you too long, so take the time to do them. By taking the time to do the exercises, you'll reinforce what you learned in the unit and strengthen your foundation before moving on to the next unit.

At the end of each part is a lab assignment that lets you practice all the skills you learned in the part. These assignments allow you to practice several skills at a time, which will help prepare you for creating HTML documents all on your own. The Lab Assignments are designed to lead you through the process of creating your own Web site on a topic and purpose that suits *your* needs. Like the unit exercises, the lab assignments don't take too much time, but completing them provides you with a strong foundation for the upcoming units and lessons.

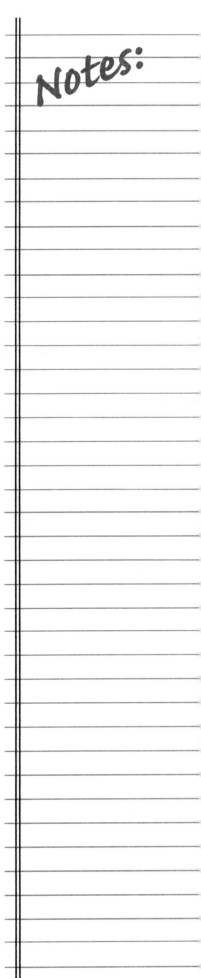
Notes:

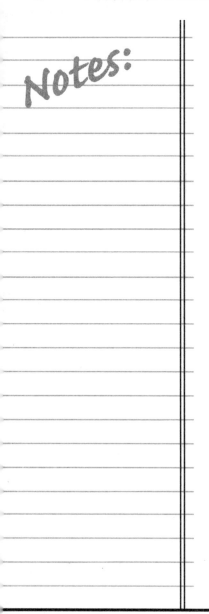

The icon crew

Throughout this book, we've sprinkled icons to draw your attention to special information.

The On the CD icon appears in two general places in each unit. First, the On the CD icon appears at the beginning of each unit and indicates the files that are provided for you to use. Second, the On the CD icon appears in the step-by-step instructions whenever you're supposed to open a file and use it for the activity, exercise, or assignment.

The sample file will be on drive C under the html101 directory and the unit folder corresponding to the unit you're in. If you're in Unit 72, you look in the unit72 folder for the files. Of course, if you're in Unit 72, you're also probably reading our follow-up book, *The Return of the Son of HTML 101 VII* — you only have 16 units to complete in this *Dummies 101* book.

Just like when your teachers told you something was on the test so you'd stop clowning around and pay attention, we use this icon to indicate a particularly important tidbit of information (which will likely show up on the test — hint, hint!).

This icon will warn you about tricky stuff that can cause problems if you don't watch out.

If you're having fun and it's all clicking for you, here's your chance to get into the topic a little deeper. Information marked by this icon is optional, but it's pretty useful if you're up to it.

The Notes column has two purposes: The first is for you to make notes to yourself. How are you going to learn if you don't make notes to yourself? Second, we're going to put little notes in that column as well to help you get started. Anything we put in the Notes column is useful, but not critical, information to help you out. For example, you'll see alternate (and possibly faster) ways of entering commands in the Notes column.

Dummies 101 CD-ROM Installation Instructions

The CD-ROM in the back of this book contains both exercise files and programs. The exercise files are sample HTML documents and graphic files that you use while following along with the lessons in the book. The programs are integrated with the lessons in the book and are necessary to get the full benefit of working through the exercises. If you have an Internet service provider and Netscape Navigator on your computer, however, you may choose to work with your current version rather than installing and registering for AT&T WorldNet Service.

Note: To use the software on this CD, you must already have Microsoft Windows 3.1x or Windows 95 installed on your computer. Microsoft Windows is sold at many computer stores. Windows is *not* included on this CD.

In order to install the programs and exercise files included on the CD, you first must install the *Dummies 101: HTML* Launching Pad. With Windows 95 or Windows 3.1*x* running, follow these steps:

1 **Insert the *Dummies 101* CD-ROM (label side up) into your computer's CD-ROM drive.**

Be careful to touch only the edges of the CD-ROM. (The CD-ROM drive is the one that pops out with a recessed circle in the drawer.)

In Windows 95, the Launching Pad should appear automatically if your computer's AutoPlay feature is working. (If it doesn't appear automatically, simply go to Step 2.)You can make the Launching Pad disappear for now by clicking the Close button, which is located in the upper right corner of the window.

2 **Windows 95 users: Click the Start button and choose <u>R</u>un.**

Windows 3.1*x* users: Click File⇨Run in the Windows Program Manager.

3 **Type d:\setup in the text box of the Run dialog box; then click OK or press Enter.**

Note: If your CD-ROM drive is not drive D on your computer, please substitute the appropriate letter before the colon.

If you are working in Windows 95, you see a message that confirms that an item named Dummies 101 was created in the Programs menu on the Start button; if you are working in Windows 3.1*x*, you see a message that confirms that a program group named Dummies 101 was created in the Program Manager. Inside that group is an icon named Dummies 101- HTML Launching Pad.

4 **Click the Yes button to start the Launching Pad.**

The *Dummies 101: HTML* Launching Pad appears on-screen. The Launching Pad is a window that allows you to begin installation of all the programs and exercise files with a click of your mouse button. For instructions on using the Launching Pad to install the programs and the exercise files, please see Appendix B.

After completing this installation process, Windows 3.1*x* users can start the Launching Pad by opening the Dummies 101 program group and double-clicking the Dummies 101 - HTML Launching Pad icon; Windows 95 users can start the Launching Pad by clicking the Start button and then choosing Programs⇨Dummies 101⇨Dummies 101 - HTML Launching Pad.

If you have problems with the installation process, you can call the IDG Books Worldwide, Inc., Customer Support number: 800-762-2974 (outside the U.S.: 317-596-5261).

For more information about installing and using the AT&T WorldNet software, see Appendix B.

When you're done with the *Dummies 101* CD-ROM, store it in a safe place.

Getting Started

Tired of all this talk and ready to get rolling with the good stuff? Good for you! The first thing you need to do is install the CD contents onto your hard drive. Appendix B provides specifics about the CD and instructions on how to install it.

Good luck, and let us know how it goes. After you've finished the book (or before hand, if you want), drop us a note at debray@raycomm.com or ejray@raycomm.com and tell us what you think. If we can do something different and make HTML even easier in the next edition, please tell us. Of course, if we did something particularly well, we'd like to know that, too.

Getting Started

Part 1

In this part . . .

Welcome! Just to make sure you walked into the right book, we're here to present the basics (and then some) of HTML. If you're in the wrong book, please take your stuff and quietly leave via the back cover.

This part isn't the most technically difficult of the bunch — it does, however, present some of the basic concepts that you'll really need to get the most out of the book, in addition to introducing you to some of the software you'll be using.

In this part, we help you become familiar with HTML and the software you use to create HTML documents. In the first unit, you get acquainted with HTML terminology and learn what HTML is all about. In the second part, you learn what HTML is, how to open and use the main programs needed for creating HTML documents, and how to enter and manipulate text and HTML tags.

Getting Acquainted with HTML

Objectives for This Unit

✓ Finding out what you can do with HTML

✓ Understanding this HTML stuff

HTML allows you to create documents — with all sorts of nifty features — that can be viewed by anyone on the planet at any time. HTML, along with the World Wide Web and the Internet, has changed the role of computers from being a tool to being a communications medium that connects millions of people around the world. Learning HTML will enable you to become a key member of the Internet community and provide information to people around the world. Now if that isn't enough to get you pumped up about learning HTML, we don't know what is!

This brief unit covers what HTML is and what you can use it for. You learn the basics about HTML and some of the terminology, which gives you a good foundation to start creating HTML documents. In no time at all, you'll be moving ahead to the next units and creating your own HTML documents.

What is HTML?

HTML is what you use to create those nifty pages you see when you're surfing the World Wide Web (WWW or Web). All the elements you see on Web pages — paragraphs of text, cool backgrounds, lists of information, spiffy graphics, neato colors, and so on — are presented with HTML. What's important about HTML is that it allows you to create documents that you can

a server waits for you to tell it what information you want, finds the information, and brings it to your computer

Progress Check

If you can do the following, you've mastered this lesson:

❑ Describe to someone the two things you can use HTML for.

❑ Describe what a WWW server does.

❑ Describe the HTML publishing process.

publish on a WWW server — in other words, you can put your documents "out there" instead of simply viewing them on your own computer. The most common place to see HTML documents is on the World Wide Web, but you can also see HTML documents, or Web pages, on company internal networks, called *intranets*.

So, what's a server? A *server* is sort of like a waiter at a restaurant. You order the food you want ("Yeah, I'll have the Super Duper Doowhichie Meal, a side of Frothy Potatoes, and a large Orange-Grape Soda, please."), and the waiter brings it to you (if he can carry it, that is). Likewise, a server waits for you to tell it what information you want, finds the information, and brings it to your computer.

To publish documents on the Internet, you need access to a server you can put things on. Most Internet service providers can provide you with Web space where you can publish your HTML documents. Or you may be able to access Web space through your employer's Internet service account. (Check with your boss before doing so, though.) In the meantime, you can test and use your HTML documents directly from your computer's hard drive. If you're not on a network, nobody else can see your documents, and you can practice and perfect your technique before opening your creations to the whole world.

Take a look at Figure 1-1, which shows the process of publishing HTML documents. At the left side of the drawing, you see that the actual activity of creating the HTML document takes place on your computer, without having to bring a server into the picture at all.

Looking at the center and right of Figure 1-1, however, you see that by putting your document on a server after you've finished creating it, other people, either on the Internet or within your company, will be able to read your document as well.

You may prefer to create an HTML document (just to see what the hype is about) and then just keep it to yourself. If that's what you want to do, you don't need to worry about having access to a server. All you need is your computer, the necessary software (good choices come with this book!), and the time and patience to learn the skills.

If you decide at any time — now or later — to publish your document for others to see, you can do that without much additional work. Simply get the instructions from your system administrator, follow them, and *voilà!* your document is there for the world to see.

Lesson 1-2

What Does HTML Stand For?

HTML stands for *HyperText Markup Language* — a mouthful by anyone's standards. We'll look at one term at a time.

Understanding "Text"

"Text" refers to any element you can place on a page

In HTML, *text* refers to any element you can place on a page. You can include things like words, graphics, art, and lines in your documents. In most cases, you combine all these things to achieve the effects you want.

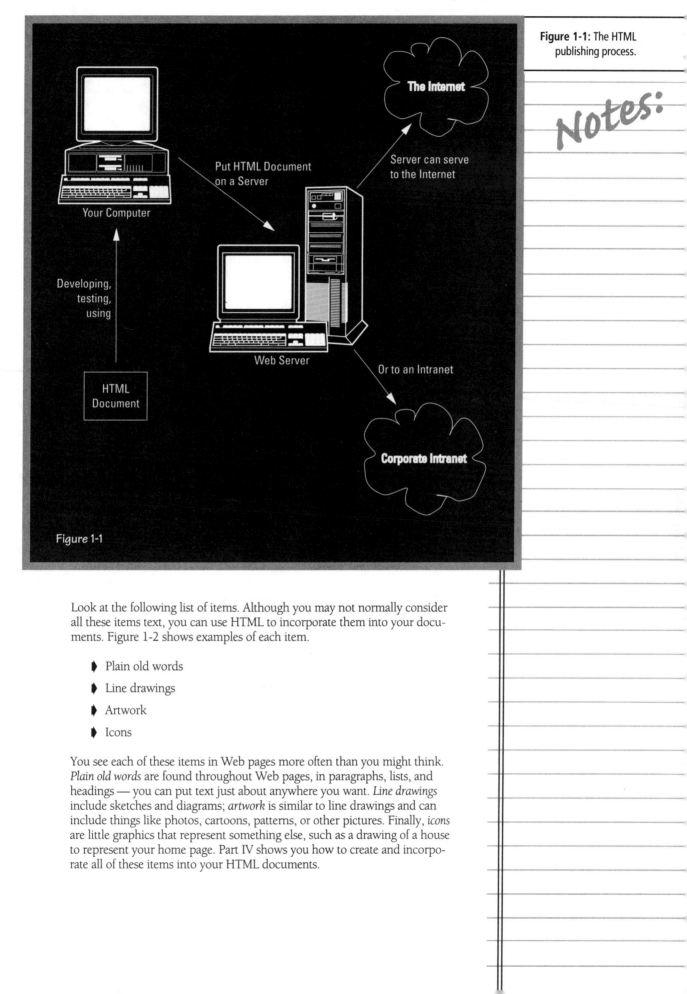

Figure 1-1: The HTML publishing process.

Notes:

Look at the following list of items. Although you may not normally consider all these items text, you can use HTML to incorporate them into your documents. Figure 1-2 shows examples of each item.

- Plain old words
- Line drawings
- Artwork
- Icons

You see each of these items in Web pages more often than you might think. *Plain old words* are found throughout Web pages, in paragraphs, lists, and headings — you can put text just about anywhere you want. *Line drawings* include sketches and diagrams; *artwork* is similar to line drawings and can include things like photos, cartoons, patterns, or other pictures. Finally, *icons* are little graphics that represent something else, such as a drawing of a house to represent your home page. Part IV shows you how to create and incorporate all of these items into your HTML documents.

Figure 1-2: Examples of items that could be in an HTML document, including words, a line drawing, artwork, and an icon.

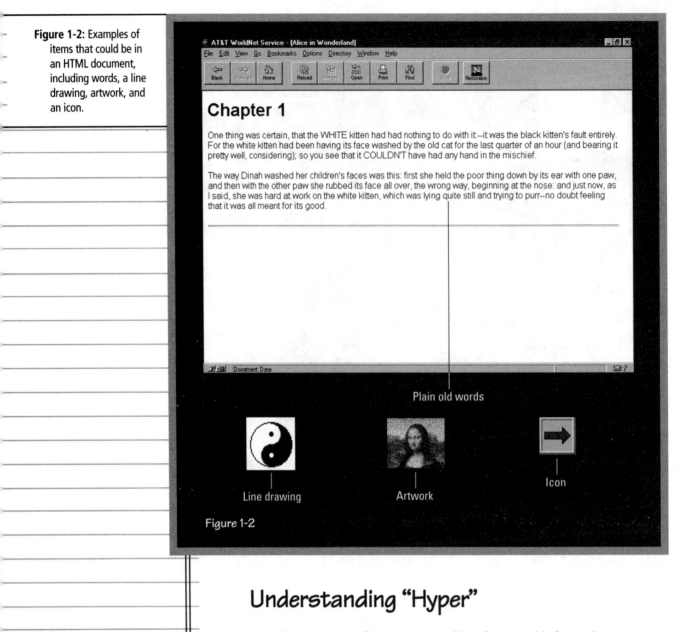

Figure 1-2

Understanding "Hyper"

The *Hyper* part of *HyperText* is just like a five-year-old after a cake, ice cream, and three-soda afternoon — jumping from place to place without ever hitting the ground in the middle. Hypertext allows you to read a document by jumping from one place in a document to another place in a document rather than progressing in a straight line from the beginning to the end (as you would read a novel). Hypertext also allows you to jump from one document to a completely different document, without having to read through one to get to the other.

Reading by skipping from topic to topic or from page to page can be quite handy. Suppose that you're looking for specific information on how to keep your kitty from climbing trees (or actually, keep you from spending your Saturday on a tall ladder). If you were reading a book on the topic, you'd most likely look in the index, find several page numbers, and then have to wade through several chapters or at least several paragraphs of information before you found exactly what you were looking for — time-consuming to say the least.

Having the opportunity to leap from topic to topic, as you do in hypertext documents, allows you to navigate through information without having to wade through irrelevant, unnecessary, or boring stuff. This can save you a *lot*

Notes:

of time. Just think, you find information on cats and see the word "climbing" in blue, underlined text. You click on it and immediately see more information about cats and climbing. You see another blue, underlined link to Joe's Discount Ladder sales. Sigh. But at least you got the information quickly. Such is life with hypertext.

You can make just about anything in an HTML document hyper (and you don't even have to feed it ice cream and cake!). You can make text, lines, graphics, or art hyper because all you're doing is adding a link from one thing to another thing.

You can easily tell where the links are when you view HTML documents on the Web. Text links appear in different colors — say, if the regular text is black, the link might appear in bright blue. Graphical links often have a border around them, which signifies that the graphic links to a related piece of information. After you visit the link, the link changes color (for example, the link changes from bright blue to red) to help let you know which links you've visited and which links you haven't.

The following exercise should help get you thinking hyper. If you think it'll help, drink a six-pack of highly caffeinated cola first.

1 **Grab a pencil and piece of scrap paper and then take your favorite activity and write a paragraph or so about it.**

2 **Underline three or four key ideas, facts, or thoughts in your paragraph.**

3 **Now write a couple of lines about each of the ideas you identified in the last step.**

4 **Draw a line to connect the terms with the new bits of information.**

Each of your lines represents a hypertext link. If you repeat steps 2 through 4, your hypertext links will start getting interesting because they might link back to other pieces of text you've already written or to pieces of information not even vaguely connected to the first paragraph.

This process is known as *manual hypertext.* Believe it or not, some novelists are now writing their books with this technique. You see a highlighted term, and you can just jump off to another page and read about it.

Your next step is to see how HTML lets you do hypertext without having to do all of this manual stuff. That's what computers are for, anyway.

Understanding "Markup Languages"

The *Markup Language* part of HTML enables you to identify the parts of a document (headings, paragraphs, lists, and so on) rather than specifying what the parts look like (14 point, Times New Roman, Bold). The system you use is comprised of codes, called *tags,* that are read by Web browsing software, or *browsers.* The tags and the browser program determine how each element appears, so you don't have to worry about applying bold or italic, or about changing fonts or font sizes.

In the following table, the items in the left column name document parts; the items in the right column specify what each part might look like in a browser. *Remember:* The exact appearance of each element will vary slightly from browser to browser.

don't worry about how to format anything; just label text as a document part by applying a tag

Figure 1-3: A sample document in Netscape.

Figure 1-4: A sample document in Lynx, a text-only browser.

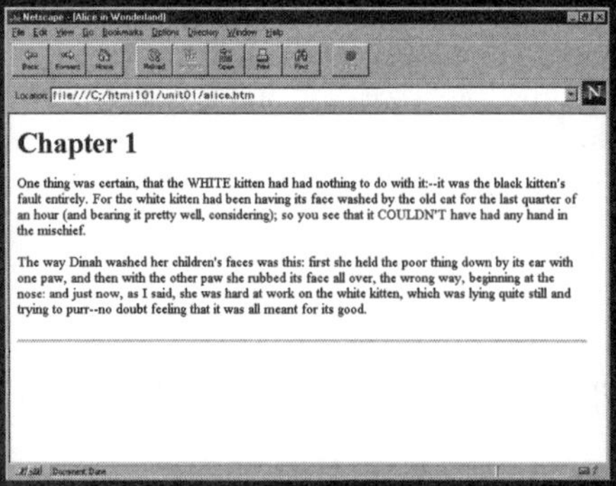

Figure 1-3

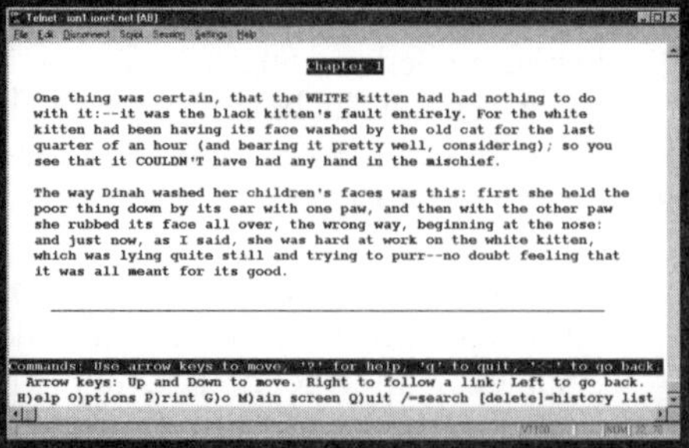

Figure 1-4

Notes:

Markup Language is a system of codes, called tags, that you use to identify parts of a document (headings, paragraphs, lists, and so on)

the readers' browsing software determines what the text looks like

Document Elements	Possible Element Appearance
Heading level 1	Times New Roman 36 point, bold
Bulleted list	Each line indented .25 inch, with bullet character
Block quote	Times New Roman 10 point, 1 inch indent from each margin

Suppose that you want to use *Light, Fluffy, Popcorn Balls* as a heading. If you were using a word-processing program, you'd probably choose a font, such as Times New Roman, make the type bigger, say 36 point, and add a style, such as bold. Choosing a font, making it bigger, and adding a style are ways you can make this piece of text look like a heading. If you want to make *Light, Fluffy, Popcorn Balls* into a heading by using HTML, however, you'd simply apply a heading level 1 tag to the text. (We'll show you how to do that in following units — it's easy, so don't worry.)

Just keep in mind that HTML is a structural language — you just label pieces of the document by what they are. You label a heading as a heading and a paragraph as a paragraph. For example, a tag indicates that a heading will appear in a certain spot, but that tag does not dictate that the heading appears in 12-point, bold type. In contrast, a word processor uses a formatting language — you label pieces of the document by how they look. You apply boldface and a larger size to headings and indentation and a smaller size to paragraphs.

One thing you need to keep in mind as you're creating HTML documents is that you cannot ensure the exact appearance that your readers see. For example, a heading level 1 in Netscape might appear a little differently than it does in another browser. The elements will be similar, but you may not know exactly what the text looks like.

Because almost anyone on the Internet can surf the Net and view Web pages, you cannot assume that your readers will have specific software or even a certain kind of computer. HTML allows you to present information that can be easily understood by many computers and browsers, but you lose the ability to precisely control the appearance of your document.

Take a look at the two screens in Figures 1-3 and 1-4, which show the same information in two different browsers. The first screen shows a page in Netscape, and the second shows the same page in Lynx, a text-only browser. Notice that although the information on the page is the same and each page was created using HTML, the pages are quite different.

Mirror, mirror on the wall — how will it look to one and all?

HTML documents are designed to be viewed by browsing software. And as is the case with most other computer applications, a number of browsers are available to choose from. Browsers are available for computers running Windows, for Macintosh computers, and for UNIX computers — not to mention the different browsers available for each of these platforms.

Keep in mind that it's the *browser* (and the reader) that determines what the document looks like — you, the HTML author, don't have much control over document appearance. Each browser may display your HTML document a little differently. The details of font, size, and formatting of a specific document element are completely determined by the setup of the browser accessing a document. For example, your browser might display a heading in 24-point Times New Roman Bold, while your best friend's browser might display the same heading in 20-point Arial Bold. The heading is similar — it's bigger than normal text and it's bold — but it's not exactly the same.

Many people are accustomed to word-processing programs and desktop-publishing software that allow you to control precisely how a final product appears. Breaking out of that mind-set into the "it'll look something vaguely like what I see here" mind-set of HTML can be difficult at first.

On the bright side, documents viewed in the same browser used on different platforms (for example, Netscape for Windows versus Netscape for Macs) will look similar, if not the same. Bigger differences will be apparent among different browsers (for example, Netscape, Internet Explorer, Mosaic, and Lynx).

If you can, view your HTML documents on as many different browsers as possible. This way, you can get a better idea of how different readers might see your documents.

☑ Progress Check

If you can do the following, you've mastered this lesson:

❑ Identify what HTML stands for.

❑ Name four things that you can consider text items with HTML.

❑ Describe what *hyper* means and what it allows you to do.

❑ Describe what the *markup language* allows you to do.

❑ Name four items that can be displayed in a browser by using HTML and that may also be used as hyperlink activation points.

❑ Describe the difference between document elements and formatting that changes document appearance.

Unit 1 Quiz

This short quiz can help you remember what you learned in Unit 1. For each question, circle the letter of the correct answer or answers.

1. **HTML stands for**

   A. HyperTerminal Manual Language.

   B. How To Make Lollipops.

   C. HyperText Markup Language.

   D. HyperText MarkedOn Language.

   E. HeavilyTechnical Machine Language.

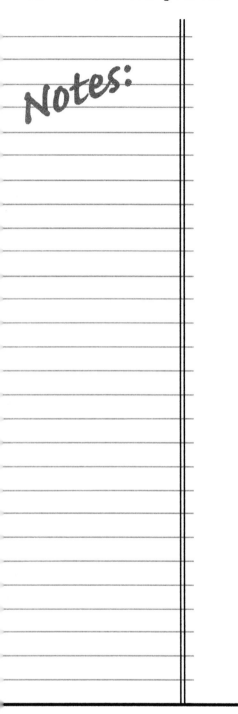

2. **What is HTML used for?**

    A. Publishing on the WWW

    B. Publishing on an intranet

    C. Publishing books

    D. Publishing with a waiter

    E. Both A and B

3. **Which of the following statements is true?**

    A. Using HTML is similar to using a word-processing program.

    B. In HTML, to make a heading, all you do is make the point size larger and hit the Bold button on the toolbar.

    C. You cannot absolutely determine what readers see on their browsers.

    D. In HTML, you still have to format text, even though the document elements are already defined by the browser.

    E. Both C and D

4. **Publishing an HTML document means that you**

    A. Submit it to an HTML publisher you found in the phone book and hope for the best.

    B. Leave it on your computer but tell everyone about it.

    C. Put it on a WWW server.

    D. Publish a book on How To Make Lollipops.

    E. Put it on an HTML server.

5. **You can precisely control HTML document formatting by doing which of the following?**

    A. Applying lots of formatting commands

    B. Simply using the proper HTML markup

    C. Telling the reader exactly what software to use

    D. Making sure that everyone reads your document from his or her own computer but doesn't change anything

    E. None of the above

Unit 1 Exercise

1. Make a list of three document elements.

2. Make a list of things that are document formatting, not document elements.

3. Explain what's special about HTML as compared to regular word-processing programs.

Unit 2

Launching and Using the Software You Need

Prerequisites

▶ Completing Unit 1

▶ Installing the software (see Appendix B)

▶ Having a working knowledge of Windows — either 3.1*x* or 95 (Where possible, we provided this type of information in the margin notes to help you out.)

Objectives for This Unit

✓ Starting and using WebEdit and Netscape

✓ Creating, saving, and testing your HTML document

✓ Closing your document

✓ Exiting WebEdit and Netscape

on the CD
▶ openme.htm
▶ firstone.htm

This unit gets you started using the software included on the CD in the back of the book. Think of this unit as putting gas in your car before taking a long trip: You won't find too much HTML here, but taking care of the basics up front makes for fewer hassles along the way.

Everything you do in this unit will help you more easily create HTML documents and test them to make sure that they work. You learn how to start and use WebEdit (an HTML authoring program) and Netscape (a Web browser). You see how to use these programs to create new documents and test them, as well as how to open existing documents and close them. You also practice moving around in your documents.

After you master this stuff, you'll be well on your way to your first Computer Geek merit badge!

Lesson 2-1   # Getting to Know WebEdit

To begin this lesson, make sure that you've completed the prerequisites. If you're not there yet (or if you haven't had your morning coffee), go get that stuff taken care of now.

on the test

This lesson teaches you about WebEdit, which is a program used to create and edit HTML documents. WebEdit and other similar programs are commonly called *editors* because you use them to create or edit documents. In this lesson, you learn how to start WebEdit and become familiar with some of its features.

The following exercises show you how to start WebEdit Windows 95 and Windows 3.1x. (If you have not yet installed the Launching Pad from the CD, see Appendix B.)

Starting WebEdit in Windows 95

If you're using Windows 95, use the following instructions to locate and start WebEdit. If you're using Windows 3.1x, skip down to the next section.

1 **Click the Start button (it's at the bottom-left corner of the screen).**

The Start menu pops up on-screen.

2 **Point your cursor at Programs (probably the first menu item) and click.**

Another menu appears.

3 **Choose Nesbitt Software on the new menu.**

4 **Click Nesbitt Software or use the down arrow to highlight Nesbitt Software and then press Enter.**

5 **Click WebEdit from this menu to start the program.**

When you open WebEdit, a dialog box appears stating that the program is shareware and that you should register it. You should, but for right now, just click Continue Without Registering and dive right in.

You will probably also see a License Agreement dialog box the first time you open WebEdit. This box provides you with the terms and conditions for using WebEdit, whether or not you decide to register the software.

Starting WebEdit in Windows 3.1x

If you're using Windows 3.1x, use the following instructions to locate and start WebEdit.

1 **Open the Nesbitt Software group in Program Manager.**

This group should be right on top if you just installed the CD. If you can see the icons within the group, Nesbitt Software is open; otherwise, double-click the icon labeled Nesbitt Software.

2 **Double-click the WebEdit icon to start the program.**

When you open WebEdit, you get a dialog box telling you that the program is shareware and that you should register it. You should, but for right now, simply click Continue Without Registering and dive right in. You will probably also see a License Agreement dialog box the first time you open WebEdit. This box provides you with the terms and conditions for using WebEdit, whether or not you decide to register the software.

WebEdit icon

register WebEdit

Notes:

Honor System Software

As much as you might think that the world is going down the tubes, some people out there still believe that most people are good and trustworthy. That belief is fundamental to the concept of *shareware*.

Regular software — the kind you buy in stores — generally costs a lot and comes in those fancy shrink-wrapped boxes. Of course, that fancy shrink-wrap also means that you don't get to try out the software or even look at it before you plunk down the old charge card.

Shareware, on the other hand, is freely distributed. In most cases, you can copy the disks and send them to all your friends without even having to worry about the software police coming after you. You install it, try it, and use it; if you like it and plan to continue using the software, then you buy it.

Many shareware programs, such as WebEdit and Paint Shop Pro on the CD in this book, are outstanding and easily as good as most of the more traditional programs. The authors believe so firmly in the quality of their software that they think you'll pay for it even after you've tried it.

After you've had a chance to work through this book, if you plan to continue using either Paint Shop Pro or WebEdit, please register them. Go to the Help menu and look for the Purchasing or Ordering options.

If you decide not to use the software, simply delete it from your computer and don't worry about it. No loss to you; no loss to the writers.

Pretty cool concept, isn't it?

Finding your way around WebEdit

The WebEdit screen provides quite a few menu options and choices, but don't worry — you don't need to learn *everything* right now. Take a look at Figure 2-1, which shows the WebEdit window. Table 2-1 describes the basic components of the WebEdit window. Relax, you won't be tested on this material!

Table 2-1	The Pieces of WebEdit
Part of Screen	*What It Does*
Title bar	Shows you the name of the document you're editing
Control menu	Provides options for minimizing, maximizing, moving, and closing windows
Minimize, Restore, and Close buttons	*Minimizes* (change from full screen to an icon), *restores* (change from full screen to partial screen), and *closes* windows
Menu bar	Provides access to all WebEdit functions when you click various menu names

(continued)

Figure 2-1: The WebEdit window, ready for action.

Close button
Restore button
Minimize button

Tabs
Control menu
Title bar
Menu bar
Formatting bar
Drop-down menu bar

Status bar   Document window

Figure 2-1

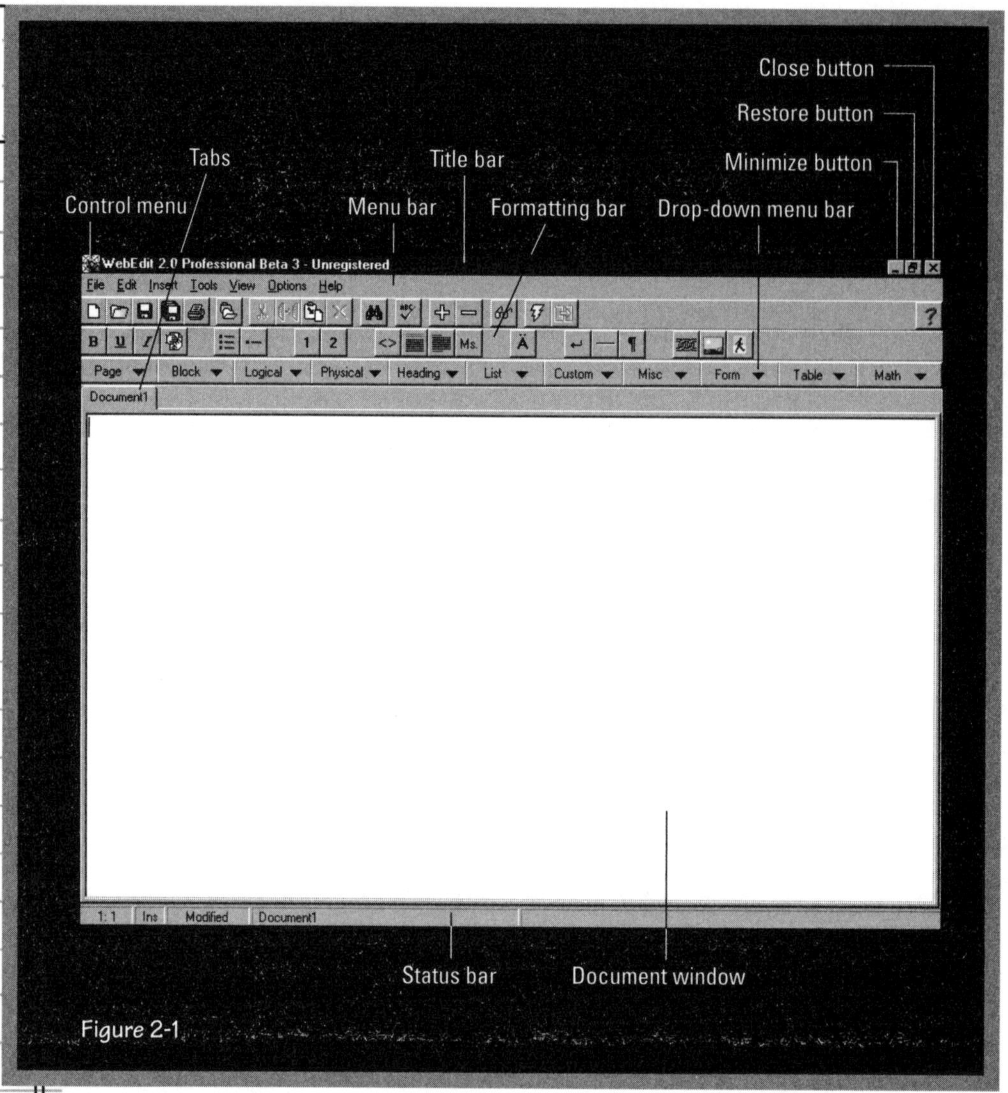

Table 2-1 *(continued)*

Part of Screen	What It Does
Formatting bar	Provides shortcuts to most of the main formatting commands you need. Simply click a button to access a command.
Drop-down menu bar	Provides a fairly quick way of inputting many commands; menus are organized by HTML tag type.
Tabs	Show you the names of the documents you have open as well as the main document you're working on. Simply click the tab to move to a different document.
Document window	Where you do the real work of creating HTML
Scroll bar	Allows you to scroll up or down to see the parts of your document that aren't visible on-screen
Status bar	Provides some information about the document and where your cursor is in the document

Notes:

Getting to Know Netscape   Lesson 2-2

This lesson teaches you about Netscape, which is a program used to view HTML documents. (The version of Netscape included on the CD in this book was redistributed by the AT&T WorldNet service, so that's the name you'll see on the program. You may also use version of Netscape that you have previously installed on your computer.) Netscape and other similar programs are commonly called *browsers* because they're what you use to browse through Web sites. In this lesson, you learn how to start your browser and become familiar with some of its features.

Starting Netscape in Windows 95

Starting Netscape is just about the same as starting WebEdit. Follow these steps to start the version of Netscape included with AT&T WorldNet Service:

1 Click the Start button.

A menu pops up on-screen.

2 Click Programs (probably the first menu item).

A new menu appears. AT&T WorldNet Service is one of the choices. (See Appendix B for complete installation instructions.)

3 Choose AT&T WorldNet Service on the new menu.

4 Click AT&T WorldNet Service to start Netscape.

If this is the first time you've used Netscape and AT&T WorldNet Service, you may see a License Agreement dialog box. Simply read through it and click Accept. You won't see the dialog box again.

Starting Netscape in Windows 3.1x

Starting Netscape by using Windows 3.1x is similar to starting WebEdit by using Windows 3.1x. Simply follow these steps:

1 Open the AT&T WorldNet Service group in Program Manager.

This group should be right on top if you just installed the CD. If you can see the icons within the group, it's open; otherwise, double-click the icon labeled AT&T WorldNet Service.

2 Double-click the AT&T WorldNet Service icon to run the program.

The first time you use Netscape, you'll probably see a License Agreement dialog box. Simply read through it and click Accept. You won't see the dialog box again.

Finding your way around Netscape

Netscape is not nearly as complex-looking as WebEdit, mostly because you can't make any changes to the documents — you can just view them. Figure 2-2 shows you the Netscape window, and Table 2-2 provides a brief not-on-the-test overview of what the different parts of the Netscape window are and what you can do with them.

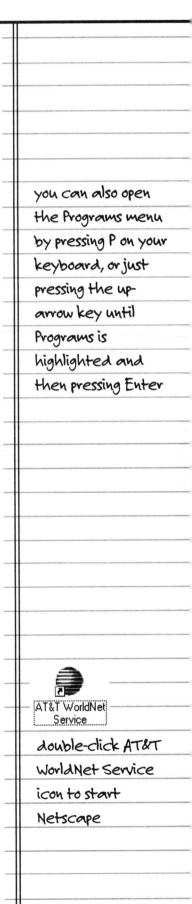

you can also open the Programs menu by pressing P on your keyboard, or just pressing the up-arrow key until Programs is highlighted and then pressing Enter

double-click AT&T WorldNet Service icon to start Netscape

Figure 2-2: Anatomy of the Netscape window.

Notes:

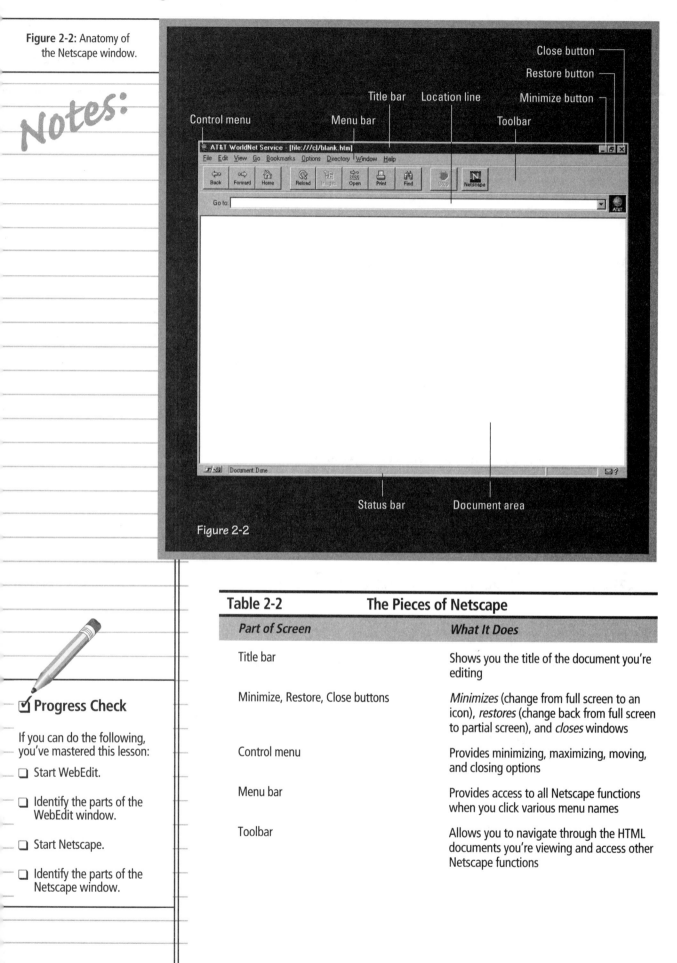

Figure 2-2

Table 2-2   The Pieces of Netscape

Part of Screen	What It Does
Title bar	Shows you the title of the document you're editing
Minimize, Restore, Close buttons	*Minimizes* (change from full screen to an icon), *restores* (change back from full screen to partial screen), and *closes* windows
Control menu	Provides minimizing, maximizing, moving, and closing options
Menu bar	Provides access to all Netscape functions when you click various menu names
Toolbar	Allows you to navigate through the HTML documents you're viewing and access other Netscape functions

☑ **Progress Check**

If you can do the following, you've mastered this lesson:

❑ Start WebEdit.

❑ Identify the parts of the WebEdit window.

❑ Start Netscape.

❑ Identify the parts of the Netscape window.

Part of Screen	What It Does
Location line	Shows the filename or the Internet address of the document you're viewing
Document area	The area where you view the HTML document
Status bar	Shows a little information about the document

Opening a Document

Lesson 2-3

The first step you take every time you want to work on an HTML document is to open a document in WebEdit. You can either create a new document or open an existing document. This lesson shows you how to create new and open existing documents — the process is the same for both Windows 95 and 3.1x users.

Creating a new document

The process for creating a new document is easy. Simply follow these instructions:

1 **Make sure that WebEdit is open.**

2 **Choose File from the menu bar.**

The menu bar is up top and starts with File, Edit, View, Insert. . . .

3 **Click New.**

A new (empty) file should now appear on-screen.

Opening an existing document

The process for opening an existing document is very similar to opening a new document. Use the following instructions:

1 **In WebEdit, choose File from the menu bar.**

2 **Click Open.**

The File Open dialog box appears.

Ctrl+O is the keyboard command for displaying the File Open dialog box. You also can press the Open button.

3 **Locate the box marked "Look in" and select drive C from the drop-down menu.**

▭

Open button

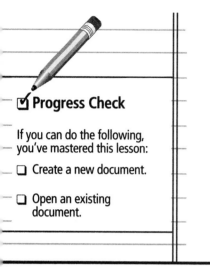

4 **Open the html101 folder.**

You may have to move back up to the top level of drive C to see the html101 folder. To move up a level, click the button with two dots (..) on it if you're using Windows 95 or double-click `c:\` if you're using Windows 3.1x. After you're at the top level of drive C, simply double-click the HTML101 folder to open it.

5 **Open the unit02 folder.**

6 **Click once on** `openme.htm` **and then click Open.**

There! You're done. As you can see, the hardest part is navigating among all the folders on your computer, not actually opening the document.

Lesson 2-4 | Saving a Document

Notes:

This lesson shows you how to save your document in WebEdit. Saving a document simply places it on your computer's hard disk (memory) so that you can reuse it and so that Netscape can use it, too.

The first time you save a document, you have to tell WebEdit where on your computer it should store the document, and you have to name your document.

on the CD

1 **Make sure that the openme.htm document is still displayed on-screen, or if you're picking back up here, open openme.htm now from the \html101\unit02 folder.**

2 **From the menu bar, choose File⇨Save As.**

3 **Find the html101\unit02 folder (which is where you'll save your document) and click it so that it appears in the Save As dialog box.**

4 **In the File Name field, type** firstone.htm.

heads up

The filename isn't particularly critical, but do not use spaces and make sure that you include the .htm at the end; otherwise, Netscape will have problems figuring out that firstone is an HTML document. Technically, Windows 95 users could use a .html extension, but all the examples in this book use just .htm, so the short version is your best choice as you work through the examples. If you're using Windows 3.1x, you can only use only eight characters before the period and three after, so you *have* to use .htm.

5 **Click the arrow next to the Save As Type field and select** `"HTM files (*.htm)"`.

`"HTM files (*.htm)"` should be the second choice in the list.

6 **Click the Save button.**

Yes, you want to replace the existing file. (The computer just doesn't want you to accidentally mess up.)

That's it. Now your document is safely stored on the computer's hard disk. For now, go ahead and leave this document open.

Save button

From now on with this document, because you've already named it, you can save the document by doing one of the following:

▶ Click the Save button.

▶ Press Ctrl+S.

▶ Choose File⇨Save.

You may wonder how often you should save your documents. You have to answer that for yourself. The more frequently you save, the less work you lose if the power goes out, if your computer chokes on too much information, or if your cat accidentally sits on the power switch. If you can afford to recreate 15 minutes of work, save every 15 minutes. If you'd rather only re-create 5 minutes of work after some catastrophe occurs, you should save every 5 minutes. Murphy is watching you!

SOS, or Save Our Stuff!

Saving, opening, and general file management (to use the techie term) techniques are a little picky when you're dealing with HTML. If you're an old hand at word processors, presentation programs, or really almost anything else on your computer, you've become accustomed to being able to just chuck your files onto Ye Old Hard Disk, anywhere, and deal with finding them later.

Here's the non-techie, 5-cent explanation of why saving files is different in HTML: Later in this book you learn how to make links between documents and include graphics in your HTML documents. Making links and including graphics require that you describe exactly where the other files (other documents, images to include, and so on) are. The easiest way to describe the location is to save all the documents in the same folder, which is what we have you do in this book. (It's like telling people where to find anything — it's easier to explain that the tools are right there in the same place they're already looking than it is to clearly explain that they're in the other bucket, on the right and up a little.)

The files for each unit are located in a folder named for the unit (you expected that, right?). Throughout the book, you *should save your documents in the same folder.* If you're working in Unit 7, for example, you open files from \html101\unit7 and save all of your files back into the unit7 folder. In some cases, the document that you edit, change, and save back into the folder will replace one of the files loaded off the CD. No problem! That's the way it works, and you're not messing anything up.

Worst case scenario: You accidentally delete the entire text of a document and then save the (now empty) document back in its proper place. Poof, there goes the file, your hard work, and darn it, now what do you do? Well, we can't give you your work back, but you can very easily replace the file by doing what's called a "Custom Install" from the CD. It's all set up to replace any accidentally-deleted or damaged files, one by one, as you choose. Cool, huh?

See Appendix B for the complete scoop on the custom installation procedure.

✅ **Progress Check**

If you can do the following, you've mastered this lesson:

❑ Save a document under a new name in a folder.

❑ Save a document with the .htm extension.

save documents in the same folder as the unit you're working on

Lesson 2-5

Testing a Document

Testing a document is the process of loading your document into Netscape so that you can get an idea of what your document looks like, determine that the hypertext links work, and proofread your work. Remember that your document will look somewhat different from browser to browser. However, you should always test your document — probably several times — to make sure that you've entered the HTML code correctly. Many times, you can catch errors more easily in browsers than you can in editors. No real test is involved (unlike the end of this unit, in which you'll be rigorously tested on every last word in here).

To test your document, follow these instructions:

1 **Make sure that Netscape is open.**

If Netscape is open but not visible, you can find it by pressing Alt+Tab to switch windows or by using the Windows 95 taskbar.

2 **In Netscape, choose <u>File</u>⇨Open <u>File</u>.**

Opening a file is slightly different from opening a regular address on the Web, so you may have a couple of changes to adjust to here if you're an old hand at surfing the Net. Even if you're new to AT&T WorldNet Service or to Netscape, you'll know stuff that nobody else in your office does after we're through here.

on the CD

3 **Find the \html101\unit02 folder, in which you saved your first document from the preceding lesson.**

You will probably need to click the Up One Level button (folder with two dots and an up arrow) a couple of times, select the html101 folder, and then select unit02.

4 **Click once on the document you just created** (firstone.htm) **and then click Open.**

If you're just picking up with this lesson and skipped the last one, you can open firstone.htm from your unit02 folder.

You should now see your document open in Netscape. Not bad, Webmaster-in-Training!

5 **Switch to WebEdit.**

You've got this one down, right? Simply press Alt+Tab or use the Windows 95 Taskbar.

6 **Immediately after the words** Your comments?**, type:** This is very easy!

    <P>Your comments? This is very easy!

You're just making a minor modification to the document so you can see how to test subsequent changes.

7 **Save your document.**

Remember, you can save your document in several ways, but Ctrl+S or clicking the diskette icon is probably the easiest.

8 **Switch to Netscape.**

Now you're back, but the document looks just the same. That's because Netscape doesn't know that you made any changes. You have to tell Netscape to open the latest-saved document.

Alt+Tab = switch windows

\html101\unit02\ firstone.htm

Save button

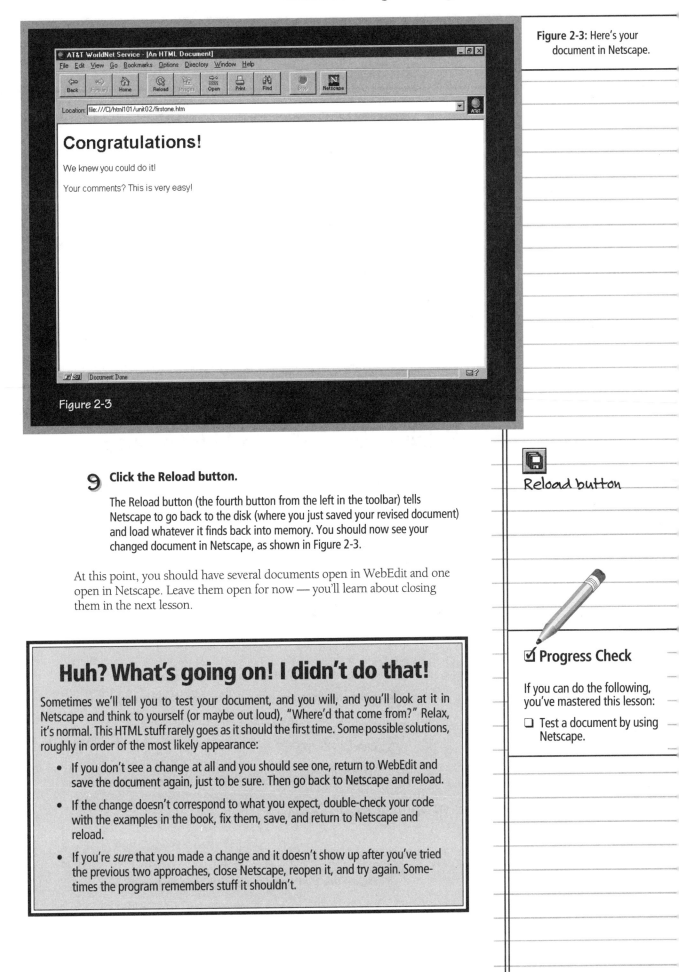

Figure 2-3

Figure 2-3: Here's your document in Netscape.

9 **Click the Reload button.**

The Reload button (the fourth button from the left in the toolbar) tells Netscape to go back to the disk (where you just saved your revised document) and load whatever it finds back into memory. You should now see your changed document in Netscape, as shown in Figure 2-3.

At this point, you should have several documents open in WebEdit and one open in Netscape. Leave them open for now — you'll learn about closing them in the next lesson.

Reload button

Huh? What's going on! I didn't do that!

Sometimes we'll tell you to test your document, and you will, and you'll look at it in Netscape and think to yourself (or maybe out loud), "Where'd that come from?" Relax, it's normal. This HTML stuff rarely goes as it should the first time. Some possible solutions, roughly in order of the most likely appearance:

- If you don't see a change at all and you should see one, return to WebEdit and save the document again, just to be sure. Then go back to Netscape and reload.

- If the change doesn't correspond to what you expect, double-check your code with the examples in the book, fix them, save, and return to Netscape and reload.

- If you're *sure* that you made a change and it doesn't show up after you've tried the previous two approaches, close Netscape, reopen it, and try again. Sometimes the program remembers stuff it shouldn't.

☑ **Progress Check**

If you can do the following, you've mastered this lesson:

❑ Test a document by using Netscape.

Lesson 2-6

Closing a Document

you also can choose Ctrl+F4 to close a document

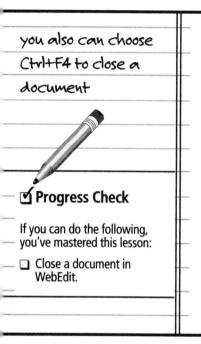

☑ **Progress Check**

If you can do the following, you've mastered this lesson:

❑ Close a document in WebEdit.

When you're ready to stop for a while, you should probably close your document. Because Netscape can't change the document, you don't have to worry about saving it or making sure a power surge doesn't eat the file. You do, however, need to save changes and close the document in WebEdit.

1 **Go to WebEdit.**

2 **Choose**  **File⇨Close.**

Suppose that you made changes to the document since the last time you saved. (You haven't, but we're just supposing.) In that case, a dialog box appears asking whether you want to save the changes to the document before you close it. WebEdit won't let you mess up and lose changes you would want to save.

The document's gone. Slick, isn't it? Actually, the document isn't gone, it's just sitting on your disk waiting for you.

Go ahead and repeat the File⇨Close sequence until all the open files in WebEdit are closed.

Lesson 2-7

Exiting WebEdit and Netscape

in Windows 3.1x, you can exit WebEdit by double-clicking upper left corner of WebEdit window

in Windows 95, click the Close button (the small x) at the upper right to close WebEdit

Exiting these programs is like exiting any other program in Windows. Because you're just bailing out of these programs, it doesn't make any difference which one you exit first. We generally exit out of WebEdit (read: stop working) and then conduct research on the Internet (read: surf the Net) for a while in our browsers.

Exiting WebEdit

To exit WebEdit, follow these instructions:

1 **Make sure that WebEdit is displayed on-screen.**

2 **Save and close any open documents, if necessary.**
Refer to Lessons 2-4 and 2-6, if you need a quick review.

3 **Choose**  **File⇨Exit.**
WebEdit closes.

Exiting Netscape

Now, to exit Netscape . . .

1 **Make sure that Netscape is displayed on-screen.**

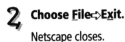

2 **Choose File⇨Exit.**

Netscape closes.

That didn't hurt too bad, did it?

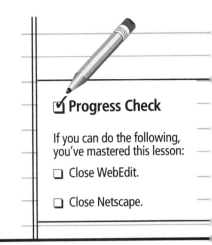

☑ Progress Check

If you can do the following,
you've mastered this lesson:

❑ Close WebEdit.

❑ Close Netscape.

Unit 2 Quiz

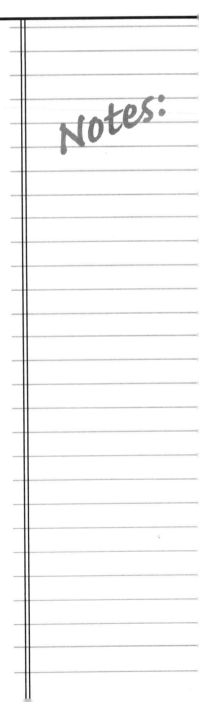

This short quiz is designed to help you remember what you learned in Unit 2.
For each of the following questions, circle the letter of the correct answer or
answers.

1. **To create a new document in WebEdit, do the following:**

   A. Choose File⇨Open (or press Ctrl+O).

   B. Double-click the upper left corner of the WebEdit window.

   C. Choose File⇨New (or press Ctrl+N).

   D. Call the neighborhood computer geek.

   E. Click the Start button.

2. **To open an existing document in WebEdit, do the following:**

   A. Choose File⇨Open (or Ctrl+O).

   B. Press Ctrl+S.

   C. Say "Open Sesame."

   D. Click 📂

   E. Double-click in the document window.

3. **WebEdit is used to create HTML documents, and Netscape is used
   to view HTML documents.**

   A. True

   B. False

   C. Not true

   D. Not false

   E. Both A and D

4. **"Reloading" means to**

   A. Reinstall the software from the CD.

   B. Double-click the Load button.

   C. Load the file into Netscape twice.

D. Load the latest-saved version of the file into Netscape.

E. Get another cup of coffee.

5. **The Taskbar is**

A. The long do-whichie at the bottom of the Windows 95 screen.

B. A list of jobs for your spouse to do.

C. The gray bar at the top of the WebEdit screen that has "File," "Edit," "Insert," and so on.

D. The gray bar at the top of the WebEdit screen that has cute little square buttons.

E. The big white space in WebEdit that you type in.

Unit 2 Exercise

on the CD

1. Open the document you've been working on in WebEdit (probably firstone.htm in the unit2 folder).

2. Add another couple of lines in the middle about how easy this whole process is.

3. Save your document.

4. Open Netscape.

5. Test your document in Netscape.

6. Close WebEdit and Netscape.

Part I Review

Unit 1 Summary

- **HTML.** HyperText Markup Language provides a set of markup tags that Web browsers use to identify different parts of a document, such as headings, paragraphs, and lists. You generally use HTML to specify parts of a document rather than the precise way those elements will appear.

- **Publishing.** You use HTML to publish documents on a server so that other people in your company or on the Internet can see your documents.

- **Developing.** You create and test your HTML documents at the privacy of your own computer. Only after you perfect your creation do you move it out to a server for the world to see, if that is, in fact, what you want to do.

Unit 2 Summary

- **WebEdit.** WebEdit is one of many editing programs available to help you create HTML documents. Throughout this book, you use WebEdit when you're creating HTML documents. You start WebEdit by double-clicking the WebEdit icon.

- **Netscape Navigator.** Netscape is a Web — or HTML — browser, and you use it to view and test your HTML documents. Double-clicking the AT&T WorldNet Service icon starts Netscape.

- **Opening.** You do essentially the same thing in either WebEdit or Netscape to open a document. You choose File➪Open to bring up the File Open dialog box. Then you use the dialog box to move through the files and folders on your computer to find the one you want to open.

- **Saving.** You can change your documents only in WebEdit; therefore, you only need to save your work in WebEdit. You choose File➪Save or click the little diskette icon to save the document. The first time you save a document, you also need to give it a name and identify the folder in which you want it to be stored.

- **Testing.** To "test" your HTML documents, you view them in your Web browser (Netscape), make whatever changes are necessary in WebEdit, save your changes, and then reload your document in Netscape.

- **Closing.** You should close your document from WebEdit after you're finished making changes to it. Choose File➪Close to close the document. You don't have to close documents in Netscape.

- **Exiting.** To exit WebEdit and Netscape, you double-click the upper left corner of the window or choose File➪Exit. From Windows 95, you click the Close (x) button at the upper right corner of the window.

Part I Test

The questions on this test cover all the material from Part I, Units 1 and 2. Good luck!

True   False

Each statement is either true or false.

T   F   1. HyperText Markup Language allows you to determine the exact fonts and formatting your readers will see.

T   F   2. HTML is most useful for publishing on paper, but it also can be used for the World Wide Web or intranets.

T   F   3. Putting your HTML document "out there" on the Web is an optional part of the HTML document development process.

T   F   4. You can use Netscape to edit HTML documents.

T   F   5. The easiest way to test your documents is to exit Netscape, reopen it, and then open your file again.

T   F   6. If you exit WebEdit without saving your document, you lose your changes you made since the last time you saved.

T   F   7. Reloading helps WebEdit better manage your documents.

T   F   8. "Text" in the context of HTML refers to only words you can put in paragraphs.

T   F   9. A Markup Language is a system of codes, called tags, that identifies parts of a document.

T   F   10. When exiting WebEdit and the AT&T WorldNet browser, you must exit the browser first so that you do not change any information that's been saved.

Multiple Choice

For each of the following questions, circle the correct answer or answers. Remember, you may find more than one correct answer for each question.

11. **HyperText allows you to**

   A. Read a document from the beginning straight through to the end.

   B. Consume three sodas and keep smiling.

   C. Structure documents so that they can be read by moving from one piece of information to one or more related pieces.

   D. Use tags to identify specific parts of your document.

12. **HyperText Markup Language tags look like which of the following?**

   A. `<TITLE></TITLE>`

   B. `[TITLE][/TITLE]`

   C. `.Title ./title`

   D. `<\TITLE><\TITLE>`

Part I Test

13. **A WWW server allows you to do what with your documents?**

    A. Make them available to anyone on the Internet or an intranet.

    B. Charge people 25 cents for each time they request a document.

    C. Format your documents for electronic distribution.

    D. E-mail your HTML documents to other readers.

14. **You can use WebEdit to do which of the following?**

    A. Create HTML documents

    B. Edit HTML documents

    C. View HTML documents

    D. Serve HTML documents

15. **In Netscape, the location line serves what function?**

    A. Shows the location of your cursor on the page.

    B. Shows the filename or the Internet address of the document you're viewing.

    C. Makes sure that both the editor and browser are located in the correct directory.

    D. Load tests your computer and operating system.

16. **With shareware software, you**

    A. Install it in your Temp directory.

    B. Have access to it only if someone else isn't using it — kind of like the old telephone party lines.

    C. Install it, try it, use it, and if you like it and plan to continue using it, then you buy it.

    D. Install it on two disk drives that share the software.

17. **Before you can view one of your own documents in Netscape, you must**

    A. Put the document on a server.

    B. Exit WebEdit.

    C. Connect to the Internet.

    D. Save the document from your editing program.

18. **After you finish using the document in Netscape, you**

    A. Must save the document before you exit.

    B. Must close Netscape so you can continue to edit the document.

    C. Don't have to do anything special, but it might be a good chance to knock off work early and surf the Internet.

    D. Need to return to WebEdit to save your document.

19. **The most common place to see HTML documents is on the World Wide Web, but**

    A. You also can see them on your personal computer.

    B. You also can see them on company internal networks, often called *intranets*.

    C. You can see them only by shining a bright light on them.

    D. Both A and B

20. **Using HTML, you'd mark a heading by**

    A. Using a tag that specifies the text should appear as a heading.

    B. Adding bold and increasing the font size.

    C. Changing the font to a heading-type font.

    D. Using a tag that specifies the text should appear in a specified color.

Part I Lab Assignment

This is the first of several lab assignments — you'll find one at the end of each part of this book. These lab assignments give you the opportunity to apply the things you learned in each part to real-life situations. We won't tell you how to do things; we want you to figure out how to do them yourself. These are the true tests of what you learned.

At this point, you have a good grasp of the basics, and you should feel confident about completing this lab assignment. The steps you are asked to complete are similar to ones you've already successfully completed. You won't find any surprises here, so just relax and do your best.

For this lab assignment, you use both WebEdit and Netscape, in addition to reviewing some of the documents you used in this part.

Step 1: Start your programs

Start WebEdit and Netscape.

Step 2: Open a document

Open up one of the sample documents you used in this part in WebEdit. Now open the same document in Netscape.

Step 3: Save and test your documents

Use the appropriate program(s) to change, save (under a new name), and test the document.

Step 4: Cool!

Good for you! That's it!

Building Your First HTML Documents

Part II

In this part . . .

Fire up the computer and warm up your typing fingers. Take the phone off the hook and lock the door. Turn off the mail and newspaper delivery. Well, maybe all that isn't necessary, but in this part, you start building your first HTML documents, and you won't want distractions. Yes, ordering pizza is acceptable as long as you don't get pepperoni on the keys.

This part introduces you to the *tags* that you'll use to create HTML documents — in brief, tags plus text yields an HTML document. The process isn't terribly difficult, but it does require a little attention to detail as far as making sure that you've typed the tags correctly. (Hence the need to warm up the typing fingers.)

After you work on the basics of *tagging* the documents, you use some of those tags to make headings, lists, and to add other cool formatting to your HTML documents. Finally, you learn to make links to other documents and Web sites so that people can click text in your HTML document and — voilà! (or violin!) — they're in another document, and it's all your fault.

Better get busy — the fun starts here!

Unit 3

Basic HTML Tagging

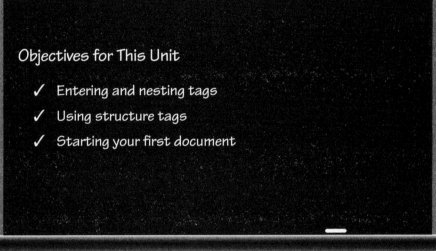

Objectives for This Unit

- ✓ Entering and nesting tags
- ✓ Using structure tags
- ✓ Starting your first document

Prerequisites

- ▶ Understanding HTML terminology (Lessons 1-1 and 1-2)
- ▶ Opening WebEdit and Netscape (Lessons 2-1 and 2-2)
- ▶ Opening a new document in WebEdit (Lesson 2-3, Opening a Document)
- ▶ Saving a document in WebEdit (Lesson 2-4)
- ▶ Testing a document in Netscape (Lesson 2-5)

Part I showed you how to use the editing and viewing software included on the CD and the basics of working with text. In this unit, you start creating your first HTML document by using the skills you learned in Part I.

In this unit, you learn how to enter those funny-looking HTML tags correctly, and you learn how and where to include the essential tags in your document. Learning these skills is very important because you will use them every time you create an HTML document.

Entering HTML Tags

Lesson 3-1

Tags are the HTML codes you apply to text that determine document elements. Before you get to the fun stuff, though, you need to know how to enter tags correctly. If you don't enter tags correctly, your document could end up with a lampshade on its title bar — or at least end up looking nothing like you wanted it to look.

Entering tags is pretty easy, but you do need to pay attention to a few things. First, you enter all HTML tags using little pointed bracket dealies (*angle-brackets* for you purists), like this:

```
<OPENING HTML TAG> </CLOSING HTML TAG>
```

Tag = HTML code that determines document elements

Second, all closing tags start with a forward slash (/). Browsers won't recognize a closing tag if it does not have the slash and will continue the style you applied until it sees a closing tag. We recommend entering both the opening tag and closing tag at the same time so that you don't forget to enter the closing tag. We have it on reliable authority that people often forget the closing tag. (Right, co-author?)

Third, almost every HTML tag appears in pairs, called *paired tags* (exceptions do exist, and we point them out later). Everything that you want the tag to affect goes between the two tags, like this:

```
<OPENING HTML TAG> interesting info </CLOSING HTML TAG>
```

What's great about HTML is that you don't have to worry about where all the text and tags appear on the page. You can enter your text and tags like the following samples, for example, or any combination you can think of.

```
<OPENING HTML TAG>
interesting info can go like this
</CLOSING HTML TAG>
```

or

```
<OPENING HTML TAG>
 interesting          info can
also
 go                   like this </CLOSING HTML TAG>
```

Notice that we use all caps for the tags. Using all caps doesn't affect whether your browser recognizes your HTML tags, but you'll find that tags are much easier to see if they're in all caps and, therefore, easier to edit. (Not to mention that the HTML specifications say that they're all supposed to be in all caps. So there!)

Go ahead and start experimenting with entering opening tags, closing tags, and text in between the two. (Don't jump ahead yet and try to test the results in your browser — simply practice entering the tags and text.)

1 **Make sure that WebEdit and Netscape are open.**

2 **In WebEdit, create a new document.**

3 **Enter** `<TAG></TAG>` **on the first line.**

Feels pretty odd starting and ending your words with those brackets, but you get used to it after a while. Did you remember the closing tag? Go ahead and type in the tags again, just for practice.

4 **Enter the following information between the tags:** My dog has fleas.

```
<TAG>My dog has fleas</TAG>
```

5 **Press Enter a couple of times to get to a new line.**

6 **Enter the following tags:** <TAG> </TAG>

7 **Now put your cursor between the two tags and enter** My dog got a flea bath.

```
<TAG>My dog has fleas.</TAG>
```

```
<TAG>My dog got a flea bath.</TAG>
```

If you want, practice entering text and tags before moving on to the next lesson. When you're done, you can leave this document open.

Now that you've got the hang of this tagging business, you're ready to learn how to use multiple tags. On to the next lesson!

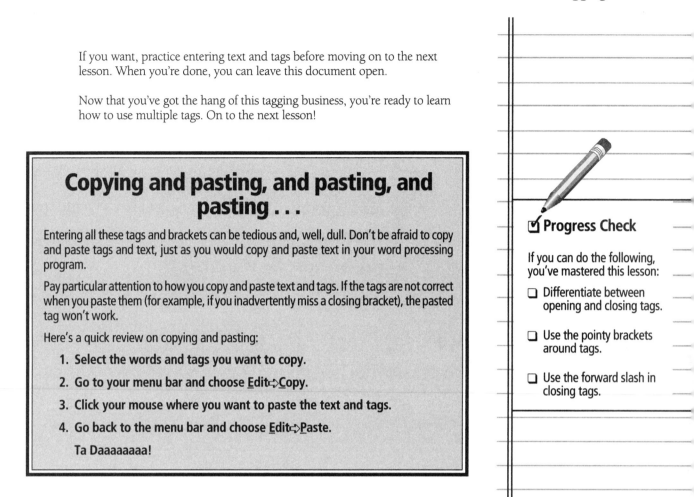

Copying and pasting, and pasting, and pasting . . .

Entering all these tags and brackets can be tedious and, well, dull. Don't be afraid to copy and paste tags and text, just as you would copy and paste text in your word processing program.

Pay particular attention to how you copy and paste text and tags. If the tags are not correct when you paste them (for example, if you inadvertently miss a closing bracket), the pasted tag won't work.

Here's a quick review on copying and pasting:

1. **Select the words and tags you want to copy.**

2. **Go to your menu bar and choose Edit⇨Copy.**

3. **Click your mouse where you want to paste the text and tags.**

4. **Go back to the menu bar and choose Edit⇨Paste.**

   Ta Daaaaaaaa!

☑ **Progress Check**

If you can do the following, you've mastered this lesson:

❑ Differentiate between opening and closing tags.

❑ Use the pointy brackets around tags.

❑ Use the forward slash in closing tags.

Nesting Tags
Lesson 3-2

Sometimes you'll want to apply more than one tag to text. For example, you may want to make a first-level heading, which you'd mark with <H1></H1>, and then you may want to make the heading italicized, which you'd mark with <I></I>. All you do is *nest* the tags, as shown in the following steps. (You don't need to actually do this now — you practice this later in the lesson.)

1 **Type your text:** How to Tune a Fish

2 **Add the <H1> . . . </H1> tags, like this:**

```
<H1>How to Tune a Fish</H1>
```

3 **Nest the <I> . . . </I> tags inside the heading tags, like this:**

```
<H1><I>How to Tune a Fish</I></H1>
```

<H1> means heading level 1

In this example, the tags for italic are nested inside the heading tags. What you need to remember is that whichever tag you start with, you also end with; the tag that is placed at the front of the text is also placed at the end of the text. A good acronym for this is FILO — that is, First In Last Out, meaning the first tag on the left is the same as the last tag on the right.

<I> means italic

Use the following steps to practice nesting tags:

1 **Make sure that the document you started in Lesson 3-1 is still open, or if you're just starting with this lesson, start a new document in WebEdit.**

2 **Press Enter a few times to get to a new line.**

3 **Enter heading tags.**

```
<H1></H1>
```

4 **Nest italics tags between the heading tags.**

```
<H1><I></I></H1>
```

5 **Enter the text between the italics tags.**

```
<H1><I>How to Make a Marshmallow Sandwich</I></H1>
```

on the test

You should always enter your tags in pairs, and you should always add to the tags one thing at a time. *Don't* try to build your text and tags by starting at the beginning of the line and typing across. You'll start making mistakes — trust us, we did.

Okay! Good job. That's the basics of nesting tags — and you've learned two tags!

Go ahead and close this document when you're done. You work with a new document in the next lesson.

WebEdit Shortcuts

After hours and hours of typing HTML tags (or even after minutes and minutes), applying tags to text can become pretty monotonous. Well, you're in luck! WebEdit offers drop-down menus and fancy buttons that apply the tag for you. Nifty, huh?

The easiest way to get accustomed to using the shortcuts is to just try them out. In general, you'll select the text you want to apply a tag to and then click a button or select a menu.

If you want to apply <I></I> tags to text, for example, highlight the text and click the Italic button (an italicized *I*). If you're not sure whether a button does what you want it to, you can hover for an answer — move the cursor over the button and don't click anything. A little box will pop up with a brief description of what the button does.

Whole sets of shortcuts lurk under the buttons labeled Page, Block, Logical, Physical, Heading, List, Custom, Misc, Form, Table, and Math. Click, for example, the Heading button and then select the type of heading from the list. If you get a dialog box asking for more information, click OK to skip past it for now.

Remember, if it doesn't work as you expect, there's always Edit➪Undo or Ctrl+Z.

Two words of warning: First, you should probably work through much of the book before you dive into the shortcuts in WebEdit. In HTML, it really does help to know how it works before you use the shortcuts.

Second, WebEdit includes all kinds of non-standard extensions to HTML that some browsers support and some don't. We'll tip you off to some non-standard stuff throughout this book, but if you're planning to really delve into this HTML business, we'd recommend getting a reference book, such as *HTML For Dummies* by Ed Tittel (published by IDG Books Worldwide, Inc.). You might also want to check out the *HTML For Dummies Quick Reference* by yours truly (published by IDG Books Worldwide, Inc.) for a reference about standard and non-standard tags.

☑ **Progress Check**

If you can do the following, you've mastered this lesson:

❑ Enter tags in pairs.

❑ Nest tags.

Starting Your First Document

Now that you've mastered the art of entering tags and nesting tags, you're ready to start your first real, law-abiding HTML document.

on the test

Every HTML document you start should contain a few basic *structure* tags. These tags don't affect the appearance or content of a document, but they do help browsers identify *document characteristics*. For example, structure tags help browsers know that the document is in fact an HTML document and provide browsers with names of document headings. Including structure tags is essential because HTML specifications say that they need to be included, not to mention that most browsers need these tags to be able to display your document.

You should include four structure tags in every HTML document:

```
<HTML>...</HTML>
<HEAD>...</HEAD>
<TITLE>...</TITLE>
<BODY>...</BODY>
```

Including the <HTML> tag

The first structure tag is the <HTML> tag. This tag defines the document as an HTML document. If you don't include this tag, the browser may not recognize the document as HTML and therefore may not be able to read the tags as tags. If the browser can't read the tags, the document would appear similar to how it appears in your browser — very texty and very taggy.

You use the <HTML> tag to start your document, like this:

```
<HTML>
</HTML>
```

Including the <HEAD> and <TITLE> tags

The next structure tags you need to include are the <HEAD> and <TITLE> tags. The <HEAD> tag is what many browsers use to identify or reference the document. Without it, some browsers cannot open and display your HTML document. The <TITLE> tag is usually used in conjunction with the <HEAD> tag, and it simply gives a title to your document. The information — title — that you put between the <TITLE>...</TITLE> tags appears in the title bar of the browser.

You will add the <HEAD> and <TITLE> tags to your document, like this:

```
<HTML>
<HEAD><TITLE>Peeling a Grape</TITLE></HEAD>
</HTML>
```

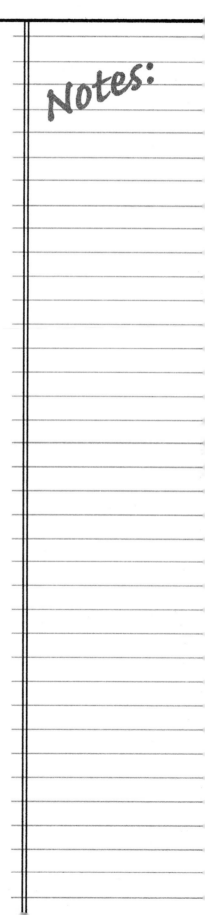

Notes:

Including the <BODY> tag

The <BODY> tag is the last structure tag you need to include. This tag indicates that all the information within the opening and closing tags are part of the document body. This is the first tag that actually affects the content of your document and is not just part of the document's title or heading information.

You add the <BODY> tag to your document, like this:

```
<HTML>
<HEAD><TITLE>Peeling a Grape</TITLE></HEAD>
<BODY>
. . . all the stuff about peeling grapes will go here
</BODY>
</HTML>
```

Notice that what we've been doing in these examples is nesting tags inside other tags. The <HEAD> tags are nested with the <HTML> tags; the <TITLE> tags are nested within the <HEAD> tags, and the <HEAD>, <TITLE>, and <BODY> tags are all nested within the <HTML> tags. Nifty, huh?

Use the following steps to practice starting a document using the structure tags:

1 **Open a new document in WebEdit.**

2 **Start your HTML document using the <HTML> tags:**

```
<HTML>
</HTML>
```

3 **Nest the <HEAD> and <TITLE> tags between the <HTML> tags:**

```
<HTML>
<HEAD><TITLE> </TITLE></HEAD>
</HTML>
```

4 **Add the title** Doing HTML Is Fun **to the document:**

```
<HTML>
<HEAD><TITLE>Doing HTML Is Fun</TITLE></HEAD>
</HTML>
```

5 **Add the <BODY> tags:**

```
<HTML>
<HEAD><TITLE>Doing HTML Is Fun</TITLE></HEAD>
<BODY>
</BODY>
</HTML>
```

6 **Add text between the body tags:** Hey! I did it! I started my first HTML document!

```
<HTML>
<HEAD><TITLE>Doing HTML Is Fun</TITLE></HEAD>
<BODY>
Hey! I did it! I started my first HTML document!
</BODY>
</HTML>
```

⊞

This button gives you a good start on the structure tags

☑ **Progress Check**

If you can do the following, you've mastered this lesson:

❑ Name the four structure tags.

❑ Use the four structure tags to start an HTML document.

❑ Test your structure tags (with some text in them) in Netscape.

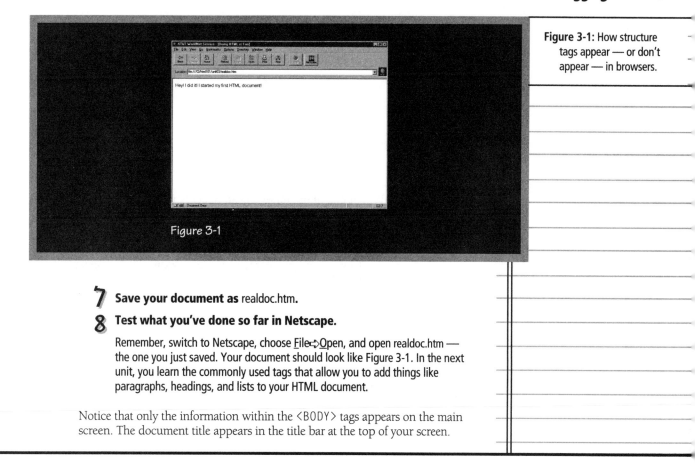

Figure 3-1: How structure tags appear — or don't appear — in browsers.

Figure 3-1

7 **Save your document as** realdoc.htm.

8 **Test what you've done so far in Netscape.**

Remember, switch to Netscape, choose File⇨Open, and open realdoc.htm — the one you just saved. Your document should look like Figure 3-1. In the next unit, you learn the commonly used tags that allow you to add things like paragraphs, headings, and lists to your HTML document.

Notice that only the information within the <BODY> tags appears on the main screen. The document title appears in the title bar at the top of your screen.

Unit 3 Quiz

This short quiz can help you remember what you learned in Unit 3. For each question, circle the letter of the correct answer or answers.

1. **The <HEAD> tag is used**

    A. By the browser to identify or reference the document.

    B. By the editor to show you where the document starts.

    C. As a place to put your thinking cap.

    D. To top off a beer.

    E. To make a heading in your document.

2. **Which two structure tags are necessary but don't really affect the appearance of your document?**

    A. <HEAD> and <BODY>

    B. <BODY> and <TITLE>

    C. <HEAD> and <TITLE>

    D. <TITLE> and <BODY>

    E. All of the above

3. **In what order do you nest tags in your document?**

    A. `<HEAD><BODY>, </HEAD>, </BODY>`

    B. `<HEAD><TITLE></TITLE></HEAD>`

    C. `<H1></H2><H3></H4>`

    D. In any order you want

    E. None of the above

4. **Which one of the following statements is true?**

    A. The opening tag must have a front slash in it.

    B. HTML tags should use rounded brackets.

    C. The way you space out text and tags is extremely important.

    D. Everything you want a tag to affect must go between the opening and closing tag.

    E. All of the above

5. **Nesting means**

    A. To clean the house before family visits.

    B. To build small trinkets with twigs, leaves, and scraps of trash.

    C. To place one set of tags in between another set of tags.

    D. To place more than one tag within a set of pointed brackets.

    E. To scope out a place for your cat to have kittens.

Unit 3 Exercise

1. Start a new document in WebEdit.

2. Enter the document structure tags, a title, and the text, I'm done with Unit 3! (Try to do this without peeking at Lesson 3-3!)

3. Save and test your document.

Unit 4

Using Common HTML Tags

Objectives for This Unit

- ✓ Making headings
- ✓ Making paragraphs
- ✓ Emphasizing text
- ✓ Making lists
- ✓ Using horizontal rules

Prerequisites

▶ Creating a new document
(Lesson 2-3)

▶ Saving a document
(Lesson 2-4)

▶ Testing a document
(Lesson 2-5)

▶ Entering text and tags
(Lesson 3-1)

on the CD

▶ head.htm
▶ getajob2.htm
▶ getajob3.htm
▶ getajob4.htm
▶ getajob5.htm
▶ getajob6.htm

Unit 3 showed you how to include structure tags in your HTML documents. Now you learn how to include some of the most commonly used HTML tags — the ones you'll use in almost every document you create. You'll learn how to make paragraphs, headings, and lists, as well as do some neat things like set off text and add *rules* (jargon for lines) to your documents.

We also show you how to use these common tags to help make online reading easier. Reading online is much different from reading paper versions of the same information. For example, the resolution on a monitor is not nearly as clear as the resolution of print on paper. Also, the black text on white background of a computer screen is more glaring than black text on white paper. The result? Readers' eyes get tired faster, and your readers are less likely to read through information that is poorly presented. For these reasons, you need to make doubly sure that you present the information effectively — you'll learn how, using the tags presented in this unit.

Lesson 4-1

Making Headings

Notes:

Some of the most useful — essential, really — tags you can include in your documents are heading tags. Using HTML, you can include six levels of headings, <H1> through <H6>. (You used the <H1> tag in Lesson 3-2, so you already have a head(ing) start!) <H1> is the largest of the headings, and <H6> is the smallest of the headings.

on the test

Using headings in your HTML documents is very important. Headings make reading easier by grouping information into major points and subpoints. If you don't use headings to group information, your readers will get lost in seas of text and generally won't take the time to wade through it. Use headings frequently throughout your HTML documents to group information and to help ease reading. Your readers probably won't notice that you use headings effectively, but they will certainly notice if you *don't*.

You enter heading tags just like you'd enter any other paired tag:

```
<H1>...</H1>
<H2>...</H2>
<H3>...</H3>
<H4>...</H4>
<H5>...</H5>
<H6>...</H6>
```

(The "..." represents where text will be between the tags.)

In the following steps, you try out some of these headings and see how they appear in WebEdit.

on the CD

when using the Heading buttons, ignore the formatting questions in the dialog box for now and click OK to cruise on through

1 **Open WebEdit and Netscape.**

2 **In WebEdit, open head.htm — this file contains the full structure tags.**

3 **Type <H1></H1> between the <BODY> tags.**

```
<BODY>
<H1></H1>
</BODY>
```

4 **Enter the following heading text between the heading tags:**

```
<BODY>
<H1>Applying for a Job</H1>
</BODY>
```

5 **Add a second-level heading:**

```
<BODY>
<H1>Applying for a Job</H1>
<H2>Creating a Resume</H2>
</BODY>
```

type the pair of tags and then add the text between them

Remember to type the pair of tags first and *then* add the text between them.

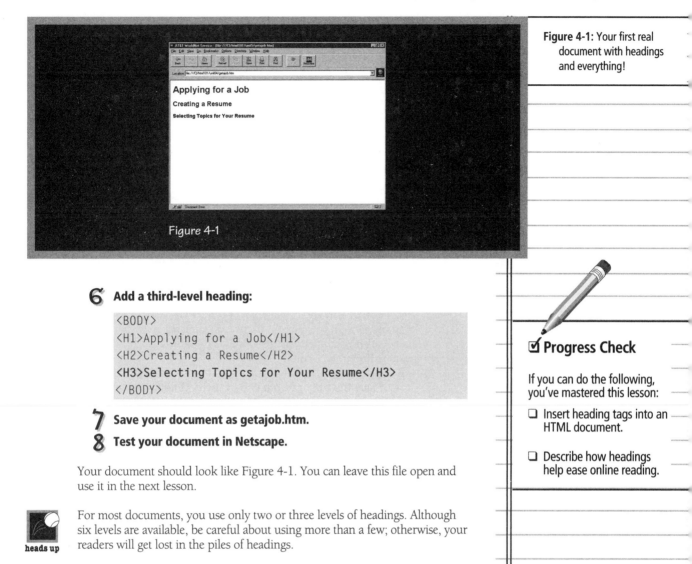

Figure 4-1

Figure 4-1: Your first real document with headings and everything!

6 **Add a third-level heading:**

```
<BODY>
<H1>Applying for a Job</H1>
<H2>Creating a Resume</H2>
<H3>Selecting Topics for Your Resume</H3>
</BODY>
```

7 **Save your document as getajob.htm.**

8 **Test your document in Netscape.**

Your document should look like Figure 4-1. You can leave this file open and use it in the next lesson.

heads up

For most documents, you use only two or three levels of headings. Although six levels are available, be careful about using more than a few; otherwise, your readers will get lost in the piles of headings.

☑ Progress Check

If you can do the following, you've mastered this lesson:

❑ Insert heading tags into an HTML document.

❑ Describe how headings help ease online reading.

Making Paragraphs

Lesson 4-2

After you create a good framework for your document by making headings, you want to add information to your page. You can do so in a number of ways, one of the most common of which is making paragraphs by using the `<P>...</P>` tags. Technically, the paragraph tag is a paired tag — you use both the `<P>` and the `</P>` — but the closing paragraph tag is not absolutely essential as it is in other paired tags. In other words, if you goof up and forget the closing tag here, your paragraph information will still look like a paragraph.

use short paragraphs

You can use short paragraphs to help ease reading. Although long paragraphs can be perfectly acceptable when writing for paper copies, the reduced readability of online documents makes long paragraphs particularly difficult to read. Short paragraphs are easier to read than long paragraphs, so readers are more likely to read them. And, of course, you'll want to use any tactic you can to keep readers glued to your page. Try sticking to short paragraphs that discuss one topic each. Remember: Long paragraphs contribute to the seas of text syndrome.

Figure 4-2: Your page with paragraphs and headings.

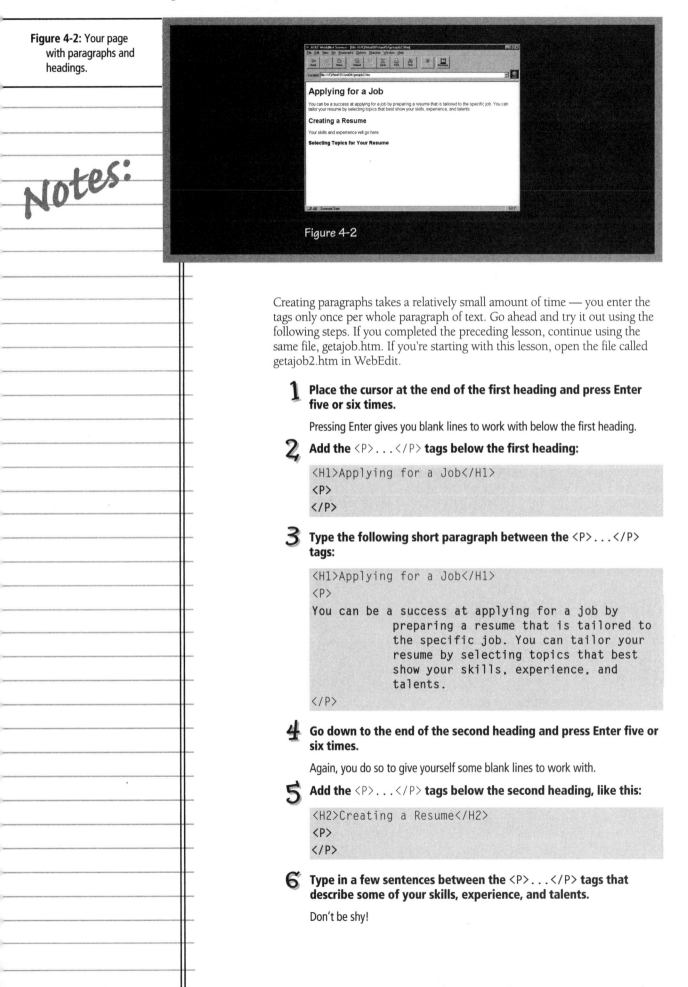

Figure 4-2

Creating paragraphs takes a relatively small amount of time — you enter the tags only once per whole paragraph of text. Go ahead and try it out using the following steps. If you completed the preceding lesson, continue using the same file, getajob.htm. If you're starting with this lesson, open the file called getajob2.htm in WebEdit.

1 **Place the cursor at the end of the first heading and press Enter five or six times.**

Pressing Enter gives you blank lines to work with below the first heading.

2 **Add the** `<P>...</P>` **tags below the first heading:**

```
<H1>Applying for a Job</H1>
<P>
</P>
```

3 **Type the following short paragraph between the** `<P>...</P>` **tags:**

```
<H1>Applying for a Job</H1>
<P>
You can be a success at applying for a job by
            preparing a resume that is tailored to
            the specific job. You can tailor your
            resume by selecting topics that best
            show your skills, experience, and
            talents.
</P>
```

4 **Go down to the end of the second heading and press Enter five or six times.**

Again, you do so to give yourself some blank lines to work with.

5 **Add the** `<P>...</P>` **tags below the second heading, like this:**

```
<H2>Creating a Resume</H2>
<P>
</P>
```

6 **Type in a few sentences between the** `<P>...</P>` **tags that describe some of your skills, experience, and talents.**

Don't be shy!

Notes:

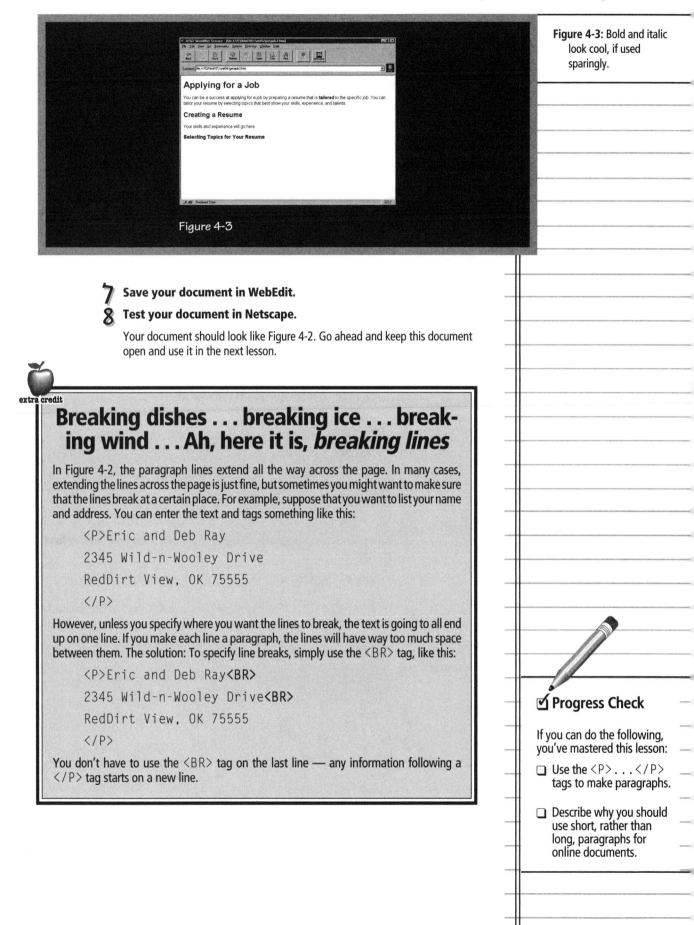

Figure 4-3: Bold and italic look cool, if used sparingly.

Figure 4-3

7 **Save your document in WebEdit.**

8 **Test your document in Netscape.**

Your document should look like Figure 4-2. Go ahead and keep this document open and use it in the next lesson.

extra credit

Breaking dishes . . . breaking ice . . . breaking wind . . . Ah, here it is, *breaking lines*

In Figure 4-2, the paragraph lines extend all the way across the page. In many cases, extending the lines across the page is just fine, but sometimes you might want to make sure that the lines break at a certain place. For example, suppose that you want to list your name and address. You can enter the text and tags something like this:

```
<P>Eric and Deb Ray

2345 Wild-n-Wooley Drive

RedDirt View, OK 75555

</P>
```

However, unless you specify where you want the lines to break, the text is going to all end up on one line. If you make each line a paragraph, the lines will have way too much space between them. The solution: To specify line breaks, simply use the <BR> tag, like this:

```
<P>Eric and Deb Ray<BR>

2345 Wild-n-Wooley Drive<BR>

RedDirt View, OK 75555

</P>
```

You don't have to use the <BR> tag on the last line — any information following a </P> tag starts on a new line.

☑ Progress Check

If you can do the following, you've mastered this lesson:

❏ Use the <P> . . . </P> tags to make paragraphs.

❏ Describe why you should use short, rather than long, paragraphs for online documents.

Lesson 4-3 Emphasizing Text

Now that you have some paragraph text in your HTML document, you probably want to tweak the text so that specified words stand out — we call this *emphasizing text*. In HTML, you can emphasize text by applying bold tags, `<B>...</B>`, or italics tags, `<I>...</I>`.

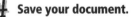

You can help ease reading by *not* using these effects too frequently. These tags should only be used for their intended purpose — to emphasize a word or words. Using them too frequently minimizes their effect. Also, long strings of bold or italicized words are difficult to read online, so use these sparingly.

To use the `<B>...</B>` and `<I>...</I>` tags, you simply insert them around the word or words you want to emphasize, as shown in the following instructions. If you're continuing from the preceding lesson, open the document you've been working on. If you're just starting now, open the document called getajob3.htm in WebEdit.

1 Look at the paragraph under the first heading.

```
<P>
You can be a success at applying for a job by
preparing a resume that is tailored to the specific
job. You can tailor your resume by selecting topics
that best show your skills, experience, and talents.
</P>
```

2 Add the `<B>...</B>` tags around the word "tailored" in the first sentence:

```
<B>tailored</B>
```

3 Add the `<I>...</I>` tags around the word "best" in the second sentence:

```
<I>best</I>
```

Placing the tags right up against the words they affect is generally best. However, if you don't, you won't have any major problems.

4 Save your document.

5 Test your document in Netscape.

Your document should look like Figure 4-3. You can use this document in the next lesson, so go ahead and leave it open.

Some browsers don't show bold and italics effectively. Instead, the browser may show the emphasis as underlined, in *reverse video* (for example, white text on black background), or it might ignore the tag entirely. Remember that as the writer, you don't have a whole lot of control over what your readers see. If you want to be sure that the text appears emphasized, you may want to use the following tags, which ensure that the browser applies some sort of emphasis to the text:

`<B>...</B> = bold`

`<I>...</I> = italic`

✓ Progress Check

If you can do the following, you've mastered this lesson:

❑ Make text bold by using the `<B>...</B>` tags.

❑ Italicize text by using the `<I>...</I>` tags.

❑ Describe how often you should (or should not) include text emphasis.

❑ Describe why you might want to use the alternate text emphasis tags, `<EM> ...</EM>` and `<STRONG>... </STRONG>`.

- <EM>...</EM> adds emphasis, usually as italics.
- <STRONG>...</STRONG> adds strong emphasis, usually as bold.

Recess

You're cooking now! You not only know how to enter tags, but you also know what some of the tags are. Time for a break, though. We're going to visit our rock garden and relax. (Have you ever noticed that waiting for rocks to sprout is even better than watching paint dry?) Next up, making lists (so that you can list the contents of your rock garden).

Making Lists   Lesson 4-4

So now you have a couple of headings, paragraphs below the headings, and some text emphasized within the paragraphs. In this lesson, you learn how to put information into both numbered and bulleted lists. *Numbered lists* are commonly used to list information (like instructions) that needs to be completed in a specific order. *Bulleted lists* are commonly used to list information that doesn't need to be in a specific order.

Putting information into lists, rather than just putting it into paragraphs, is an excellent way of helping your readers get through information. Would you rather read through several paragraphs of information or scan at a glance information in a bulleted list? We thought you'd vote for the latter, too. Also, making lists is a great way for you, the writer, to organize your information and provide easy-to-find links to other pages. (We get to links in Unit 5.)

on the test

You need to keep a few things in mind when making lists:

- Be sure to start each list item with the same part of speech — like a noun, verb, adjective, or gerund (those verbs with -ing endings). For the most part, the part of speech you use doesn't matter as long as you're consistent.

- Be sure to put the most important information first in case your readers don't read the entire list. If they're going to miss something, you want it to be the less important stuff.

- Be sure that the lists are not too long. Lists containing more than about seven items are often as hard to read as (gag!) long paragraphs.

To make bulleted lists, you have to do two things:

- Specify whether the list should be *ordered* (numbered), <OL>... </OL>, or *unordered* (bulleted), <UL>...</UL>

- Specify each line item, <LI>, which is a *non-paired tag*. A non-paired tag doesn't require a closing tag.

The following instructions show you how to make a bulleted list. (You complete the same steps for making a numbered list, but you use the <OL>...</OL> tags instead.) If you just completed Lessons 4-1 through 4-3, continue using the same document in WebEdit. If not, open the document called getajob4.htm in WebEdit.

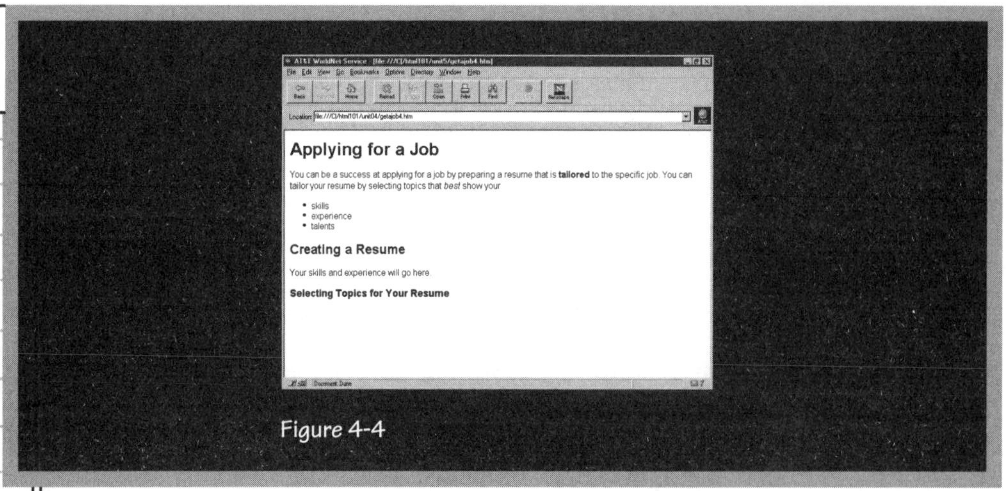

Figure 4-4: More fun than a shopping list!

Figure 4-4

Notes:

1 **Look at the paragraph under the first heading.**

```
<P>
You can be a success at applying for a job by
preparing a resume that is tailored to the specific
job. You can tailor your resume by selecting topics
that best show your skills, experience, and talents.
</P>
```

2 **Consider what information in that paragraph may be better presented by using a bulleted list.**

Hint: How about the last three words of the second sentence?

3 **Cut the three words you're going to put in a list (from *skills* to *talents*) and paste them on a blank line *after* the `</P>`. (Lists are *not* contained within paragraphs.)**

While you're at it, you might also make sure that you have a blank line or two above and below the list.

4 **Put each word on a line by itself and delete the punctuation.**

5 **Place your cursor before the word *experience* and press Enter. Place your cursor before the word *talents* and press Enter.**

You'll have something like this:

```
skills
experience
talents
```

6 **Specify that you want an unordered (bulleted) list by inserting the `<UL>...</UL>` tags above and below the list:**

```
<UL>
skills
experience
talents
</UL>
```

`<UL>...</UL> =`
`bulleted list`

Figure 4-5: Cool rules.

7 **Specify each line of the list by inserting the** `<LI>` **tag before each of the list items:**

```
<UL>
<LI>skills
<LI>experience
<LI>talents
</UL>
```

8 **Save your document.**

9 **Test your document in Netscape.**

You should have something that looks like Figure 4-4.

Using Horizontal Rules

Lesson 4-5

One last common HTML tag is the `<HR>` tag, which simply puts a *horizontal rule* — a line — across the page. Horizontal rules are another page element that you can get too carried away with. Limit how many rules you use on a page and use them only where they help readers find information or help readers wade through a long section of information.

The following steps show you how to insert a horizontal rule in your HTML document. If you've been working along in this unit, use the same document in WebEdit, which should be getting pretty crowded by now. If you're just joining in now, open getajob5.htm in WebEdit.

1 **Go down to the bottom of the document, right above the** `</BODY>` **tag.**

2 **Insert a space above the** `</BODY>` **tag.**

You're a pro at this by now.

3 **Enter the** `<HR>` **tag.**

4 **Save your document.**

5 **Test your document in Netscape.**

Your document should look something like Figure 4-5. Notice the rule at the bottom of the page. If, for whatever reason, your document doesn't look like the figures in this unit, check your code against the code provided in getajob6.htm.

Congratulations! You are now an official expert on some of the more common (and useful) HTML tags!

☑ **Progress Check**

If you can do the following, you've mastered this lesson:

❑ Use both `<OL>`... `</OL>` and `<UL>`... `</UL>` tags.

❑ Describe the difference between the `<OL>` and `<UL>` tags.

❑ Use `<LI>` tags.

❑ Define non-paired tag.

❑ List three ways to help make effective lists.

❑ Discuss when lists are more effective than paragraphs.

<HR> is a non-paired tag

☑ Progress Check

If you can do the following, you've mastered this lesson:

❑ Use the <HR> tag to create a horizontal rule.

❑ List two occasions when you might use a horizontal rule.

❑ Describe whether <HR> is a paired or non-paired tag.

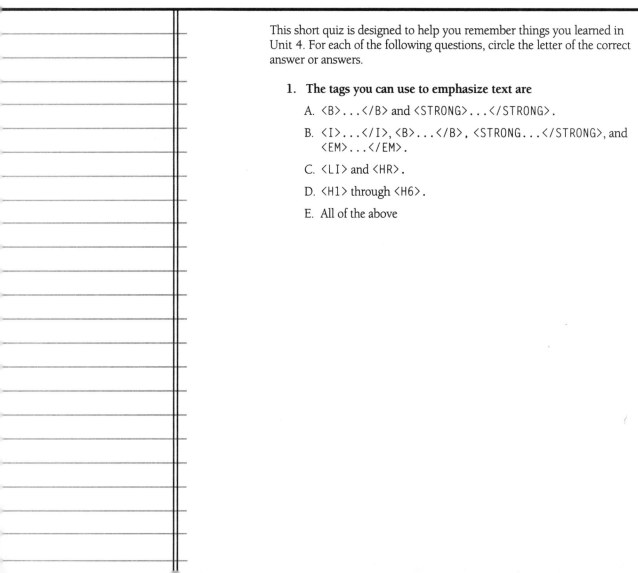

Figure 4-5

Unit 4 Quiz

This short quiz is designed to help you remember things you learned in Unit 4. For each of the following questions, circle the letter of the correct answer or answers.

1. **The tags you can use to emphasize text are**

    A. <B>...</B> and <STRONG>...</STRONG>.

    B. <I>...</I>, <B>...</B>, <STRONG...</STRONG>, and <EM>...</EM>.

    C. <LI> and <HR>.

    D. <H1> through <H6>.

    E. All of the above

Notes:

2. **The difference between paired and non-paired tags is that**

   A. Paired tags are married.

   B. Nonpaired tags aren't legal.

   C. Paired tags use both the opening and closing tags; nonpaired tags use only the opening tag.

   D. Nonpaired tags use both the opening and closing tags; paired tags use only the opening tag.

   E. There is no such thing as a nonpaired tag.

3. **Lists are sometimes better than paragraphs because**

   A. They provide at-a-glance information.

   B. They are easier to read.

   C. They can help you organize information.

   D. All of the above

   E. None of the above

4. **Some non-paired tags discussed in this unit are**

   A. `<H1>` and `<H6>`.

   B. `<OL>` and `<UL>`.

   C. `<LI>` and `<HR>`.

   D. `<OI>` and `<UI>`.

   E. `<P>` and `</P>`.

5. **The correct place to put boldface tags is**

   A. Directly before and after the text.

   B. Only before the text, because it's a non-paired tag.

   C. Only after the text, because it's a non-paired tag.

   D. Directly after the `</BODY>` tag.

   E. Boldface tags are inserted automatically wherever necessary.

6. **The processes for making ordered and unordered lists is the same except**

   A. You have to call in an ordered list, like you do a pizza for delivery.

   B. You don't use `<LI>` in ordered lists.

   C. You must choose what the bullet will look like.

   D. You have to use different tags to specify which type of list you want.

   E. The process is exactly the same.

7. **Which one of the following statements is true?**

   A. Headings can help group information.

   B. Headings can help ease online reading.

   C. You can create six levels of headings using HTML.

   D. `<H1>...</H1>` is the largest of the headings; `<H6>...</H6>` is the smallest.

   E. All of the above

Unit 4 Exercise

1. Create a short HTML biography or resume for yourself.
2. Save and test your document in Netscape.
3. Compare your Web page to the one in \html101\unit04.

   This document should include:

   ◗ All structure tags

   ◗ A first-level heading called "My Goals for the Year"

   ◗ A second-level heading about one of your goals

   ◗ A paragraph about that goal

   ◗ A list (either ordered or unordered)

   ◗ A few words that are emphasized

   ◗ A horizontal rule

Making Links and Anchors

Prerequisites

- Knowing about Hypertext (Unit 1)
- Being able to use WebEdit and Netscape (Unit 2)
- Being familiar with the basics of HTML (Unit 3 and Unit 4)

Objectives for This Unit

✓ Linking your document to other documents

✓ Linking your document to other Web sites

✓ Linking to specific places within documents

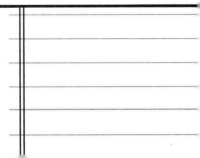

on the CD

- anchor.htm
- wood.htm
- oakstuff.htm
- trees.htm

Ahoy there! In this unit, you learn all about making links. A *link* is what connects one piece of information to another — it's the *hyper* part of HTML you learned about in Unit 1. You click a word or graphic and all of a sudden find that you've jumped to another specified part of a document entirely. Using HTML, you can link to information within the same HTML document, link to information in another HTML document, or link to information in another Web site.

To make these links, you use the *anchor tag*, ⟨A⟩...⟨/A⟩. The anchor tag has two purposes: It marks the word or graphic that you want to use as a link, and in some cases, it marks the word or graphic that you want information to link to. Lesson 5-1 introduces you to the anchor tag and shows you how to use it.

Along the way of learning how to make links by using anchors, you learn how to create links to other documents, other Web sites, and even to other places within your HTML document. Making links is one of the coolest things you can do using HTML, so park yourself in your seat and enjoy the ride!

anchors identify places from which or to which you can link

Making Links

Lesson 5-1

Making links is no different from making other cool effects with HTML — you simply apply tags to text. To make links, you use the anchor tags, ⟨A⟩...⟨/A⟩. The only difference between anchor tags and other tags you've learned so far is that instead of the tag making the text look different on your

Notes:

readers' browsers, the anchor tag allows readers to do something — link to other information.

- Link to other HTML documents on your computer
- Link to documents on the Web
- Link to specific locations within documents (instead of just linking to the document as a whole).

We discuss the how-tos of these link options in Lessons 5-2 through 5-5. For right now, you'll be learning terminology and the basics of making links.

To make a link, you have to do three things:

- Identify the text you want to use as a link to other information
- Indicate a link to some location
- Specify the address you're linking to

We take these items one at a time.

Applying the anchor tag

The anchor tag, `<A>...</A>`, is applied just like any other paired tag, with the opening tag at the beginning of the text it affects and the closing tag (the one with the /) at the end. The following example shows you how anchor tags set off the words that will eventually be links. Don't type now — you'll practice these tags throughout the rest of the unit. Kick back, put your feet up, and read along.

```
<UL>
<LI><A>skills</A>
<LI><A>experience</A>
<LI><A>talents</A>
</UL>
```

Pretty basic stuff — but you're not done. Anchor tags don't do anything alone — it's kind of like Fred Astaire without Ginger Rogers, peanut butter without jelly, or liver without onions (yuck!). Anchor tags must have an attribute with them.

Adding an attribute

After you mark your anchor text, you include an attribute, which in this case, indicates that the anchor is going to link to somewhere. An *attribute* is part of an HTML tag that specifies additional information — in this case, where the anchor links to. You use two main attributes with anchor tags:

- `HREF=` lets you jump from somewhere in one document to another location in the same document, another document, or another Web site. To do this, you need to include the location you want to jump to in the anchor you are jumping from. Doing so is easier than it sounds.

HREF= goes where
the reader jumps
from

◆ NAME= lets you specify a target within a document to which you can link. To do this, you not only need to specify the HREF= attribute with the anchor you're linking from, but you also need to provide an additional anchor tag with the NAME= attribute to identify the anchor you're linking to.

The attributes will fit in the initial anchor tag as shown in the following example. For now, just read through the example; you'll have plenty of opportunity to practice adding the anchor tags and attributes later in this unit.

```
<UL>
<LI><A HREF="???">skills</A>
<LI><A HREF="???">experience</A>
<LI><A HREF="???">talents</A>
</UL>
```

You'll learn what goes in the "???" part in the next section.

So far, so good — but you're still not done. You've indicated that the anchor is going to link somewhere, but you still need to indicate *where* the link goes.

Specifying the address

After you mark the anchor and include the necessary attribute, you have to specify the address you want to link to. Specifying a link is kind of like writing a letter — you have to write the letter, put it in an envelope, and stick an address on it. If you don't use an address, the letter won't be delivered anywhere.

When you create links, you can apply the anchor tag and put in an attribute, but if you don't specify an address, your link won't work. (Obviously, there has to be something at that address. In this case, you'll have to make sure that a document exists. More about this in Lesson 5-4.)

The addresses you use with HTML are called URLs. *URL* stands for Uniform Resource Locator and is pronounced either "You-are-ell" or "Earl." (We'll go with "You-are-ell" throughout this book.) A URL is simply an address on the Internet.

URLs can be either absolute or relative, depending on how much information you need to provide. Say what? For example, you'd probably give really detailed directions to your house to someone who has never visited your town. On the other hand, you might give someone only partial directions if he or she is already familiar with the area. That is, you'd tell Aunt Mabel whom you haven't seen in ten years to go to your city, your street, and then your house. But someone from the same vicinity wouldn't need the city, and your neighbor wouldn't need the city or the street. Just give the necessary information.

URLs are very similar to these directions — *absolute* (complete) or *relative* (partial). If you're creating a document that you want to publish on the Internet, you give out the absolute URL so that anyone, anywhere in the world, can find the page. On the other hand, if you're creating links to other files within the same folder (or directory), you may include only a relative URL because you're already in the right area.

NAME= goes somewhere in document and indicates where a reader's jump will end

place the attribute in initial tag only

URL = address on Internet

absolute URL = complete address

relative URL = partial address

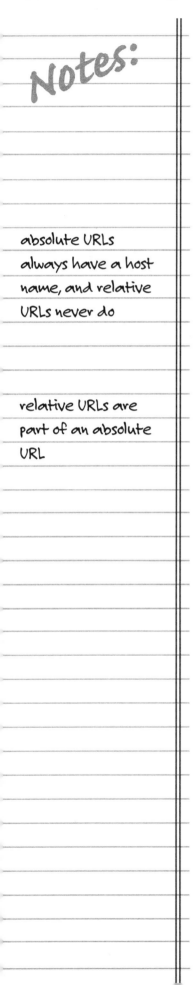

So what do these URLs look like? They're kind of funny looking if you're not familiar with them. Here's the breakdown of an absolute URL for a fictitious university.

```
http://www.gostate.edu/teams/winning.htm
```

The `http://` is called the *protocol indicator,* which tells the server how to send the information. For example, you could send a package overnight to your Aunt Flo by using any number of overnight delivery services. Well, the Internet can use any number of protocols to send information from one computer to another. `Http://` just happens to be the protocol used by Web servers and browsers that allows them to talk to each other. If you're creating Web pages, people point to them using `http://` + something.

The `www.gostate.edu` is the name (address) of the host computer that holds the document. Remember that when you publish an HTML document, you really place it on a computer that holds it until someone calls up the document's URL. This computer has an address that is common to all documents it stores. It "hosts" all of these documents for people to access.

The `teams` part is the directory name. You may not have to show a directory name at all, or you may have several, representing directories inside of directories inside of directories (or folders inside of folders inside of folders).

The `winning.htm` part is the actual name of the file located on the host computer. Sometimes you won't have to give a filename — the server will just give out the default file in the directory.

Table 5-1 provides examples of absolute and relative URLs. Absolute URLs always have a host name. Relative URLs never do.

Table 5-1   Samples of URLs (Uniform Resource Locators)

Absolute URL Samples	*Relative URL Samples*
`http://www.gostate.edu/teams/losing.htm`	`/teams/losing.htm`
`http://www.yahoo.com/`	`search.htm`
`http://idgbooks.com/`	`html101/books/`

Now that you know about URLs and that they are used in links to point people to a specific place, you need to know how to include a URL in the link. To add the URL to the attribute, you insert the URL in place of the `"???"`, as we did in this example:

```
<UL>
<LI><A HREF="documentname.htm">skills</A>
<LI><A HREF="folder/documentname.htm">experience</A>
<LI><A HREF="http://www.idgbooks.com/">talents</A>
</UL>
```

heads up

The quotation marks are essential for your links to work.

Try making links by using the following steps:

1 **In WebEdit, open anchor.htm.**

2 **Add the anchor tags, `<A>...</A>`, around each word in the list.**

```
<UL>
<LI><A>Management Experience</A>
<LI><A>Writing Experience</A>
<LI><A>Design Experience</A>
</UL>
```

remember to add tags in pairs

3 **Add the `HREF=` attribute inside the initial anchor tag.**

```
<UL>
<LI><A HREF= >Management Experience</A>
<LI><A HREF= >Writing Experience</A>
<LI><A HREF= >Design Experience</A>
</UL>
```

remember to use quotation marks around the URL

4 **Add URLs (mgmt.htm, write.htm, design.htm) to the `HREF=` attributes.**

```
<UL>
<LI><A HREF="mgmt.htm">Management Experience</A>
<LI><A HREF="write.htm">Writing Experience</A>
<LI><A HREF="design.htm">Design Experience</A>
</UL>
```

It looks like the URLs — `mgmt.htm`, `write.htm`, and `design.htm` — are completely arbitrary. They are. We made them up. Actually, we read ahead and know that these examples will work, so we used them.

5 **Save the document.**

6 **Take a look at your document so far in Netscape.**

Although you put in the anchors and attributes to make a link, you haven't actually linked these to anything yet. (For example, mgmt.htm is not yet an actual document to link to.) Therefore, the links won't work. You'll learn how to make the links work in the next lessons in this unit.

Your document should look like Figure 5-1. Double-check your HTML code, if your document doesn't look right. When you're done, close this file — you'll be using a new file in the next lesson.

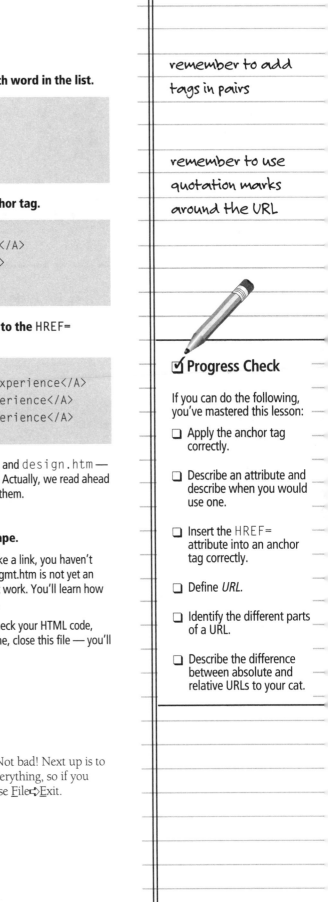

☑ Progress Check

If you can do the following, you've mastered this lesson:

❑ Apply the anchor tag correctly.

❑ Describe an attribute and describe when you would use one.

❑ Insert the `HREF=` attribute into an anchor tag correctly.

❑ Define *URL*.

❑ Identify the different parts of a URL.

❑ Describe the difference between absolute and relative URLs to your cat.

Recess

Whew! Break time. You've now put in your first links. Not bad! Next up is to get into a little more detail on the links. You've saved everything, so if you need to exit and come back later, feel free. Simply choose File➪Exit.

Figure 5-1: Your new links should look like this example. (You'll see color and probably underlines on your screen where we have only underlines here in the picture.)

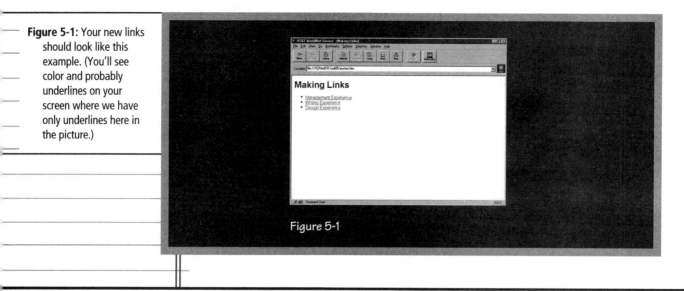

Figure 5-1

Lesson 5-2

Linking to Another HTML Document

Notes:

In Lesson 5-1, you learned all about using anchors and attributes to make links. In this lesson, you learn how to actually link your document to another HTML document. The process is no different from the one you tried out in Lesson 5-1, but this time you link to an actual document.

on the CD

1 **Open wood.htm in WebEdit.**

2 **Also open oakstuff.htm.**

3 **Switch to wood.htm by clicking the gray tab labeled** wood.html **toward the upper left of the screen.**

4 **Add the anchor tags, <A>...</A>, to the word** Oak:

```
<UL>
<LI><A>Oak</A>
<LI>Maple
<LI>Pine
</UL>
```

5 **Add the** HREF= **attribute to the anchor tag:**

```
<UL>
<LI><A HREF= >Oak</A>
<LI>Maple
<LI>Pine
</UL>
```

6 **Add the URL of the second document you opened, oakstuff.htm, to the** HREF= **attribute:**

```
<UL>
<LI><A HREF="oakstuff.htm">Oak</A>
<LI>Maple
<LI>Pine
</UL>
```

don't forget to include quotes (" ") around the URL

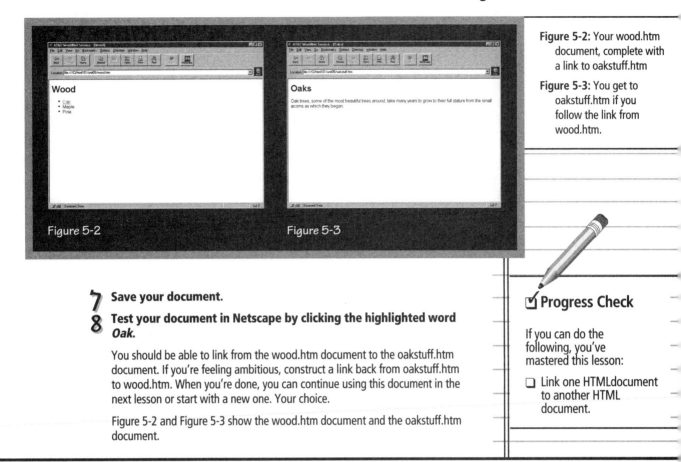

Figure 5-2: Your wood.htm document, complete with a link to oakstuff.htm

Figure 5-3: You get to oakstuff.htm if you follow the link from wood.htm.

Figure 5-2   Figure 5-3

7 **Save your document.**

8 **Test your document in Netscape by clicking the highlighted word *Oak*.**

You should be able to link from the wood.htm document to the oakstuff.htm document. If you're feeling ambitious, construct a link back from oakstuff.htm to wood.htm. When you're done, you can continue using this document in the next lesson or start with a new one. Your choice.

Figure 5-2 and Figure 5-3 show the wood.htm document and the oakstuff.htm document.

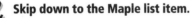

☑ Progress Check

If you can do the following, you've mastered this lesson:

❏ Link one HTMLdocument to another HTML document.

Linking to Another Web Site

Lesson 5-3

You learned how to link to another HTML document. In this lesson, you're going to apply the same steps and learn how to link to another Web site. Before you dive in, be sure that you've reopened WebEdit and Netscape, if necessary.

on the CD

1 **Make sure that the document wood.htm is open in WebEdit.**

If you want to start with a clean slate, open wood2.htm instead of continuing from the previous lesson. If you start with wood2.htm, save it as wood.htm so you continue working with the same filenames throughout the lesson.

You may need to click the gray tab marked `wood.htm` to bring that document to the top.

2 **Skip down to the Maple list item.**

3 **Add anchor tags, `<A>...</A>`, around the word *Maple*:**

```
<UL>
<LI><A HREF="oakstuff.htm">Oak</A>
<LI><A>Maple</A>
<LI>Pine
</UL>
```

Figure 5-4: This figure shows your wood.htm document, now with two links in it.

Figure 5-5: If your maple link works, you'll get to this site.

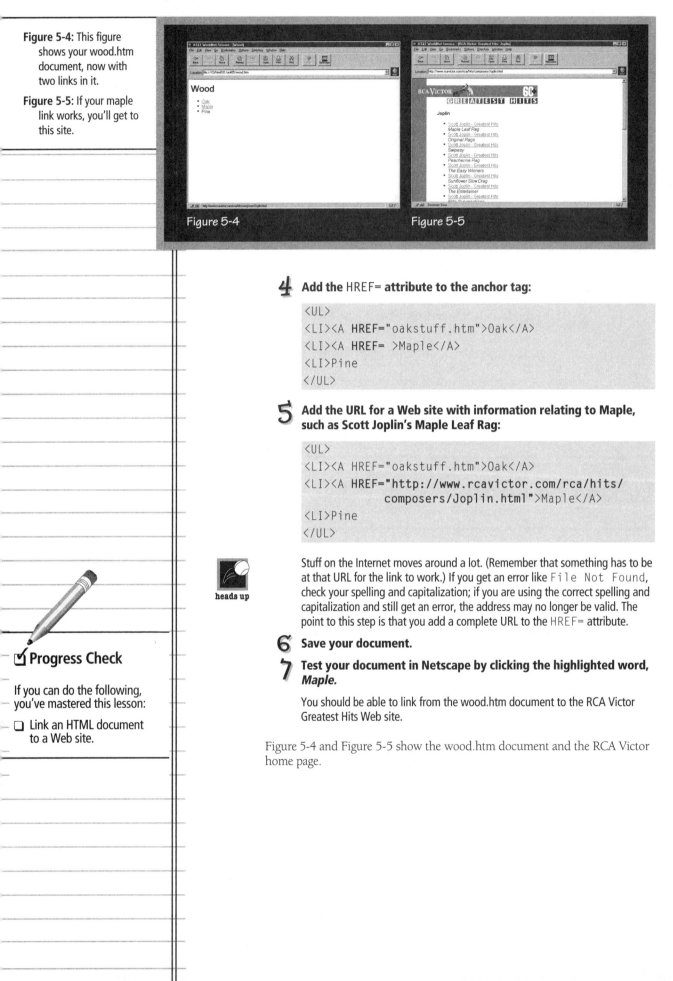

Figure 5-4   Figure 5-5

4 **Add the HREF= attribute to the anchor tag:**

```
<UL>
<LI><A HREF="oakstuff.htm">Oak</A>
<LI><A HREF= >Maple</A>
<LI>Pine
</UL>
```

5 **Add the URL for a Web site with information relating to Maple, such as Scott Joplin's Maple Leaf Rag:**

```
<UL>
<LI><A HREF="oakstuff.htm">Oak</A>
<LI><A HREF="http://www.rcavictor.com/rca/hits/
            composers/Joplin.html">Maple</A>
<LI>Pine
</UL>
```

heads up

Stuff on the Internet moves around a lot. (Remember that something has to be at that URL for the link to work.) If you get an error like `File Not Found`, check your spelling and capitalization; if you are using the correct spelling and capitalization and still get an error, the address may no longer be valid. The point to this step is that you add a complete URL to the `HREF=` attribute.

6 **Save your document.**

7 **Test your document in Netscape by clicking the highlighted word, Maple.**

You should be able to link from the wood.htm document to the RCA Victor Greatest Hits Web site.

Figure 5-4 and Figure 5-5 show the wood.htm document and the RCA Victor home page.

✓ **Progress Check**

If you can do the following, you've mastered this lesson:

❏ Link an HTML document to a Web site.

Linking to Specific Locations within Documents

Lesson 5-4

In the last two lessons, you learned how to link your document to other HTML documents and to other Web sites. In this lesson, you learn how to make a link from one place in an HTML document to another place in an HTML document.

So far, you've been using the HREF= attribute. In this lesson, you use the NAME= attribute that we introduced at the beginning of the unit. The NAME= attribute helps you to link to a specific location within a document — either the same document or another document entirely. If you're linking to a specific place within a document, you need to do two things:

- ◗ Use the HREF= attribute to mark the place you're linking from, as you've been doing so far.
- ◗ Use the NAME= attribute to mark the specific place you're linking to. If the place you're linking to isn't marked, the link won't work.

You use the NAME= attribute in the same way you use the HREF= attribute, including it in the initial anchor tag. The following steps show you how to insert a NAME= anchor and how to link to it.

on the CD

1 **Open the document called trees.htm. If you are not continuing from the preceding lesson, you need to open wood3.htm and resave it under the name wood.htm.**

2 **Make sure that the document trees.htm is on top because that's the one you'll be working with first.**

Click the gray tab marked `trees.htm`, if necessary.

3 **Skip down to the second level heading with *Pine* in it and find the *Pine* in the next line.**

4 **Add anchor tags, `<A>...</A>`, around the word Pine:**

```
<H2>Pine</H2>
<A>Pine</A> trees also provide good wood for a
        variety of purposes.
```

5 **Add the NAME= attribute to the initial anchor tag:**

```
<H2>Pine</H2>
<A NAME= >Pine</A> trees also provide good wood for
        a variety of purposes.
```

6 **Add the name for the NAME= attribute.**

```
<H2>Pine</H2>
<A NAME="pine">Pine</A> trees also provide good
        wood for a variety of purposes.
```

All you're doing here is giving a name to a random point in the document. The random point happens to be the word *Pine*, so go ahead and add *pine* to the NAME= attribute.

on the CD

7 **Switch to your second document, wood.htm.**

Click the gray tab marked `wood.htm`.

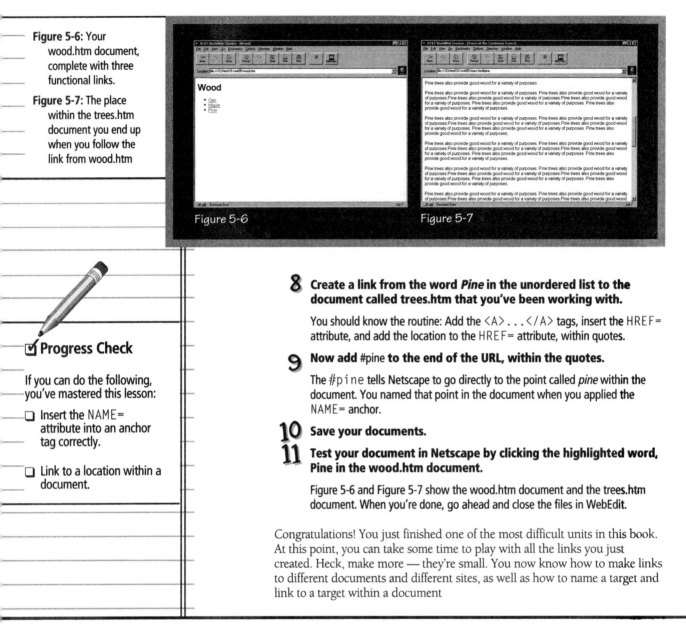

Figure 5-6: Your wood.htm document, complete with three functional links.

Figure 5-7: The place within the trees.htm document you end up when you follow the link from wood.htm

Figure 5-6   Figure 5-7

✏️ **Progress Check**

If you can do the following, you've mastered this lesson:

❑ Insert the NAME= attribute into an anchor tag correctly.

❑ Link to a location within a document.

---

8 **Create a link from the word *Pine* in the unordered list to the document called trees.htm that you've been working with.**

You should know the routine: Add the ⟨A⟩...⟨/A⟩ tags, insert the HREF= attribute, and add the location to the HREF= attribute, within quotes.

9 **Now add #pine to the end of the URL, within the quotes.**

The #pine tells Netscape to go directly to the point called *pine* within the document. You named that point in the document when you applied the NAME= anchor.

10 **Save your documents.**

11 **Test your document in Netscape by clicking the highlighted word, Pine in the wood.htm document.**

Figure 5-6 and Figure 5-7 show the wood.htm document and the trees.htm document. When you're done, go ahead and close the files in WebEdit.

Congratulations! You just finished one of the most difficult units in this book. At this point, you can take some time to play with all the links you just created. Heck, make more — they're small. You now know how to make links to different documents and different sites, as well as how to name a target and link to a target within a document

---

Unit 5 Quiz

This short quiz is designed to help you remember things you learned in Unit 5. For each of the following questions, circle the letter of the correct answer or answers.

1. **An anchor tag is**

   A. A large iron object you throw in the water.

   B. One of those scratchy tags in the back of your shirt.

   C. An HTML tag that is the basis for creating links.

   D. An HTML tag that anchors the information so you can't link to or from it.

   E. The thing you insert your seat belt into in the car.

2. **An attribute is**

   A. A peculiarity of HTML.

   B. The gray tabs in WebEdit that arrange your open documents.

   C. An HTML tag that is the basis for creating links.

   D. Part of an HTML tag that specifies additional information.

   E. The heavy things that hang at the bottom of a cuckoo clock.

3. **You can use anchors and attributes to**

   A. Link to other HTML documents in the same folder or directory.

   B. Link to documents on the Web.

   C. Link to specific locations within documents.

   D. All of the above.

   E. Only A and B.

4. **Anchor tags must be used with**

   A. Only ADDRESS= attributes.

   B. Anything except paired tags.

   C. Attributes.

   D. Ships and boats.

   E. Cars and trucks.

5. **The HREF= attribute is used to**

   A. Create links within the same document.

   B. Create links only to other documents and Web sites.

   C. Referee hockey games.

   D. Create links to heading tags only.

   E. None of the above.

6. **The NAME= attribute is used to**

   A. Identify a specific place within a document so links can point to it.

   B. Create links to other documents and Web sites.

   C. Name documents.

   D. Create links to title tags only.

   E. None of the above.

7. **When linking to a specific place within a document, you have to do which two things?**

   A. Use <TITLE>...</TITLE> tags and the NAME= attribute.

   B. Verify that everything in your document is spelled correctly and run a grammar check.

   C. Use the <BODY>...</BODY> tags and the NAME= anchor.

   D. Use the NAME= attribute to mark the place within the document and use the HREF= attribute to make a link to link from.

   E. Use the HREF= attribute to mark the place within the document and use the NAME= attribute to make a link to link from.

Notes:

Unit 5 Exercise

1. Use WebEdit to open the two documents from your html101\ unit05 folder called link1.htm and link2.htm.

2. Create a link from the link1.htm document to link2.htm.

3. Create a link from the link2.htm document to link1.htm.

4. Test your documents and links in Netscape.

Unit 3 Summary

- **Tagging:** Tagging refers to labeling different parts of your document by putting `<TAG>`tags `</TAG>` around them.

- **Nesting tags:** Nesting tags refers to doubling up on tags by putting `<TAG><ANOTHER>`multiple tags`</ANOTHER></TAG>` around text. Remember, the first tag you open should be the last tag you close, as in the preceding example.

- **Structure tags:** HTML requires certain structure tags so that it knows what's going on. You have `<HTML>` around the whole document, `<HEAD>` around about-this-document-type information, `<BODY>` around the visible part of the document, and finally `<TITLE>` within the `<HEAD>...</HEAD>` tags.

Unit 4 Summary

- **Headings:** HTML allows you to label lines of text as headings. The headings are a different size than the regular text. Generally, you use mostly `<H1>`heading 1`</H1>`, `<H2>`heading 2`</H2>`, and `<H3>`heading 3`</H3>`, but you may occasionly use the fourth, fifth, and sixth level headings.

- **Paragraphs:** Regular text within your HTML document needs to be labeled as a paragraph. You do this with `<P>`paragraph`</P>` tags.

- **Emphasizing text:** You can use `<B>`boldface`</B>`, `<I>`italics`</I>`, `<STRONG>`strong emphasis`</STRONG>`, or `<EM>`emphasis`</EM>` to make select words stand out from the rest of the text. Don't overdo it, though, or nothing will stand out.

- **Lists:** People can find information much more easily if you break it up into bulleted lists (`<UL>`unordered lists`</UL>`) for material that can go in any order. If you have a sequence of steps, like instructions, use a numbered list (`<OL>`ordered list`</OL>`). Each item within each list must be labeled as a `<LI>`line item. Note that `<LI>` tags are not paired, so you only use one for each item — no closing tags here.

- **Horizontal rules:** HTML allows you to draw a line across the screen to visually make a break between sections of your document. You use a horizontal rule (`<HR>`) to do this. `<HR>` is also an unpaired tag. If you put in two tags, you get two rules.

Unit 5 Summary

- **Anchors:** Anchors are the basis for making links and are used like any other paired tag, `<A> . . . </A>`. You can use anchors to link to other HTML documents, link to documents on the Web, and link to specific locations within documents.

- **Links:** A link is the actual connection to a different piece of information. Making a link has three steps: apply the anchor tag, add an attribute, and specify the address you want to link to.

- **Attributes:** Attributes are part of an HTML tag that specifies additional information. When used to make links, attributes are used in conjunction with the anchor tags, `<A> . . . </A>`. Attributes are only included in the initial tag. The attribute used for making links is the `HREF=` attribute, and the attribute used to mark a location within an HTML document is the `NAME=` attribute.

- **URLs:** URLs are Uniform Resource Locators and are addresses on the Internet. URLs can be absolute (complete) or relative (partial). Absolute URLs contain a protocol indicator, the host name, a directory name, and filenames. Relative URLs can contain include any part but the protocol indicator and host name. URL can be pronounced either as You-Are-Ell or like old Uncle Earl.

Part II Test

The questions on this test cover all the material from Part 2, Units 3 through 5. Good luck!

True False

Each statement is either true or false.

T F 1. Nesting is what you do to make "hot spots" in Web pages.

T F 2. Of the four structure tags discussed, only the `<HEAD>` tag can be seen in the actual document.

T F 3. Tags can be either paired or nonpaired.

T F 4. Anchors do not necessarily need to be used with attributes.

T F 5. Attributes do not need to be associated with a tag.

T F 6. Absolute URLs are complete addresses.

T F 7. Two nonpaired tags discussed in this part are the `<LI>` and the `<HR>`.

T F 8. Lists must be contained within the `<P> . . . </P>` tags.

T F 9. The following is an example of nesting tags correctly: `<B><I>Birds</B> </I>`.

T F 10. The `<HTML> . . . </HTML>` tags tell the browser that the document is an HTML document.

Multiple Choice

For each of the following questions, circle the correct answer or answers. Remember, you may find more than one answer for each question.

11. The `<A> . . . </A>` tag

A. Stands for "abandon," as in "abandon this document and link to another."

B. Is the tag associated with making links.

C. Is used only if you're linking to documents on the Web.

D. Must be used in the document you're linking from as well as in the document you're linking to.

12. The `HREF=` attribute

A. Is used for linking to other HTML documents or Web sites.

B. Is used for linking to a specific place within a document or Web site.

C. Is not used for making links.

D. Is used only as a reference to words beginning with "H."

13. When making lists, you should

A. Be sure to start each list item with the same part of speech.

B. Be sure to start the list with the most important information.

C. Be sure that the lists are no more than about seven items.

D. All of the above

14. Headings make online reading easier by

A. Dividing information into major points and subpoints.

B. Putting information into smaller chunks that are easier to read.

C. Both A and B

D. Headings don't make online reading easier.

Part II Test

15. To test links in Netscape, you

    A. Must upload your documents onto a server.

    B. Save changes in WebEdit and load (or reload) the documents in Netscape.

    C. Push the Test button on the Toolbar in Netscape.

    D. Use e-mail to send the files to beta-testers.

16. When the authors took a break in Unit 5, they

    A. Made a pot of coffee.

    B. Did laundry and ate lunch.

    C. Took a smooch break.

    D. Rushed to the bookstore to buy the *HTML For Dummies Quick Reference* (published by IDG Books Worldwide) so we'd know what to do next.

17. When identifying the location you're going to link to, you have to include

    A. Parentheses around the filename.

    B. Pointed brackets around the filename.

    C. Equal signs (=) around the filename.

    D. Quotation marks around the filename.

18. When using tags, you place the text

    A. Between the two paired tags.

    B. Only after nonpaired tags.

    C. Either before or after nonpaired tags, depending on the tag.

    D. Both A and C

19. Emphasizing text should be done

    A. Frequently, because it helps ease online reading.

    B. Frequently, because it's cool.

    C. Infrequently, because too much emphasis defeats the purpose of emphasizing.

    D. Infrequently, because the tags are monotonous to enter.

20. Match the tags and attributes in the left column to the effects in the right column. Note that more choices are in the right column than in the left.

A. `<B>...</B>`

B. `<I>...</I>`

C. `HREF=`

D. `<UL>... </UL>`

E. `<TITLE>... </TITLE>`

F. `NAME=`

G. `<LI>`

H. `<HR>`

I. `<OL>... </OL>`

J. `<A>...</A>`

1. Indicates a document heading.

2. Indicates a line item.

3. Indicates a numbered list.

4. Indicates a bulleted list.

5. Indicates a horizontal rule.

6. Used for linking to another document or Web site.

7. Used for linking to a specific place within a document.

8. Marks an anchor.

9. Is one of the structure tags.

10. Makes text bold.

11. Makes text italicized.

12. Indicates a document title.

13. Makes a horizontal rule.

14. Changes the look of bullets.

Part II Lab Assignment

This is the second of your lab assignments. If you can handle this one, you can do the rest without problems. Part II is one of the most challenging in the book.

In this lab assignment, you're going to start creating your very own Web site. You need to decide on a topic for your Web site and whether you want to create a personal site or a site for a company.

To start with, pick out two topics that you want to include in your Web site. For example, you might choose to profile your company or a product, or even provide a page about your hobby. Pick two topics that (A) you're comfortable with and that (B) you're planning to include in the Web site.

The following steps will indicate what HTML elements these pages need to contain.

Step 1: Start the HTML documents

Start the two HTML documents and be sure to include all the necessary structure tags. Save them as separate files in the same folder.

Step 2: Compose document #1

In this document, include all the information about, well, topic #1. This document should contain a nice balance of headings, lists, paragraphs, horizontal rules, and text emphases. Also, include at least one link to the second document.

Step 3: Compose document #2

In this document, include all the information you want to include about topic #2. Again, use headings, lists, paragraphs, horizontal rules, and text emphasis, and include at least one link back to the first document.

Step 4: Save and test your documents

Well, do it!

This step should be pretty familiar by now. No problem, we hope.

Part II Lab Assignment

Step 5: Ask yourself some questions

- Does the link or links work?
- Do the headings add emphasis, or are they too overbearing?
- Are the lists purposefully used?
- Are the paragraphs short enough, or are they seas of text?
- Is the text emphasis used sparingly?
- Are the documents free from typos and proofreading errors?

Step 6: Pat yourself on the back

If you can reach back there, that is. . . .

In this part . . .

The first two parts of this book took you through the basics of HTML and tagging. Now that you're (hopefully) feeling comfortable with that stuff, it's time to temporarily derail your train of thought. This part, at least at the beginning, moves away from HTML *per se* and shows you how to use graphics in Web pages. Using a way-cool graphics program called Paint Shop Pro, you learn how to make your own graphics as well as how to adapt existing graphics for use on the Web.

Creating your own graphics isn't as daunting as it might sound — it can actually be pretty fun. Most of the really fancy home pages you see on the Internet rely heavily on graphics, which somebody had to create.

By the way, if you're inclined to venture out on your own, you'll be amazed at the things you can do with Paint Shop Pro and a little time. You can kill off hours and hours of spare time in the quest for that perfect graphic or effect.

Back to the topic though, Part III shows you how to use graphics effectively in your HTML documents. In the next four units, you learn how to use your graphics program, how to develop graphics and link them into your HTML documents, and how to use imagemaps (those cool clickable images). These units even contain some tips and tricks to help you make your graphics and images the best they can be.

Using Your Graphics Program

Objectives for This Unit

✓ Getting familiar with Paint Shop Pro

✓ Opening, saving, and changing graphics

✓ Creating new graphics

✓ Viewing graphics in Netscape

Prerequisites

▶ Installing Paint Shop Pro, if by chance you haven't already (See instructions in Appendix B.)

▶ Having a working knowledge of Windows — either 3.x or 95 (Where possible, we provide this type of information in the margin notes to help you out.)

on the CD
▶ sample.pcx
▶ trans.gif

To this point, you've learned skills that let you create effective Web pages — entering tags and text, nesting tags, using tags to help readers easily read your documents, just to name a few. The tags and attributes discussed so far are very useful in creating solid, usable pages. Starting with this unit, you'll learn skills that will make your Web pages explode with excitement — well, OK, maybe not explode with excitement . . . but they can certainly show your personality and creativity.

Specifically, in this unit, you'll become familiar with your graphics program, Paint Shop Pro. You can use Paint Shop Pro to create and modify graphics for use in your HTML documents. Using graphics — such as photos, sketches, icons, or artwork — is one of the easiest and most effective ways of making your HTML documents more interesting and eye-catching when viewed in browsers.

For example, would you rather look through a book that has absolutely no pictures and is just a mass of solid text, or would you rather look through a book that has many interesting, colorful pictures that show, rather than describe, a concept? We'd vote for the one with pictures. Web pages are very similar. Ones that offer a mix of nifty graphics and accompanying text are much easier and more fun to read, and offering a good mix of text and graphics is an excellent way to help ensure that your Web pages will be read and revisited, rather than skipped over.

Lesson 6-1

Starting Paint Shop Pro

Notes:

In this lesson, you get acquainted with Paint Shop Pro, the software you'll use to work with graphics. This lesson shows you how to start Paint Shop Pro and clues you in to a few of its features. In no time at all, you'll be comfortable with the software so that you can start using it to create nifty graphics for your HTML documents.

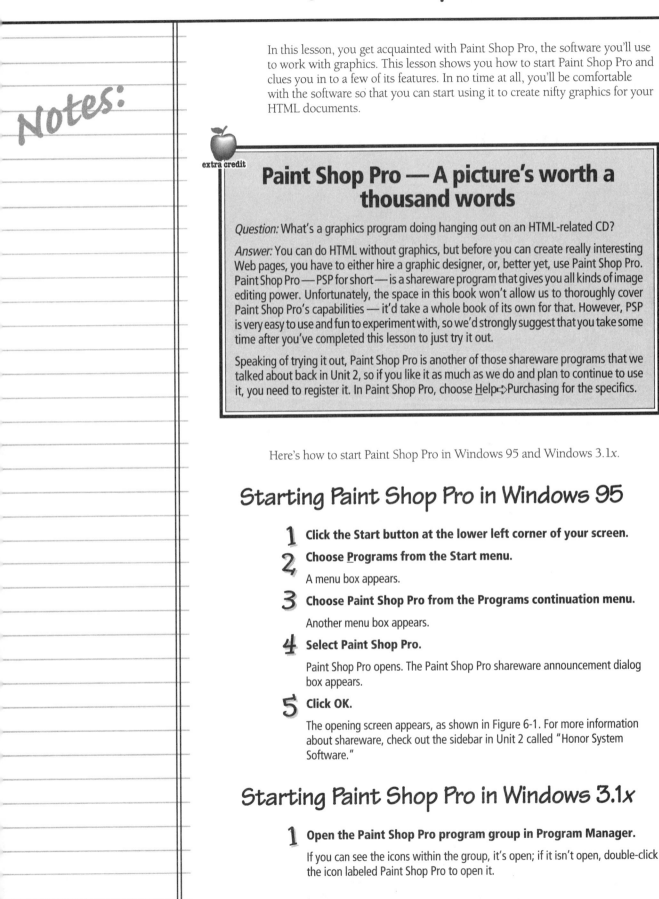

extra credit

Paint Shop Pro — A picture's worth a thousand words

Question: What's a graphics program doing hanging out on an HTML-related CD?

Answer: You can do HTML without graphics, but before you can create really interesting Web pages, you have to either hire a graphic designer, or, better yet, use Paint Shop Pro. Paint Shop Pro — PSP for short — is a shareware program that gives you all kinds of image editing power. Unfortunately, the space in this book won't allow us to thoroughly cover Paint Shop Pro's capabilities — it'd take a whole book of its own for that. However, PSP is very easy to use and fun to experiment with, so we'd strongly suggest that you take some time after you've completed this lesson to just try it out.

Speaking of trying it out, Paint Shop Pro is another of those shareware programs that we talked about back in Unit 2, so if you like it as much as we do and plan to continue to use it, you need to register it. In Paint Shop Pro, choose Help⇨Purchasing for the specifics.

Here's how to start Paint Shop Pro in Windows 95 and Windows 3.1*x*.

Starting Paint Shop Pro in Windows 95

1 Click the Start button at the lower left corner of your screen.

2 Choose Programs from the Start menu.

A menu box appears.

3 Choose Paint Shop Pro from the Programs continuation menu.

Another menu box appears.

4 Select Paint Shop Pro.

Paint Shop Pro opens. The Paint Shop Pro shareware announcement dialog box appears.

5 Click OK.

The opening screen appears, as shown in Figure 6-1. For more information about shareware, check out the sidebar in Unit 2 called "Honor System Software."

Starting Paint Shop Pro in Windows 3.1*x*

1 Open the Paint Shop Pro program group in Program Manager.

If you can see the icons within the group, it's open; if it isn't open, double-click the icon labeled Paint Shop Pro to open it.

2 **Double-click the Paint Shop Pro icon.**

Paint Shop Pro opens. The Paint Shop Pro shareware announcement dialog box appears.

3 **Click OK.**

The opening screen appears, as shown in Figure 6-1. For more information about shareware, check out the sidebar at the beginning of this lesson.

Finding your way around Paint Shop Pro

Paint Shop Pro provides several menu options and choices, several of which you'll use to create and modify graphics for your HTML documents. Figure 6-1 shows the Paint Shop Pro opening screen, and Table 6-1 gives you an overview of Paint Shop Pro features.

The first thing to do is to make sure the Select Toolbox and the Paint Toolbox are open.

If these two toolboxes are not visible, choose View in the menubar and look at the five toolbox options at the bottom of the drop-down box. Select Toolbox and Paint Toolbox should have check marks next to them, as shown in Figure 6-1. If they don't, click your mouse on the Select Toolbox. Then Choose View and select the Paint Toolbox. Also, make sure that the Toolbar option is still checked.

You can move these toolboxes around on your screen to move them out of your way. All you do is click (and hold) the blue bar at the top of the toolbox and drag the toolbox to where you want it.

See, graphics aren't so complicated. Okay, here we go!

Table 6-1	The Paint Shop Pro Main Screen
Part of Screen	**What It Does**
Title bar	Shows you the title of the graphic you're working on
Minimize, Restore, Close buttons	Let you minimize, restore (changes between full screen and partial screen), and close the window
Menubar	Lets you choose menus that offer access to all Paint Shop Pro functions
Toolbar	Gives you shortcut options to some basic Paint Shop Pro functions
Workspace	Provides space for you to view and work with graphics files
Statusbar	Provides information about the document, like graphic size and color depth, as well as where your cursor is in the document
Select Toolbox	Provides you with a variety of tools you can use to change pieces of your graphics
Paint Toolbox	Contains a variety of tools to modify your graphics, such as adding shapes, filling shapes with a color, and drawing lines

☑ Progress Check

If you can do the following, you've mastered this lesson:

❑ Start Paint Shop Pro.

❑ Describe Paint Shop Pro features.

Figure 6-1: Choosing the Select Toolbox and Paint Toolbox from the View menu.

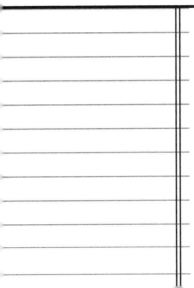

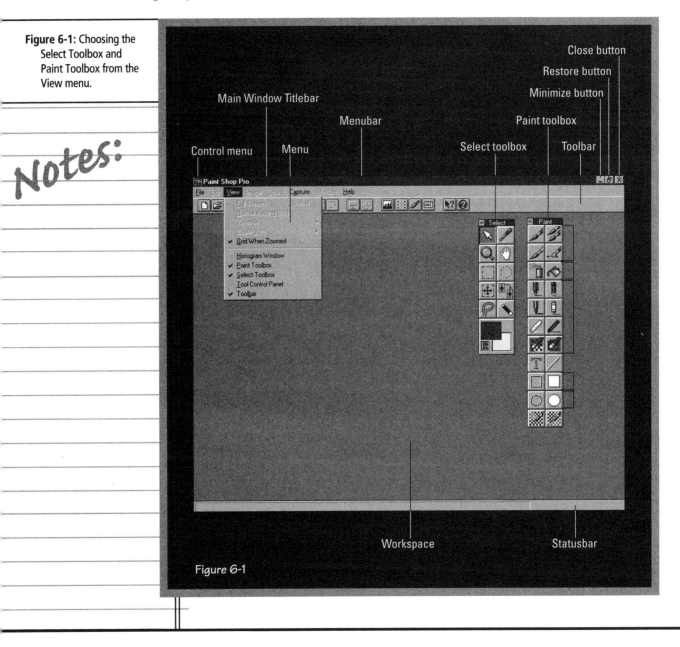

Figure 6-1

Lesson 6-2   Saving Graphics in Paint Shop Pro

In this lesson, you learn how to save graphics. Saving graphics is very similar to saving HTML documents, but you should pay attention to a few things.

Graphics that you're going to include in HTML documents must be saved in one of two formats:

- GIF (*.GIF) — pronounced like *Jif*, the peanut butter
- JPG (*.JPG) — pronounced *jay-peg*

Each of these provides a little different option for saving graphics for use in HTML documents.

About GIF files

The GIF file format is usually the best choice for saving graphics that are used in HTML documents. First, all graphical Web browsers can read GIF files; therefore, all readers who have graphical browsers will be able to see the graphics you provide. Second, GIF files are usually better for drawings or line art (but not better for photographs). Using GIF files for this type of image is important for providing crisp-looking (rather than fuzzy-looking) graphics.

Third, the GIF format gives you two special effects that JPG graphics do not. One is the choice of saving your graphic as an *interlaced* or *noninterlaced* graphic. These terms refer to how the graphic appears on your readers' screens — interlaced graphics fade in as they appear, and noninterlaced graphics appear in one big piece. Therefore, you can use GIF files to create a nifty effect that you cannot achieve using the JPG format. You learn more about making interlaced graphics in Unit 7.

The second special effect that only GIF graphics support is the ability to make a transparent graphic so that part of the graphic appears in the same color as the browser background, which helps many graphics look better. This feature is also covered in Unit 7.

GIF files come in a couple of different flavors — 87a and 89a. The numbers don't have anything to do with HTML or creating graphics. Simply keep in mind that the 89a variety is the kind that supports the special effects. You'll have a place to choose the flavor when you're saving your GIF images in this lesson. There's no reason you'd need to save as 87a, so just plan on saving all your GIF images as 89a.

About JPG files

JPG files have some important uses for Web page development as well. They can be read by many graphical browsers and are, like GIFs, compressed files.

JPG files are particularly useful for saving photographs because the format compresses the photograph file even smaller than the GIF format does. Everything else being equal, smaller files load more quickly than larger files; therefore, the JPG format is a better choice for photographs.

The downside to JPG files is that some of the detail is lost in the compression process, so graphics are often not as crisp as those saved in GIF format. Suppose that you took a picture of your favorite piece of wood furniture, which has an array of brown and deep red tones in the wood grain. If you save the document as a JPG file, the array of brown and red tones would probably appear as only a few colors — such as brown, medium brown, dark brown, deep red, and auburn — rather than the blend of colors that really exists.

Handwritten margin notes:

GIF file format is usually best for HTML documents

Save GIF images as 89a

JPG file format is great for photographs because file is compressed very small

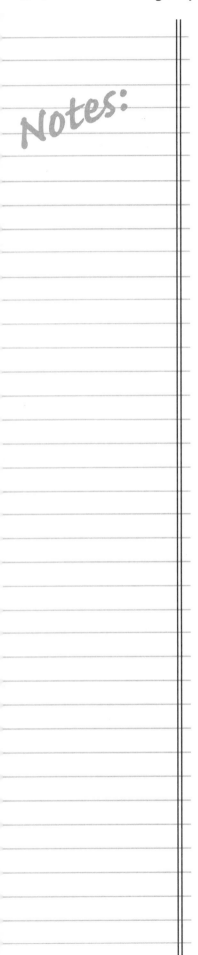

Where — oh where — do you find graphics to use?

So just where will you get graphics to use in your HTML documents? Well, you have three options.

Option #1

You could borrow existing graphics on the Web. We are not suggesting that you go out and snag a graphic that someone else created and has rights to, but some Web sites provide graphics specifically for people to use in their own documents. Here are the basic instructions for getting borrowed graphics into your documents:

```
http://www.yahoo.com/Computers_and_Internet/Multimedia
/Pictures/Clip_Art/
```

`http://www.lycos.com/` (Search for `clip art`.)

`http://www.altavista.digital.com/` (Search for `clip art`.)

If you find a graphic you can use on the Web, it will already be a GIF or JPG graphic. However, you will need to get the graphic from the Web into your HTML document. Here's how:

1. **Open Netscape and connect to the Internet.**

   If you have a modem and need to dial into a service provider, do so. If you're in an office and have a full-time Internet connection, lucky you!

2. **Connect to the Internet address of your choice.**

   Type the address in the Location: line or go to File->Open Location (Ctrl+L) and type the URL.

3. **After the graphic is completely loaded to your browser (the red Stop icon goes off), right click the graphic.**

   Right clicking brings up a pop-up menu.

4. **Click Save this Image As.**

5. **Put the file wherever you'd like on your computer.**

Remember that whoever created the cool graphic you see on the Web has the copyright to it. If the image isn't clearly labeled as one that you're free to use, don't use it.

Option #2

You can create the graphics yourself by using Paint Shop Pro or other graphics software you might have. As you find out later in this unit, you can be pretty creative with Paint Shop Pro, creating graphics such as line art, diagrams, signs, symbols, logos — just about anything you dare to draw. Don't worry, we've provided you with sample graphics files while learning about Paint Shop Pro and learning how to include graphics in your HTML documents (covered in Units 7, 8, and 9).

Option #3

If you're lucky enough to have a scanner and know how to use it, go wild, child! Enjoy! Keep those copyright laws in mind, though, as you're scanning to your heart's content. Best to use your own camera and scanner.

Specific instructions for scanning pictures and graphics varies from scanner to scanner — you have to refer to the instructions provided with the equipment.

Remember to save your files as GIF or JPG. If your scanner software won't save in the correct format, you can always open up the file in Paint Shop Pro and save it in the correct format.

The following steps show you how to save a graphic for use in an HTML document:

on the CD

1 Open sample.pcx in Paint Shop Pro.

You may have to make sure that the List Files of Type drop-down list at the bottom of the dialog box shows All Files to see sample.pcx.

2 Choose File⇨Save As.

3 Find the folder in which you want to save your files — again, we recommend saving unit06 stuff in the unit06 folder.

4 In the File Name field, type the following file name: sample.gif.

5 Choose the file type by clicking the arrow next to the List Files of Typefield and select GIF files (*.gif).

It's not enough to just put in .gif after the filename. You also have to choose the file type.

6 Select the File Sub-Format in the box below the List Files of Type box and select Version 89a Noninterlaced.

Click the little arrow on the right side of the box, if necessary. A drop-down box will appear with the proper choice.

Figure 6-2 shows the Save As dialog box and the save options you should have selected.

7 Click the OK button.

With the second and subsequent saves, you see a dialog box that asks whether you want to overwrite the existing file. Click Yes.

Good job! You just saved the graphic under a different filename. The process for saving is the same whether the document is already named or not.

You can close the document now; you use a different one in the next lesson.

heads up

As we suggested in Unit 2, saving your files frequently is a good idea. Should your computer go on the fritz and crash, you'll lose all the changes you made since the last time you saved. (At least for us, that tends to be more frustrating with graphics.)

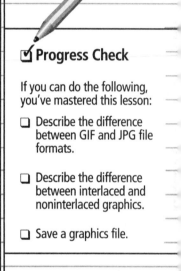

File Save icon

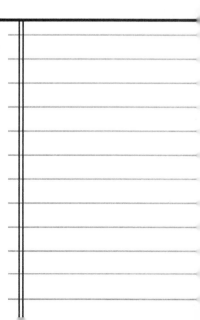

☑ Progress Check

If you can do the following, you've mastered this lesson:

❏ Describe the difference between GIF and JPG file formats.

❏ Describe the difference between interlaced and noninterlaced graphics.

❏ Save a graphics file.

Viewing Graphics in Netscape   Lesson 6-3

on the test

In the Lesson 6-2, you learned how to save graphics files. You now need to learn how to view these graphics in Netscape. Viewing graphics in Netscape is as easy as opening a file and looking at it. However, we do want to point out that graphics often look different in a browser than they do in Paint Shop Pro (and other graphics software) — you should keep this in mind as you're working with graphics that will be viewed in Web browsers.

The most dramatic difference in graphics viewed in the graphics software versus the browser is with graphics that have transparent backgrounds. A graphic that has a transparent background means that the background color of the graphic is the same color as the background of the browser. Because the two background colors are the same, all you see is the foreground objects in the graphic. You'll learn how to make transparent backgrounds in Unit 7.

Figure 6-2: The Save As dialog box with File Type and File Sub-Format selected.

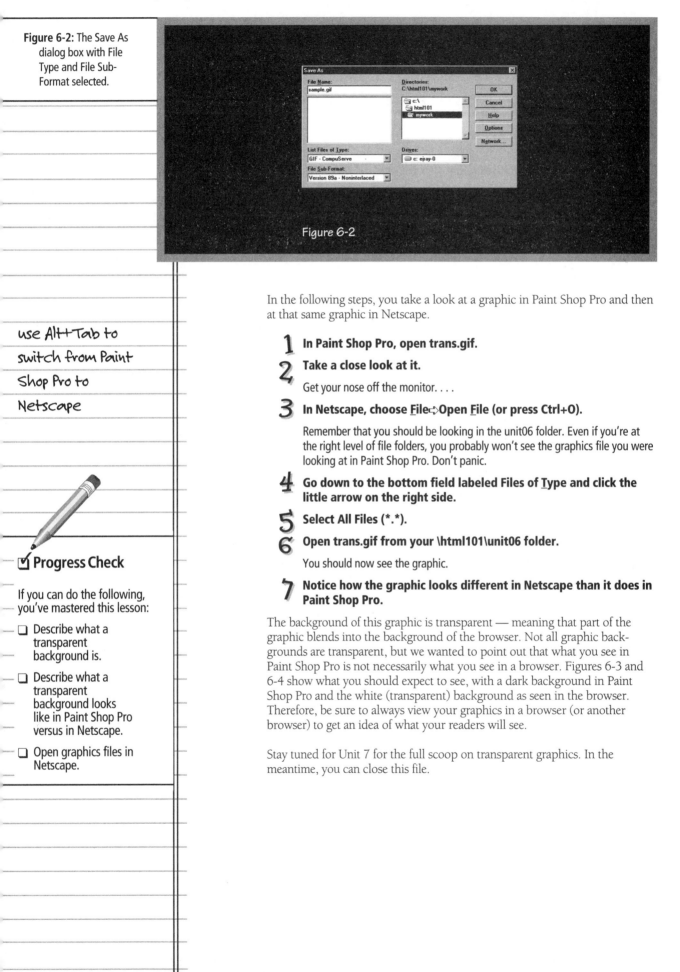

Figure 6-2

use Alt+Tab to switch from Paint Shop Pro to Netscape

Progress Check

If you can do the following, you've mastered this lesson:

❑ Describe what a transparent background is.

❑ Describe what a transparent background looks like in Paint Shop Pro versus in Netscape.

❑ Open graphics files in Netscape.

In the following steps, you take a look at a graphic in Paint Shop Pro and then at that same graphic in Netscape.

1 In Paint Shop Pro, open trans.gif.

2 Take a close look at it.

Get your nose off the monitor. . . .

3 In Netscape, choose File➪Open File (or press Ctrl+O).

Remember that you should be looking in the unit06 folder. Even if you're at the right level of file folders, you probably won't see the graphics file you were looking at in Paint Shop Pro. Don't panic.

4 Go down to the bottom field labeled Files of Type and click the little arrow on the right side.

5 Select All Files (*.*).

6 Open trans.gif from your \html101\unit06 folder.

You should now see the graphic.

7 Notice how the graphic looks different in Netscape than it does in Paint Shop Pro.

The background of this graphic is transparent — meaning that part of the graphic blends into the background of the browser. Not all graphic backgrounds are transparent, but we wanted to point out that what you see in Paint Shop Pro is not necessarily what you see in a browser. Figures 6-3 and 6-4 show what you should expect to see, with a dark background in Paint Shop Pro and the white (transparent) background as seen in the browser. Therefore, be sure to always view your graphics in a browser (or another browser) to get an idea of what your readers will see.

Stay tuned for Unit 7 for the full scoop on transparent graphics. In the meantime, you can close this file.

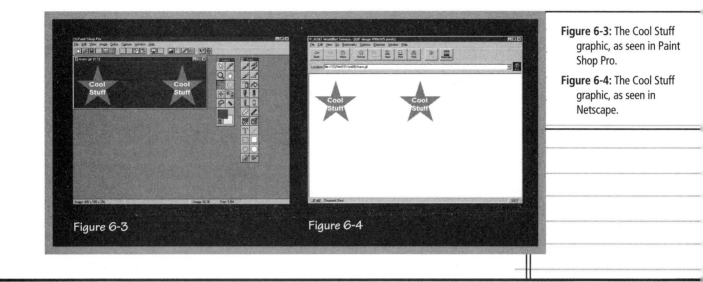

Figure 6-3: The Cool Stuff graphic, as seen in Paint Shop Pro.

Figure 6-4: The Cool Stuff graphic, as seen in Netscape.

Playing with Paint Shop Pro

Lesson 6-4

You've just learned the basics of graphics software and file formats and how to view graphics, but you haven't yet had the opportunity to play with some Paint Shop Pro features. This lesson lets you experiment with the basic features of Paint Shop Pro and will make you more comfortable with working with graphics in general.

Keep in mind that this lesson only presents some basic features of Paint Shop Pro — entire books are dedicated to this type of software, so you're only getting a tiny taste here.

1 In Paint Shop Pro, choose File⇨New.

Choose a size (320 x 240 is a good starting size) and an Image Type of 256 colors.

You will be saving this image as a GIF image, which means that it can only support 256 colors. Although that might sound like a lot of colors, it takes millions of colors to provide photographic quality. (Good thing JPG images support millions of colors, huh?) As a rule, most of your readers' computers will only be able to display 256 colors anyway, so you're not missing much.

Notice that the graphic screen does not take up all the available space. You can make the graphic screen bigger by moving your cursor to one of the gray borders (the cursor will turn into a double-arrow), clicking (and holding) the border, and dragging the border toward the edge of the screen. This procedure doesn't change the size of the graphic, but it lets you see more of the graphic at once. Changing the size will come up in the next unit.

2 Experiment with the buttons in the toolboxes by clicking a toolbox button, moving your cursor over to the graphic screen, and trying it out.

You should try out *at least* the following ones listed in Table 6-2. If you goof, Choose Edit⇨Undo to reverse the last change you made.

Tip: Place your cursor over any of the buttons in Paint Shop Pro and look at the Statusbar at the very bottom of the screen. The Statusbar displays the name of the button and gives a description of what the tool does.

3 Close your current drawing by choosing File⇨Close.

You can save your doodles if you choose. We hear that modern art sells well, if you get lucky.

Notes:

Table 6-2	Some Paint Shop Pro Features	
Toolbox Button	**Tool Name**	**Effect**
	Pointer tool	Lets you select shapes, lines, and text
	Text tool	Lets you include text in the graphic. When you select this tool, you must choose where on the page the text should appear. A dialog box appears where you then enter your text and choose your text formatting.
	Background/ Foreground tool	Lets you change the background and foreground colors. The background color refers to the background of the graphic; the foreground color refers to the color of the tool you're drawing with. You use these by double-clicking them and selecting a new color from the color palette. (If all you can get is black and white or a few select colors, Choose File➪New and select, for example, 256 colors from the dialog box.)
	Drawing tools	Lets you draw freehand with a variety of pen tip sizes and paint brush tip sizes
	Fill buttons	Lets you add colors or patterns within either small or large shapes
	Line tools	Lets you draw nonfreehand lines (these are handy, if the line needs to be straight)
	Box tools	Lets you draw either filled or non-filled squares and rectangles
	Circle tools	Lets you draw either filled or non-filled square and rectangles

Now that you've played for a few minutes — whoops, make that now that you've been working hard for a while (in case the boss is watching) — it's time to start drawing a toolbar that you can use in a Web page.

1   In Paint Shop Pro, create a new file that is 640 by 100 and 256 colors.

2   Double-click the top of the overlapping boxes in the Select palette and choose a color that contrasts with the lower of the two boxes.

You can double-click the back box to change the other color and double-click the spot to the lower left to switch the top and back colors.

3   Click the Text tool (T in the Paint Palette) and then in your new image.

Selecting the Text tool and then clicking in the image brings up the Add Text dialog box in which you can type in the text you want on your new button.

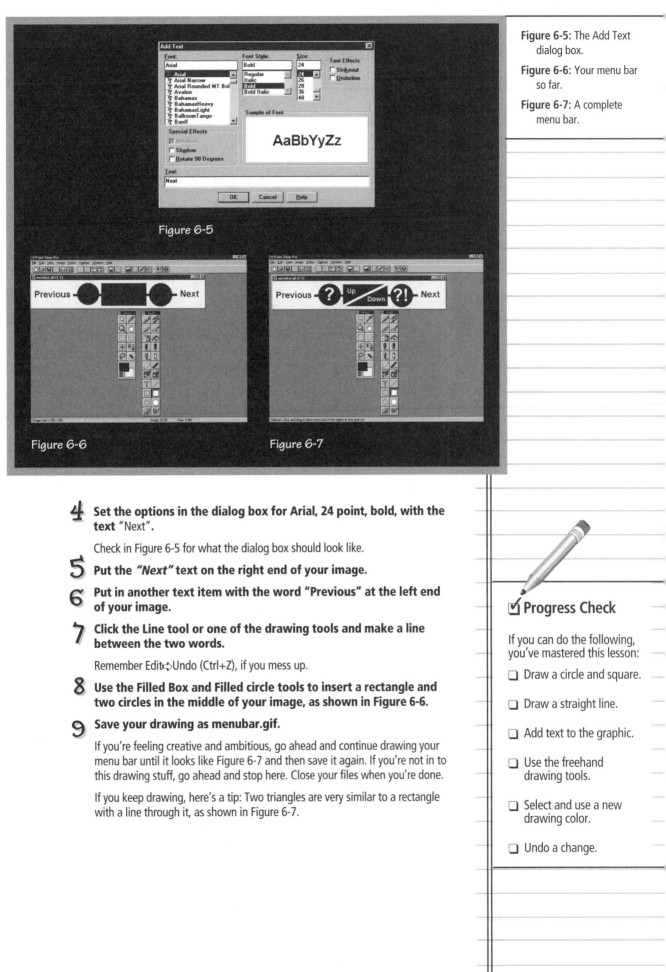

Figure 6-5: The Add Text dialog box.

Figure 6-6: Your menu bar so far.

Figure 6-7: A complete menu bar.

Figure 6-5

Figure 6-6

Figure 6-7

4 **Set the options in the dialog box for Arial, 24 point, bold, with the text** "Next".

Check in Figure 6-5 for what the dialog box should look like.

5 **Put the** *"Next"* **text on the right end of your image.**

6 **Put in another text item with the word "Previous" at the left end of your image.**

7 **Click the Line tool or one of the drawing tools and make a line between the two words.**

Remember Edit⇨Undo (Ctrl+Z), if you mess up.

8 **Use the Filled Box and Filled circle tools to insert a rectangle and two circles in the middle of your image, as shown in Figure 6-6.**

9 **Save your drawing as menubar.gif.**

If you're feeling creative and ambitious, go ahead and continue drawing your menu bar until it looks like Figure 6-7 and then save it again. If you're not in to this drawing stuff, go ahead and stop here. Close your files when you're done.

If you keep drawing, here's a tip: Two triangles are very similar to a rectangle with a line through it, as shown in Figure 6-7.

☑ Progress Check

If you can do the following, you've mastered this lesson:

❑ Draw a circle and square.

❑ Draw a straight line.

❑ Add text to the graphic.

❑ Use the freehand drawing tools.

❑ Select and use a new drawing color.

❑ Undo a change.

Unit 6 Quiz

This short quiz is designed to help you remember things you learned in Unit 6. For each of the following questions, circle the letter of the correct answer or answers.

1. **The GIF file format is best for using in HTML documents because**

   A. All graphical browsers can view GIF files.

   B. The GIF format allows you to choose either interlaced or non-interlaced.

   C. GIF files offer better details than JPG files.

   D. GIF files go best with Jelly files.

   E. A , B, and C

2. **When saving GIF files, you want to use which file sub-type?**

   A. Only interlaced

   B. Only noninterlaced

   C. 89a translucent

   D. 89a, either interlaced or noninterlaced

   E. 87a

3. **Transparent images**

   A. Disappear in Netscape.

   B. Look normal in Paint Shop Pro, but look different in Netscape.

   C. Always look interlaced in Netscape.

   D. Are always invisible in Netscape.

   E. Cannot be saved in Netscape.

4. **You should save graphics as GIF files because**

   A. Jif peanut butter is good for lunch.

   B. GIF is the file format that all graphical browsers can read.

   C. JPG cannot be read by all Web browsers.

   D. GIF is the only file format that has online documentation that can help if you get in a bind.

   E. You want to save your files in a GIFfy.

5. **You can move the toolboxes around on the Paint Shop Pro screen by**

   A. Copying and pasting them.

   B. Saving them as GIF files.

   C. Copying and pasting them into a JPG format.

   D. Clicking (and holding) the blue bar on the top and dragging them to where you want.

   E. You can't move the toolboxes.

Unit 6 Exercise

Create a new graphic (for example, a logo for that company you've always dreamed of starting) by using Paint Shop Pro. This graphic could have both filled and non-filled shapes, and you should include text in some portion of the graphic. Be creative with colors as well.

1. Start a new graphic in Paint Shop Pro.

2. Add a filled shape or two.

3. Add text.

4. Add lines.

5. Save your graphic as mylogo.gif.

6. Test your graphic in Netscape, just for the fun of it.

7. Apply for trademark status for your logo. Maybe it'll be as big as the Coca-Cola bottle shape.

Developing Graphics for HTML Documents

Prerequisites
- Opening graphics in Paint Shop Pro (Lesson 6-2)
- Saving graphics in Paint Shop Pro (Lesson 6-3)
- Viewing graphics in Netscape (Lesson 6-4)

on the CD
- unsuit.htm
- unsuit.gif
- suitable.htm
- suitable.gif
- pagehog.htm
- pagehog.gif
- subtle.htm
- subtle.gif
- dom1.gif
- trans.gif
- winchs.tif

Objectives for This Unit

✓ Understanding what suitable graphics are

✓ Resizing the physical size of graphics

✓ Making a graphic's file size as small as possible

✓ Making a graphic's background transparent

✓ Making graphics interlaced

Unit 6 showed you the basics of using Paint Shop Pro, and you even got to dabble with some of the software's features. In this unit, you find out how Paint Shop Pro can help make graphics more suitable for use in your HTML documents.

Making graphics suitable for HTML documents is important because if you use inappropriate graphics, your readers can encounter a number of irritations, such as having to wait eons for a graphic to download and not being able to view the whole graphic at once. These things may seem fairly trivial, but you'll find that they become particularly burdensome with HTML documents.

In the first lesson, you learn what suitable graphics are and why they're important. In the following lessons, you learn techniques to help make your graphics suitable.

Lesson 7-1

What Are Suitable Graphics, Anyway?

Notes:

What makes a graphic suitable for use in an HTML document, you ask? The following sections describe three concepts that help make your graphics suitable:

- Graphics should load quickly.
- Graphics should complement information.
- Graphics should be flashy.

Each of these sections provides examples that show the difference between suitable and unsuitable graphics. After you understand the difference, you'll be well on your way to learning *how* to make graphics quick, complementary, and flashy in Lessons 7-2 through 7-5.

Graphics should load quickly

Graphics need to load quickly — that is, they should come up on your computer screen quickly. The file size of the graphic (amount of disk space it takes) is directly related to how quickly a graphic loads on-screen. The larger the file, the slower it loads.

Providing graphics that load quickly is essential if you want people to browse and, more importantly, revisit your site. For example, have you ever visited a Web site that has way-slow graphics? Do you find yourself avoiding that site for that reason? We thought so.

You can help make your graphics load quickly by doing two things. First, choose a graphic that isn't too huge to begin with. Choosing a smaller graphic that loads quickly is often much more effective than choosing a large graphic that seemingly takes forever to load. Second, you can resize the graphic's file size so that it's smaller and, therefore, appears on-screen more quickly. You learn how to reduce the graphic's file size in Lesson 7-2.

Before you move on to the next section, take a few minutes to look at two sample Web pages. The first Web page gives you an example of an *unsuitable* graphic that loads too slowly. The second Web page gives you an example of a *suitable* graphic that loads quickly.

on the CD

1 **Open the file unsuit.htm (located in your \html101\unit07 folder) in Netscape.**

Wait. Wait. There it is. Finally.

on the CD

2 **Open the file suitable.htm.**

There it is. Much faster, 'eh? Go ahead and close these files and then move on to the next section.

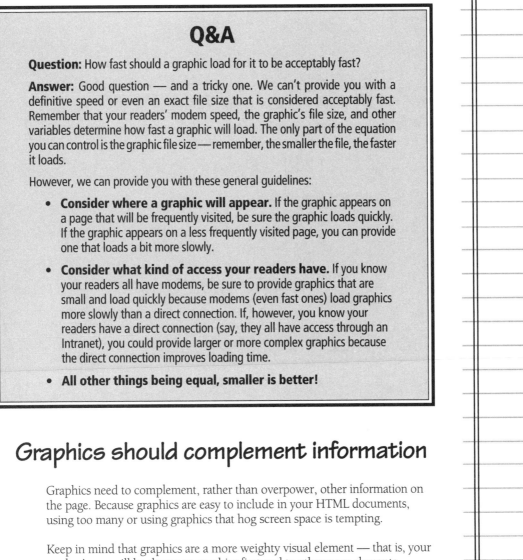

Q&A

Question: How fast should a graphic load for it to be acceptably fast?

Answer: Good question — and a tricky one. We can't provide you with a definitive speed or even an exact file size that is considered acceptably fast. Remember that your readers' modem speed, the graphic's file size, and other variables determine how fast a graphic will load. The only part of the equation you can control is the graphic file size — remember, the smaller the file, the faster it loads.

However, we can provide you with these general guidelines:

- **Consider where a graphic will appear.** If the graphic appears on a page that will be frequently visited, be sure the graphic loads quickly. If the graphic appears on a less frequently visited page, you can provide one that loads a bit more slowly.

- **Consider what kind of access your readers have.** If you know your readers all have modems, be sure to provide graphics that are small and load quickly because modems (even fast ones) load graphics more slowly than a direct connection. If, however, you know your readers have a direct connection (say, they all have access through an Intranet), you could provide larger or more complex graphics because the direct connection improves loading time.

- **All other things being equal, smaller is better!**

Graphics should complement information

Graphics need to complement, rather than overpower, other information on the page. Because graphics are easy to include in your HTML documents, using too many or using graphics that hog screen space is tempting.

Keep in mind that graphics are a more weighty visual element — that is, your readers' eyes will be drawn to graphics first and to other page elements second. Using too many or too big a graphic often detracts from the content of your document because the text, headings, lists, and so on get lost in the boldness of the graphics. The result is that readers may not get past the graphic to read the other information on the page.

One way to avoid this problem is to make sure that the graphics comfortably co-exist with other page elements. You can do this by resizing the graphic — making it a more subtle page element. You learn how to resize graphics in Lesson 7-3.

In the meantime, go through the following exercise, which gives you an example of a page-hogging graphic and a subtle, more effective graphic.

on the CD

1 **Open the file pagehog.htm in Netscape.**

Take a good look at it. Then close the file.

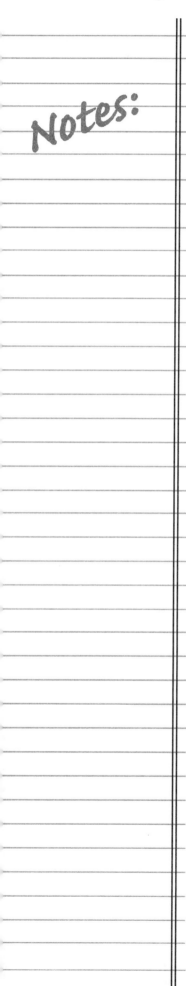

2 **Answer the following questions (you can just do this in your head).**

- How long did you look at the graphic compared to the other page elements? Did you even look at the other page elements?

- If you looked at the other page elements, what were they?

3 **Open the file subtle.htm in Netscape.**

Take a good look at it. When you're done, close the file and answer the following questions (in your head).

- How long did you look at the graphic compared to the other page elements?

- What were the other page elements?

- Did you at least notice text on the screen?

- Did the reduced size keep you from being able to tell what was depicted?

We bet that you saw a difference in the effectiveness of the graphics in the two sample files.

Graphics should be flashy

Graphics don't have to be complex, but you can make them more interesting to look at. For example, you can make the graphic's background *transparent,* which means that you get rid of the background so that only the foreground objects are visible. Or you can make the graphic appear in your readers' screens in phases (rather than appear all at one time). Both techniques add pizzazz to your graphics without increasing the file or graphic size.

You learn how to make graphics transparent in Lesson 7-4 and how to make graphics appear gradually (called *interlacing graphics*) in Lesson 7-5. For now, complete the following exercise. In the first part of the exercise, you compare a regular graphic with one that has a transparent background. In the second part, you get to see how an interlaced graphic is flashier than one that is not.

1 **Take a look at Figures 7-1 and 7-2.**

Figure 7-1 shows a graphic with a regular background. Figure 7-2 shows the same graphic with a transparent background.

2 **Sit and marvel about how cool the transparent background is. (It *does* make the graphic more effective, doesn't it?)**

3 **Open regular.htm in Netscape.**

Notice that the graphic appears on-screen all at one time — that is, evenly from top to bottom.

4 **Open interlac.htm.**

Notice that the graphic appears on-screen in waves — the cat kinda comes into focus. (Yes, that's as focused as he ever gets — he's fuzzy to begin with!) Cool, huh? Now you're ready to learn how to *do* some of these neat tricks.

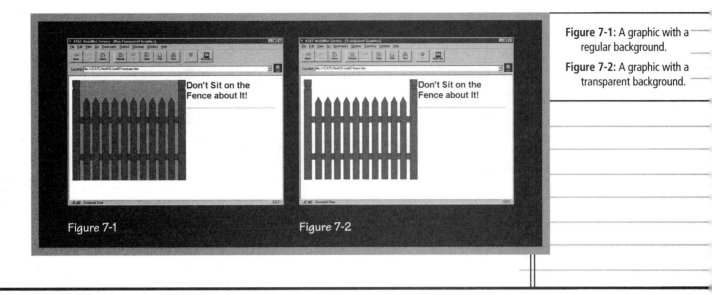

Figure 7-1: A graphic with a regular background.

Figure 7-2: A graphic with a transparent background.

Reducing a Graphic's File Size

Lesson 7-2

In Lesson 7-1, you learned that the smaller the file size, the faster the graphic loads in your readers' browsers. In this lesson, you learn how to reduce a graphic's file size without making much difference in its appearance. This way, you can use fancy or large graphics *and* have them load relatively quickly.

on the test

The best way to make a graphic as small as possible is to decrease the number of colors it uses. Think of it this way. A graphic often carries excess baggage — it may only use 16 colors, but can carry the option of using 256 colors. The extra 240 colors take up space and don't contribute to the graphic's appearance (like the extra pounds on a waistline). So all you have to do is decrease the number of colors to the number actually used, and voilà, you've made the file size smaller. (Now, if we could cast off the pounds that don't do anything and keep the muscle-type pounds, we'd be set.)

You also can decrease the number of colors used for graphics that do use a lot of colors. For example, if a graphic uses, say, 87 different colors, you can sometimes reduce the number of colors to a smaller number — say, 16 colors. The result is that the graphic won't have the color depth it had before, but it will be a smaller and, therefore, faster graphic. You have to experiment with this one, though, to be sure that reducing the colors doesn't change the graphic's appearance too drastically.

In the following exercise, you learn how to decrease the number of colors in a graphic.

on the CD

1 **Open fatcolor.gif in Paint Shop Pro.**

In the Statusbar, you can see that the current size of the image is displayed as **272 x 247 x 256**, Image: 274 x 247 x 256 (that is, 247 pixels wide by 247 pixels high by 256 colors). But if you look at the graphic, you can see that it uses only a few basic colors — red, yellow, and blue, plus white and black. No mauve or off-sky-blue colors in this graphic. Therefore, this image is a good candidate to reduce the color depth.

lean graphics load faster

decrease number of colors

Statusbar is down along bottom of screen

Figure 7-3: The Decrease color depth dialog box.

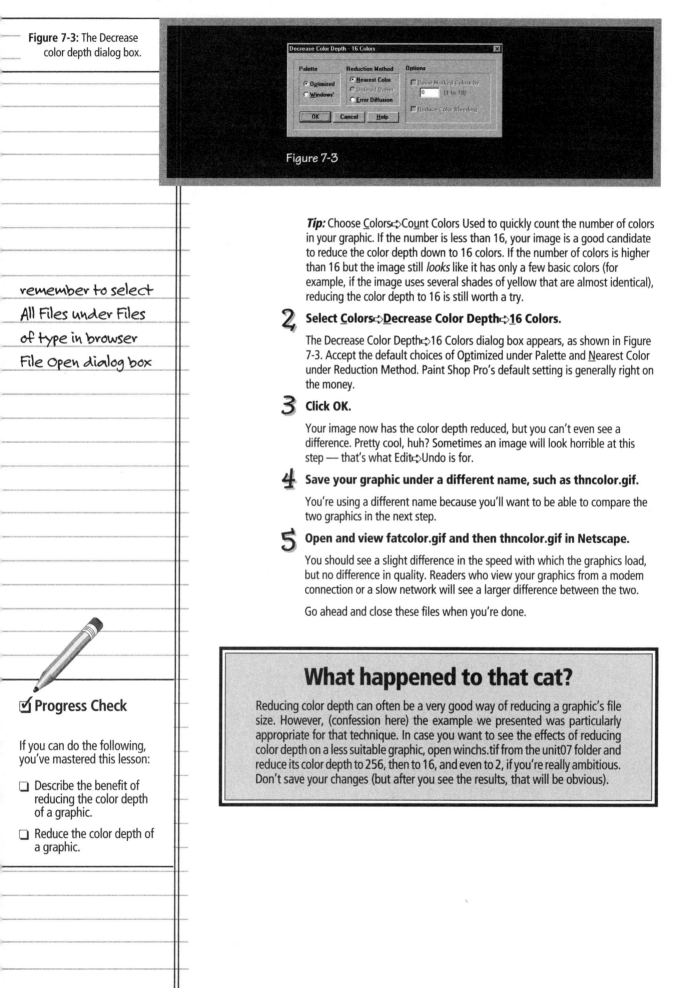

Figure 7-3

remember to select All Files under Files of type in browser File Open dialog box

Tip: Choose <u>C</u>olors⬄Co<u>u</u>nt Colors Used to quickly count the number of colors in your graphic. If the number is less than 16, your image is a good candidate to reduce the color depth down to 16 colors. If the number of colors is higher than 16 but the image still *looks* like it has only a few basic colors (for example, if the image uses several shades of yellow that are almost identical), reducing the color depth to 16 is still worth a try.

2 **Select <u>C</u>olors⬄<u>D</u>ecrease Color Depth⬄<u>1</u>6 Colors.**

The Decrease Color Depth⬄16 Colors dialog box appears, as shown in Figure 7-3. Accept the default choices of O<u>p</u>timized under Palette and <u>N</u>earest Color under Reduction Method. Paint Shop Pro's default setting is generally right on the money.

3 **Click OK.**

Your image now has the color depth reduced, but you can't even see a difference. Pretty cool, huh? Sometimes an image will look horrible at this step — that's what Edit⬄Undo is for.

4 **Save your graphic under a different name, such as thncolor.gif.**

You're using a different name because you'll want to be able to compare the two graphics in the next step.

5 **Open and view fatcolor.gif and then thncolor.gif in Netscape.**

You should see a slight difference in the speed with which the graphics load, but no difference in quality. Readers who view your graphics from a modem connection or a slow network will see a larger difference between the two.

Go ahead and close these files when you're done.

What happened to that cat?

Reducing color depth can often be a very good way of reducing a graphic's file size. However, (confession here) the example we presented was particularly appropriate for that technique. In case you want to see the effects of reducing color depth on a less suitable graphic, open winchs.tif from the unit07 folder and reduce its color depth to 256, then to 16, and even to 2, if you're really ambitious. Don't save your changes (but after you see the results, that will be obvious).

✓ **Progress Check**

If you can do the following, you've mastered this lesson:

❑ Describe the benefit of reducing the color depth of a graphic.

❑ Reduce the color depth of a graphic.

Making Graphics Bigger or Smaller   Lesson 7-3

As you learned in Lesson 7-1, one of the easiest things you can do to make a graphic effective in an HTML document is to resize the graphic to better fit the document. For example, an otherwise effective graphic may be too big or too small for the visual effect you want to achieve. The easy solution is to resize the graphic.

on the test

The size of a graphic is measured in *pixels*. A pixel is the smallest element of a graphic as it appears on a computer screen. If you look real close at your monitor, you might be able to see a bunch of tiny little dots — those are *pixels*. (If your nose is touching your monitor, you're too close!) Graphics are really the result of coloring gobs of pixels; when you view all these pixels from a little further away, they appear as a single entity.

For example, a graphic that measures 640 x 480 has 640 pixels horizontally and 480 pixels vertically on-screen. The higher the number of pixels, the better the graphic's quality. By the way, a graphic size of 640 x 480 is the absolute largest size you should plan to use for a graphic in an HTML document — you should really stick with about 580 x 400 pixels. If your graphics are any larger, you'll run the risk of the edges not fitting on your readers' computer screens.

> *gobs = technical term for chunks or blobs*

In the following steps, you learn how to decrease the size of a large graphic so that it doesn't hog screen space. You also can use the same process to increase the size of a graphic.

on the CD

1 Open dom1.gif in Paint Shop Pro.

Your screen should look like Figure 7-4. In the Statusbar at the left end, you can see that the current size of the image is displayed as `Image: 640 x 401 x 256` (that is, 640 pixels wide by 401 pixels high by 256 colors).

2 Choose Image⇨Resize.

The Resize dialog box appears, as shown in Figure 7-5.

3 Select Custom Size, if it isn't already selected.

This option allows you to specify the new dimensions of the image.

4 Select the Maintain Aspect Ratio check box.

By maintaining the aspect ratio (proportion of height to width), you ensure that the image's size changes but that the image isn't distorted. If you change the image size without selecting this option, your image could have that warped fun-house mirror look.

> *maintaining aspect ratio keeps image in proportion*

5 Enter 320 in the first Custom Size text box (for width).

6 Press Tab.

The cursor moves to the next text box, and Paint Shop Pro automatically calculates the correct height based on the width you entered, keeping the aspect ratio the same.

Tip: You can enter the height and then press Shift+Tab to have Paint Shop Pro calculate the proportional width, if you'd rather go that way.

Figure 7-4: Image before resizing.

Figure 7-5: The Resize dialog box.

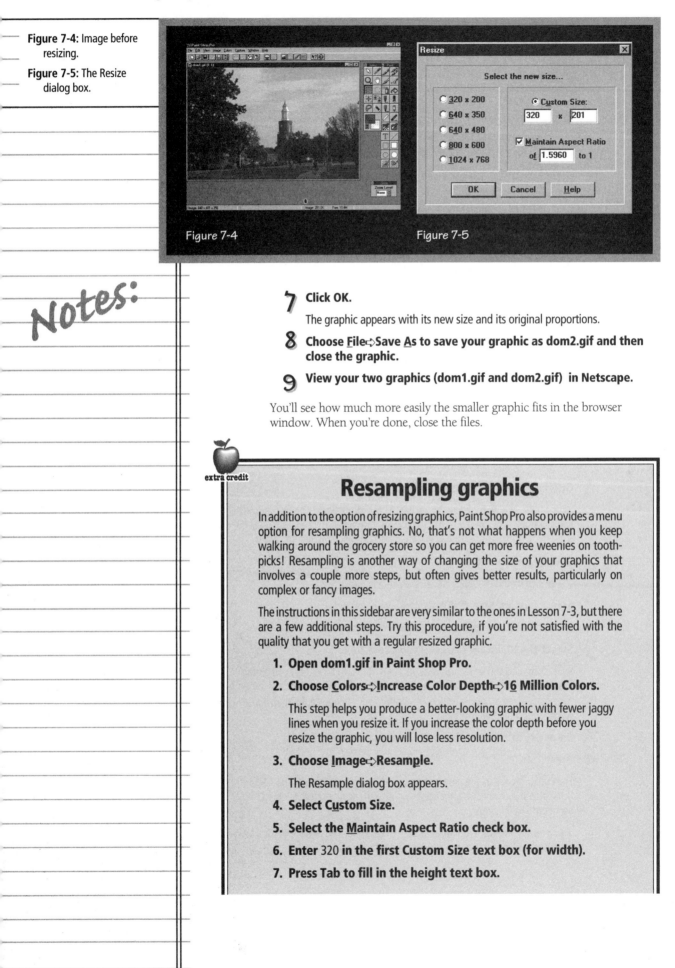

Figure 7-4   Figure 7-5

Notes:

7 Click OK.

The graphic appears with its new size and its original proportions.

8 Choose File➪Save As to save your graphic as dom2.gif and then close the graphic.

9 View your two graphics (dom1.gif and dom2.gif) in Netscape.

You'll see how much more easily the smaller graphic fits in the browser window. When you're done, close the files.

extra credit

Resampling graphics

In addition to the option of resizing graphics, Paint Shop Pro also provides a menu option for resampling graphics. No, that's not what happens when you keep walking around the grocery store so you can get more free weenies on tooth-picks! Resampling is another way of changing the size of your graphics that involves a couple more steps, but often gives better results, particularly on complex or fancy images.

The instructions in this sidebar are very similar to the ones in Lesson 7-3, but there are a few additional steps. Try this procedure, if you're not satisfied with the quality that you get with a regular resized graphic.

1. **Open dom1.gif in Paint Shop Pro.**

2. **Choose Colors➪Increase Color Depth➪16 Million Colors.**

   This step helps you produce a better-looking graphic with fewer jaggy lines when you resize it. If you increase the color depth before you resize the graphic, you will lose less resolution.

3. **Choose Image➪Resample.**

   The Resample dialog box appears.

4. **Select Custom Size.**

5. **Select the Maintain Aspect Ratio check box.**

6. **Enter 320 in the first Custom Size text box (for width).**

7. **Press Tab to fill in the height text box.**

8. Click OK.

The graphic appears with its new size and its original proportions.

9. Choose Colors⇨Decrease Color Depth⇨256 Colors.

Choosing this command reduces the graphic back down to the maximum number of colors a GIF can be saved with (and also the maximum number of colors you should use in a graphic for the Web).

10. Accept the default values in the Decrease Color Depth dialog box.

11. Choose File⇨Save As to save your graphic as dom3.gif.

12. Test your graphic in Netscape.

The quality should be slightly better than that of the one you resized in Lesson 7-3. The difference may not be apparent, depending on your monitor's quality and your eyesight.

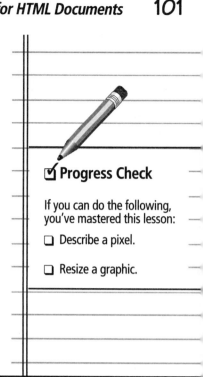

☑ **Progress Check**

If you can do the following, you've mastered this lesson:

❑ Describe a pixel.

❑ Resize a graphic.

Making a Transparent Background

Lesson 7-4

on the test

As you learned in Lesson 7-1, one of the ways to make graphics more interesting is to make the background transparent so that the color of the browser shows through. Making a background transparent makes the graphic more interesting because it helps the foreground objects stand out and visually flow into the HTML document more easily. In some cases, using a transparent background can significantly improve the graphic's effectiveness because the background won't detract from the foreground objects.

This exercise shows you how to make graphics with transparent backgrounds:

on the CD

1 Open trans.gif in Paint Shop Pro.

Notice that the graphic has a uniform background color, which is necessary to make the background transparent. Only one color can be transparent, so you need to make sure that all areas that should be transparent are colored exactly the same.

2 Open the graphic in Netscape.

Notice how the background appears just as it did in Paint Shop Pro.

3 Switch to Paint Shop Pro.

4 Select the Eyedropper tool from the Select toolbox.

5 Place the cursor on part of the image you want to be transparent — the background behind the star — and click once with the right mouse button.

This step selects the background color. If you click with the left mouse button, you select the new foreground color, which won't help much with this transparency business.

6 Choose File⇨Save As.

The Save As dialog box appears, as shown in Figure 7-6. Double-check that the file is a GIF file and that Version 89a is selected (select Version 89a Noninterlaced for this example).

uniform background color is necessary to make background transparent

Eyedropper tool

Figure 7-6: The Save As dialog box.

Figure 7-7: The GIF transparency options dialog box.

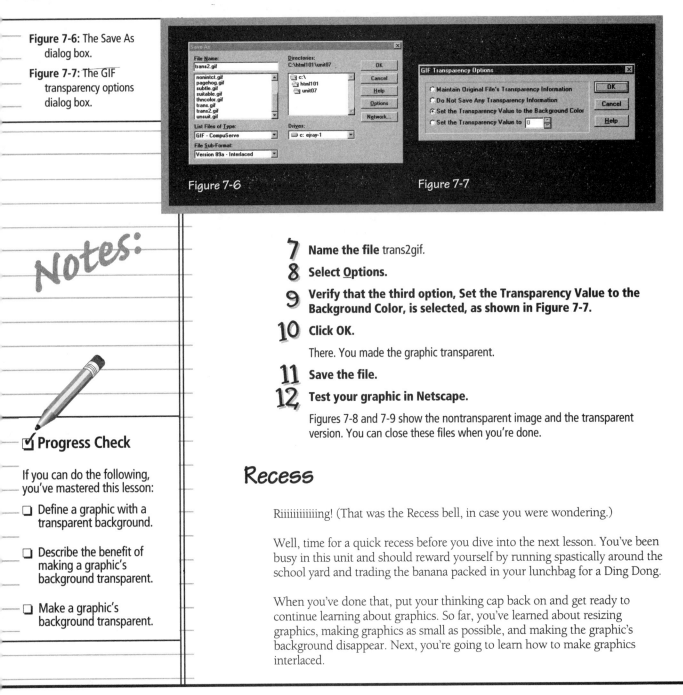

Figure 7-6

Figure 7-7

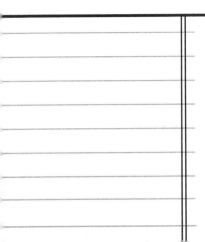

Progress Check

If you can do the following, you've mastered this lesson:

❏ Define a graphic with a transparent background.

❏ Describe the benefit of making a graphic's background transparent.

❏ Make a graphic's background transparent.

7 **Name the file** trans2gif.

8 **Select Options.**

9 **Verify that the third option, Set the Transparency Value to the Background Color, is selected, as shown in Figure 7-7.**

10 **Click OK.**

There. You made the graphic transparent.

11 **Save the file.**

12 **Test your graphic in Netscape.**

Figures 7-8 and 7-9 show the nontransparent image and the transparent version. You can close these files when you're done.

Recess

Riiiiiiiiiiiing! (That was the Recess bell, in case you were wondering.)

Well, time for a quick recess before you dive into the next lesson. You've been busy in this unit and should reward yourself by running spastically around the school yard and trading the banana packed in your lunchbag for a Ding Dong.

When you've done that, put your thinking cap back on and get ready to continue learning about graphics. So far, you've learned about resizing graphics, making graphics as small as possible, and making the graphic's background disappear. Next, you're going to learn how to make graphics interlaced.

Lesson 7-5   Making Graphics Interlaced

Another really neat thing you can do with graphics is to make them interlaced. Interlacing affects how the graphic comes up on the Web page. In Lesson 7-1, you learned that a *noninterlaced* graphic comes up on-screen in one big piece — poof, and it's there (or actually, wait, wait, wait, poof, and it's there). An *interlaced* graphic comes up in waves — more like, poooooooooof, and it's there.

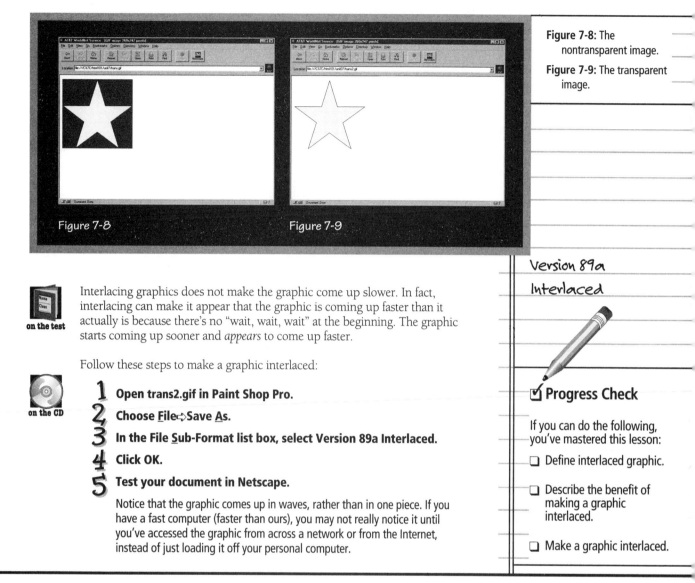

Figure 7-8

Figure 7-9

Version 89a
Interlaced

Interlacing graphics does not make the graphic come up slower. In fact, interlacing can make it appear that the graphic is coming up faster than it actually is because there's no "wait, wait, wait" at the beginning. The graphic starts coming up sooner and *appears* to come up faster.

on the test

Follow these steps to make a graphic interlaced:

on the CD

1 **Open trans2.gif in Paint Shop Pro.**

2 **Choose File⇨Save As.**

3 **In the File Sub-Format list box, select Version 89a Interlaced.**

4 **Click OK.**

5 **Test your document in Netscape.**

   Notice that the graphic comes up in waves, rather than in one piece. If you have a fast computer (faster than ours), you may not really notice it until you've accessed the graphic from across a network or from the Internet, instead of just loading it off your personal computer.

☑ **Progress Check**

If you can do the following, you've mastered this lesson:

❏ Define interlaced graphic.

❏ Describe the benefit of making a graphic interlaced.

❏ Make a graphic interlaced.

Unit 7 Quiz

This short quiz is designed to help you remember things you learned in Unit 7. For each of the following questions, circle the letter of the correct answer or answers. You can find the answers to the quiz questions in Appendix A.

1. **Three things that make graphics suitable for HTML documents are**

    A. Jeans and a T-shirt.

    B. Fast loading speed.

    C. A purpose for being there.

    D. Something interesting or flashy.

    E. B, C, and D

2. **Interlaced graphics**

   A. Combine two or more graphics into one big graphic.

   B. Weave the horizontal and vertical pixels.

   C. Show up in waves.

   D. Wave at you to say hello.

   E. Can only be viewed in Paint Shop Pro.

3. **Transparent graphics**

   A. Cannot be viewed in Netscape.

   B. Are invisible.

   C. Go poooooof when you view them in Netscape.

   D. Say cheese when you take their picture.

   E. Are graphics with a transparent background when viewed in Netscape.

4. **When you resize a graphic, you**

   A. Change the dimensions.

   B. Make the graphic file twice as big.

   C. Tickle its toes.

   D. Outgrow the existing file storage space.

   E. None of the above

5. **An interlaced graphic**

   A. Has no dimensions.

   B. Takes more storage space because it poooooofs, rather than poofs.

   C. Appears to come up faster than an noninterlaced graphic.

   D. Is much slower than a noninterlaced graphic.

   E. All of the above

Unit 7 Exercise

This exercise gives you more practice manipulating images in Paint Shop Pro.

on the CD

1. Open the file winchs.tif from your html101\unit7 folder.

   Yes, Winchester is a real cat. He's old and decrepit, but he photographs well.

2. Save it in an appropriate format for use in an HTML document.

3. Resize it so it will fit better in an HTML document.

4. Want to try making part of this image transparent?

   Hint: You'll have to color in a solid color.

Linking Graphics into Your Document

Objectives for This Unit

✓ Putting graphics in your HTML documents

✓ Using text alternatives

✓ Aligning graphics on-screen

✓ Using graphics as links in your HTML documents

✓ Using thumbnails

Prerequisites

▶ Using anchor tags and attributes to make links (Lesson 5-1)

▶ Linking to other documents (Lessons 5-2 through 5-4)

▶ Opening and saving graphics (Lessons 6-2 and 6-3)

▶ Using graphics within your HTML document (Unit 7)

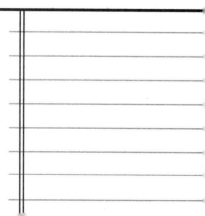

on the CD

▶ addimage.htm
▶ morrill.gif
▶ navigate.htm
▶ left.gif
▶ up.gif
▶ right.gif
▶ previous.htm
▶ main.htm
▶ next.htm
▶ tmbnail.htm
▶ buildtmb.gif
▶ build.gif
▶ win.htm
▶ winchs.gif

Look how far you've come! In the last two units, you learned how to make graphics suitable for your HTML document. In this unit, you combine what you've learned about graphics with the HTML concepts (including making anchors and links) you practiced earlier in the book. In this unit, you learn how to put graphics in your HTML document and use the graphics as anchors, how to prepare and use thumbnail (miniaturized) versions of graphics and text alternatives, and how to change the graphic's alignment on the page.

Adding Graphics to Your HTML Document

Lesson 8-1

Whooeee! It's now time (drum roll, please!) to move past those plain old boring text-only HTML documents into including graphics. Now you're ready to start playing Web-jockey with the pros. This lesson shows you how to add graphics to your HTML document, in a number of different contexts, including with different alignment, as anchors for links, and as miniaturized versions of larger images.

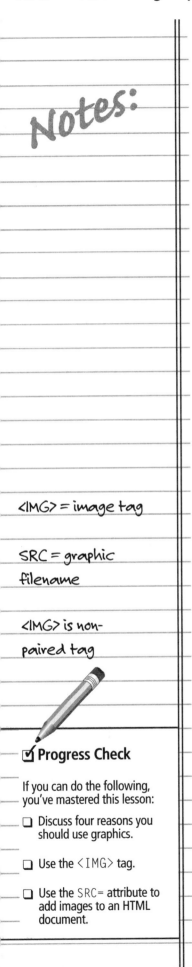

Notes:

<IMG> = image tag

SRC = graphic filename

<IMG> is non-paired tag

☑ **Progress Check**

If you can do the following, you've mastered this lesson:

❑ Discuss four reasons you should use graphics.

❑ Use the <IMG> tag.

❑ Use the SRC= attribute to add images to an HTML document.

Including graphics in your HTML document makes your Web page more effective for several reasons:

▶ Graphics make Web pages look spiffier by adding visual interest and aesthetic appeal. Graphics add color, lines, and shapes to your document that paragraphs, headings, and lists cannot bring. (Remember, as you learned in Unit 7, that you have to be sure graphics are suitable for HTML documents; otherwise, all the spiff the graphic can bring to a document will be lost.)

▶ Graphics often make communicating difficult concepts or instructions easier. For example, on a company's Web page, you might see a map showing people how to get to the office from the airport rather than step-by-step instructions.

▶ Graphics can express your corporate or personal image. You often see graphical logos used throughout a Web site to help establish a Web site theme or to establish a corporate identity. For example, if you see a bright yellow book with a funny looking guy with big glasses, you know it's a . . .*For Dummies* book because the Dummies Man represents the corporate identity.

▶ Graphics can help you compete with the Joneses. If you're creating Web pages for the Acme company, you want to be sure that you keep up with the special effects that Acme's competitors use in their Web sites.

Including graphics in your HTML documents is similar to building anchors, which you learned about in Unit 5. To place a graphic in your document, you use a tag and attributes, just as you did to make anchors.

To add a graphic to your HTML document, you have to complete two steps. (Don't actually *do* these instructions — you'll practice the process a little later in this lesson. Just sit back and read along. By the way, if the terms look unfamiliar, take a couple of minutes to review Unit 5 on making anchors and links.)

1 Apply the image tag where you want the graphic to appear.

2 Add the source attribute to indicate the graphic's filename.

In the following exercise, you add a graphic called morrill.gif to the document.

Go ahead and try this out using the steps provided:

1 In WebEdit, open addimage.htm from your \html101\unit08 folder.

2 Type <IMG> above the first paragraph of text (above the <P> tag).

Remember, the <IMG> tag is not a paired tag.

3 Add the attribute SRC="morrill.gif" to designate which image file you want to load (the SouRCe):

```
<IMG SRC="morrill.gif">
```

4 Save addimage.htm in the \html101\unit08 folder and then test your document in Netscape.

Look at Figures 8-1 and 8-2 to see the HTML code and the resulting graphic.

If the image doesn't appear, make sure that your graphic (morrill.gif) and document (addimage.htm) are in the same folder.

You can leave these documents open and use them again in the next lesson.

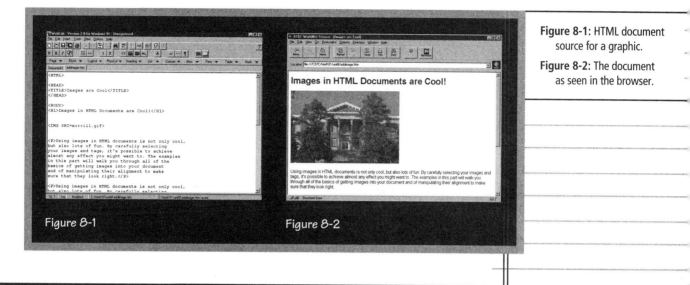

Figure 8-1: HTML document source for a graphic.

Figure 8-2: The document as seen in the browser.

Using the Text Alternative

Lesson 8-2

In this lesson, you learn how to add text to the <IMG> tag to help those readers who cannot view images or who choose not to download them. Even if you don't think that there's much call for a text substitute for a graphic, including alternative text doesn't take much time, and we strongly recommend that you do so. Why? Read on.

Suppose that your readers exercise an option in their browsers that allows them to choose not to view graphics. (In Netscape, Options➪Auto Load Images toggles this option on or off.)

People may not want to view graphics if, for example, they're paying for Internet service by the hour — they may not want to pay to sit and watch someone's slow-loading graphics, right? Heck, cost might not even be a factor — waiting for graphics to download is almost as fun as watching paint dry. Also, consider those folks who don't have graphical browsers. Providing a text alternative for these folks allows them to see a description of the graphic even though they cannot see the actual image.

To make text alternatives, you use the same process that you used to insert graphics (Lesson 8-1) and add in a step to put in the ALT text. The process looks like the following series of steps. You'll get a chance to actually work through the process yourself later in this lesson. For now, simply read through and become familiar with the process.

1 Apply the image tag where you want the graphic to appear.

2 Add the source attribute to indicate the graphic's filename.

3 Specify the alternative text to accompany the image using the ALT= attribute.

The following example shows you how to use the text alternative attribute, ALT=. Notice that the steps show you how to use the text alternative *in addition* to using a graphic.

[margin notes]

Text Alternative = using text to describe graphic

ALT= indicates alternative text

Figure 8-3: HTML document source for an image and alternative text.

Figure 8-4: The document as seen in the browser without Auto Image Loading.

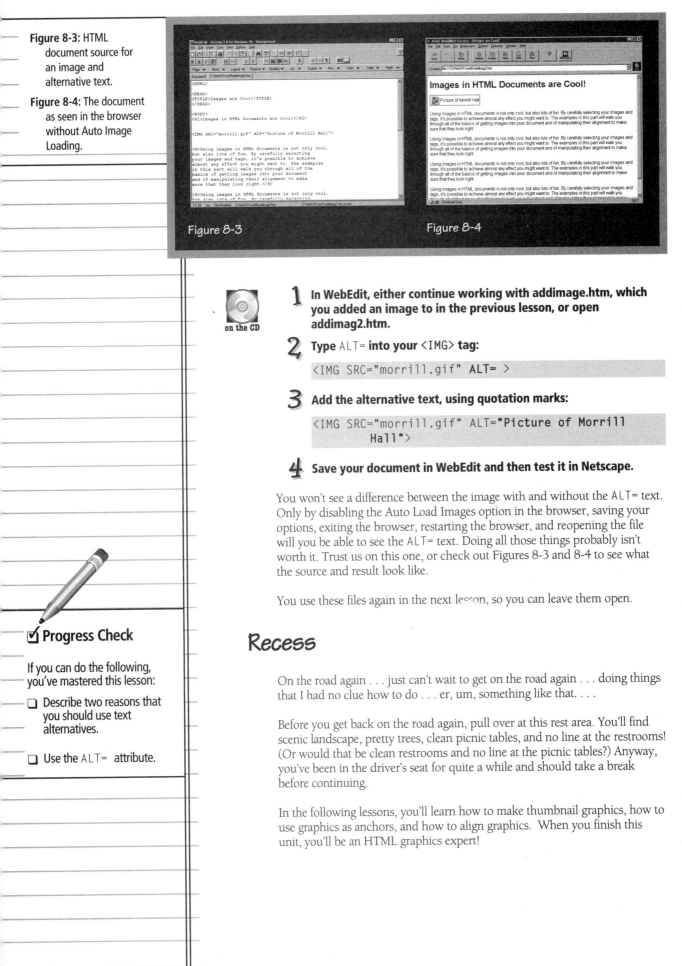

Figure 8-3   Figure 8-4

1 In WebEdit, either continue working with addimage.htm, which you added an image to in the previous lesson, or open addimag2.htm.

on the CD

2 Type ALT= into your <IMG> tag:

```
<IMG SRC="morrill.gif" ALT= >
```

3 Add the alternative text, using quotation marks:

```
<IMG SRC="morrill.gif" ALT="Picture of Morrill
          Hall">
```

4 Save your document in WebEdit and then test it in Netscape.

You won't see a difference between the image with and without the ALT= text. Only by disabling the Auto Load Images option in the browser, saving your options, exiting the browser, restarting the browser, and reopening the file will you be able to see the ALT= text. Doing all those things probably isn't worth it. Trust us on this one, or check out Figures 8-3 and 8-4 to see what the source and result look like.

You use these files again in the next lesson, so you can leave them open.

Recess

On the road again . . . just can't wait to get on the road again . . . doing things that I had no clue how to do . . . er, um, something like that. . . .

Before you get back on the road again, pull over at this rest area. You'll find scenic landscape, pretty trees, clean picnic tables, and no line at the restrooms! (Or would that be clean restrooms and no line at the picnic tables?) Anyway, you've been in the driver's seat for quite a while and should take a break before continuing.

In the following lessons, you'll learn how to make thumbnail graphics, how to use graphics as anchors, and how to align graphics. When you finish this unit, you'll be an HTML graphics expert!

☑ **Progress Check**

If you can do the following, you've mastered this lesson:

❑ Describe two reasons that you should use text alternatives.

❑ Use the ALT= attribute.

Aligning Graphics

Another really fun thing you can do with graphics is change how they are aligned on the page, either left, center, or right. You may have noticed when you completed the exercise in Lesson 8-1 that the graphic you added appeared along the left margin. Left alignment is the default, and all graphics appear on the left unless you specify otherwise.

Changing alignment is particularly handy for improving page design because — well, different alignment creates different visual effects. Using the center and right alignment options with graphics helps make graphics stand out and helps make your page design a bit more interesting. You also can specify how the text elements on the page align with the graphic, such as along the top or bottom of the graphic, to help create the effect you want.

heads up

Not all browsers support alignment attributes. If a browser doesn't support alignment attribute, it will display the graphic with left alignment. So as you're working with the alignment attributes and creating your page design, consider how the graphic will appear on the left, too.

To change graphic alignment, insert <IMG> tags and attributes, just as you have throughout this unit. The general procedure goes like the following steps. You'll do the actual steps later in this lesson:

1 Apply the image tag where you want the graphic to appear.

2 Add the source attribute to identify the file to use and the alternate text attribute to specify alternative text.

3 Include the appropriate alignment attribute.

Table 8-1 lists the most common and useful alignment attributes.

Table 8-1	Alignment Attributes
Attribute	**Effect**
ALIGN=left	Allows a graphic to float to the left margin; subsequent text wraps to the right of that image.
ALIGN=right	Aligns the graphic with the right margin and wraps the text around the left.
ALIGN=top	Aligns the text with the top of the tallest item in the line without affecting text wrap.
ALIGN=middle	Aligns the baseline (line on which the letters rest) of the current line with the middle of the graphic without affecting text wrap.
ALIGN-bottom	Aligns the bottom of the graphic with the baseline of the current line without affecting text wrap.
HSPACE=n	Controls the horizontal space (white space) around the graphic. *n* refers to the number of pixels (little dots on screen).
VSPACE=n	Controls the vertical space (white space) around the graphic. *n* refers to the number of pixels.
HEIGHT=n	Specifies the height of the image in pixels.
WIDTH=n	Specifies the width of the image in pixels.

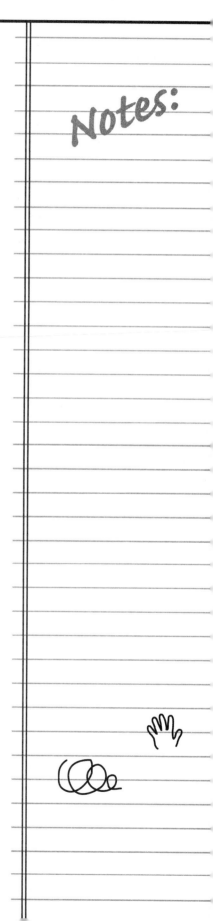

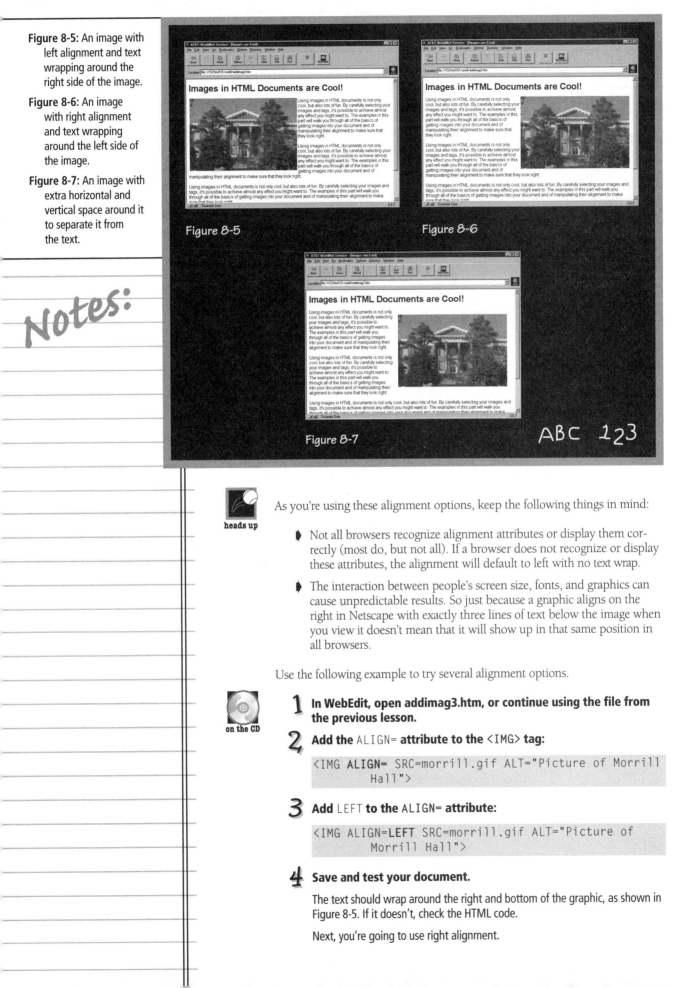

Figure 8-5: An image with left alignment and text wrapping around the right side of the image.

Figure 8-6: An image with right alignment and text wrapping around the left side of the image.

Figure 8-7: An image with extra horizontal and vertical space around it to separate it from the text.

Figure 8-5

Figure 8-6

Figure 8-7

heads up

As you're using these alignment options, keep the following things in mind:

▶ Not all browsers recognize alignment attributes or display them correctly (most do, but not all). If a browser does not recognize or display these attributes, the alignment will default to left with no text wrap.

▶ The interaction between people's screen size, fonts, and graphics can cause unpredictable results. So just because a graphic aligns on the right in Netscape with exactly three lines of text below the image when you view it doesn't mean that it will show up in that same position in all browsers.

Use the following example to try several alignment options.

on the CD

1 In WebEdit, open addimag3.htm, or continue using the file from the previous lesson.

2 Add the ALIGN= **attribute to the** <IMG> **tag:**

```
<IMG ALIGN= SRC=morrill.gif ALT="Picture of Morrill
     Hall">
```

3 Add LEFT **to the** ALIGN= **attribute:**

```
<IMG ALIGN=LEFT SRC=morrill.gif ALT="Picture of
     Morrill Hall">
```

4 Save and test your document.

The text should wrap around the right and bottom of the graphic, as shown in Figure 8-5. If it doesn't, check the HTML code.

Next, you're going to use right alignment.

5 **Switch to WebEdit to try using** RIGHT **alignment.**

6 **Change the** ALIGN= **attribute to** RIGHT.

7 **Save and test your document.**

Your graphic should be on the right side of your screen with the text wrapped around it, as shown in Figure 8-6.

Next you add space between the graphic and text.

8 **Insert two more attributes in the** <IMG> **tag by adding** HSPACE=20 **and** VSPACE=20 **to put more space between the image and the text:**

```
<IMG ALIGN=RIGHT HSPACE=20 VSPACE=20
        SRC="morrill.gif" ALT="Picture of Morrill
        Hall">
```

You can use either or both of these attributes to control the spacing between the text and image both horizontally (HSPACE) and vertically (VSPACE).

9 **Save and test your document.**

Again! Your document should have extra white space around the graphic, as shown in Figure 8-7. If it doesn't look right, check your tags and attributes.

After you're satisfied with your document, switch to WebEdit and close it. The remaining lessons use new files.

☑ **Progress Check**

If you can do the following, you've mastered this lesson:

❏ Describe why the alignment attributes are useful.

❏ Describe several ways you can align graphics.

❏ Discuss two possible problems with aligning graphics.

❏ Use the alignment attributes correctly to improve the design of your HTML document.

Using Graphics as Anchors

Lesson 8-4

In this lesson, you learn how to use a graphic as an anchor that links to other information. Using graphics as anchors is as easy as making a regular text link and then adding an image — you're simply combining steps you're already familiar with.

see Unit 5 for quick review of anchors and links

You may want to use graphics as anchors so that you can create those cute little navigation buttons. A *navigation button* is simply a small graphic that you click to link to other information. And, of course, another reason to use graphics as anchors is because they look cool.

To use graphics as anchors, you follow these general steps. Later in this lesson, you add graphics as anchors in an exercise.

1 **Place an image in your document.**

2 **Add text alternative.**

3 **Add a link around the image.**

In the following steps, you'll learn to use graphics as anchors by inserting navigation buttons into a document.

on the CD

1 **Open navigate.htm from your \html101\unit08 folder in WebEdit.**

2 **Add the graphic called left.gif at the bottom of the document, immediately above the** </BODY> **tag.**

Figure 8-8: Your
navigation icons.

Figure 8-9: Your
navigation icons now
work — note the
pointing finger in
the picture.

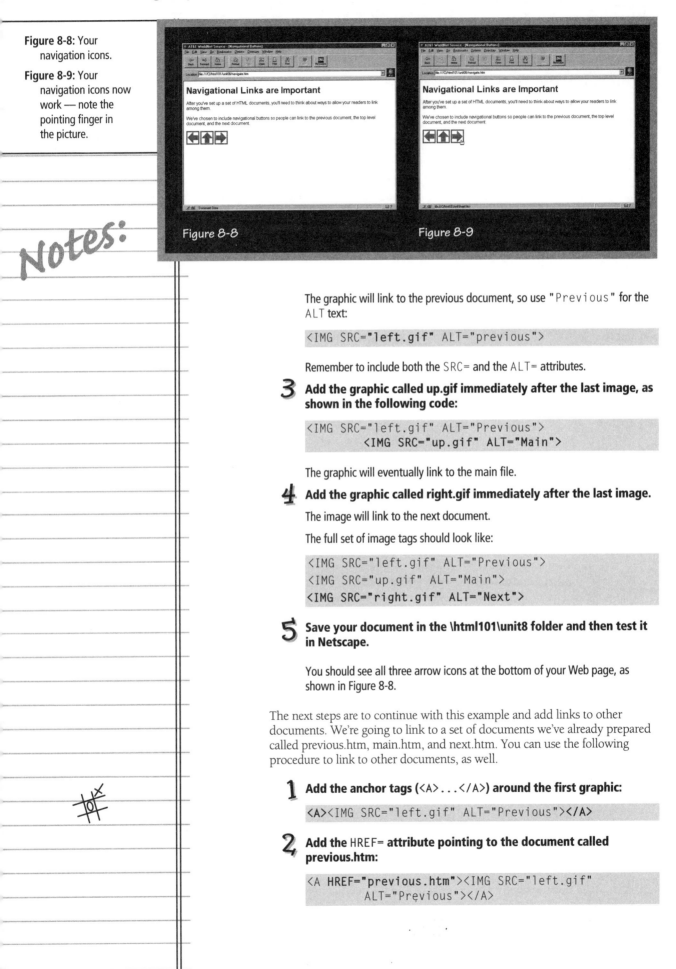

Figure 8-8   Figure 8-9

The graphic will link to the previous document, so use `"Previous"` for the
ALT text:

```
<IMG SRC="left.gif" ALT="previous">
```

Remember to include both the SRC= and the ALT= attributes.

3 **Add the graphic called up.gif immediately after the last image, as
shown in the following code:**

```
<IMG SRC="left.gif" ALT="Previous">
        <IMG SRC="up.gif" ALT="Main">
```

The graphic will eventually link to the main file.

4 **Add the graphic called right.gif immediately after the last image.**

The image will link to the next document.

The full set of image tags should look like:

```
<IMG SRC="left.gif" ALT="Previous">
<IMG SRC="up.gif" ALT="Main">
<IMG SRC="right.gif" ALT="Next">
```

5 **Save your document in the \html101\unit8 folder and then test it
in Netscape.**

You should see all three arrow icons at the bottom of your Web page, as
shown in Figure 8-8.

The next steps are to continue with this example and add links to other
documents. We're going to link to a set of documents we've already prepared
called previous.htm, main.htm, and next.htm. You can use the following
procedure to link to other documents, as well.

1 **Add the anchor tags (<A>...</A>) around the first graphic:**

```
<A><IMG SRC="left.gif" ALT="Previous"></A>
```

2 **Add the HREF= attribute pointing to the document called
previous.htm:**

```
<A HREF="previous.htm"><IMG SRC="left.gif"
        ALT="Previous"></A>
```

3 Add the anchor tags and the HREF= attribute pointing to main.htm to the second graphic:

```
<A HREF="main.htm"><IMG SRC="up.gif"
       ALT="Main"></A>
```

4 Add the anchor tags and an HREF= attribute pointing to next.htm to the third graphic:

```
<A HREF="next.htm"><IMG SRC="right.gif"
       ALT="Next"></A>
```

No sweat! You did it!

5 Now save and test your document.

Your document should look like Figure 8-9, and the links should work. If not, go back and check your code.

6 Close your document in WebEdit when you finish.

☑ **Progress Check**

If you can do the following, you've mastered this lesson:

❑ Identify the primary use of graphical anchors.

❑ Create anchors using images to link to other documents.

Using Thumbnails

Lesson 8-5

on the test

Thumbnails, as they pertain to HTML documents, are smaller copies of bigger images — as opposed to those things you chew on when you're nervous. You can include a thumbnail to spare your readers from having to wait for a large image to download. If they really want to see an image, they can; otherwise, they don't have to wait for it. It's kind of like getting one trial issue of a magazine before you subscribe for a whole year — you get a small taste of the publication without having to wade through 12 month's worth to see whether that's what you wanted.

You should use thumbnails to give your readers the option of viewing a huge graphic. All you do is insert the thumbnail graphic and a link to the large version of the graphic. That way, readers can choose to view the larger graphic by clicking the thumbnail, but they don't have to. Readers can decide, based on the thumbnail, whether or not they're interested in seeing the whole thing.

thumbnail = small version of big image

To use thumbnail graphics, you'll use the same basic steps that you used in the previous lessons in this unit for adding and linking graphics. The primary difference is that you use a smaller version of the graphic to anchor the link and then link to a larger version.

Use the following steps to include thumbnails in your document:

on the CD

1 Open tmbnail.htm in WebEdit.

2 Add an <IMG> tag immediately under the <H1>, complete with SRC= and ALT=; use buildtmb.gif as the image:

```
<IMG SRC="buildtmb.gif" ALT="Thumbnail Image">
```

3 Save and test your document.

No problem at all, right? You should see the thumbnail graphic so far.

Figure 8-10: Your thumbnail image links to a larger version of the same image.

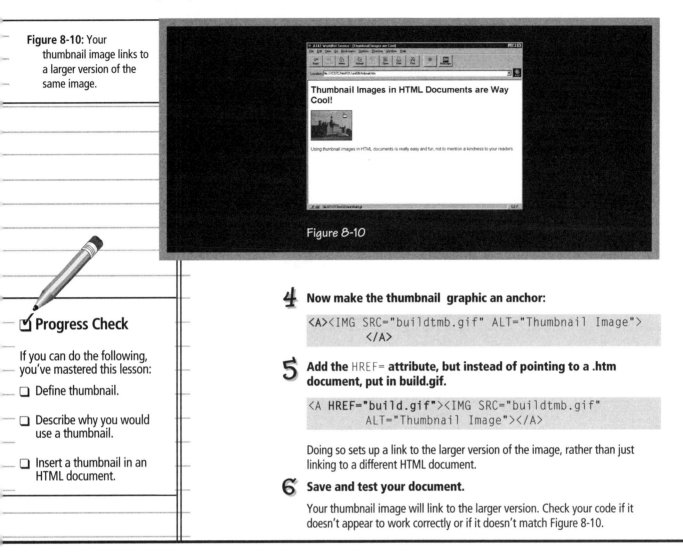

Figure 8-10

☑ Progress Check

If you can do the following, you've mastered this lesson:

❑ Define thumbnail.

❑ Describe why you would use a thumbnail.

❑ Insert a thumbnail in an HTML document.

4 Now make the thumbnail graphic an anchor:

```
<A><IMG SRC="buildtmb.gif" ALT="Thumbnail Image">
      </A>
```

5 Add the HREF= attribute, but instead of pointing to a .htm document, put in build.gif.

```
<A HREF="build.gif"><IMG SRC="buildtmb.gif"
        ALT="Thumbnail Image"></A>
```

Doing so sets up a link to the larger version of the image, rather than just linking to a different HTML document.

6 Save and test your document.

Your thumbnail image will link to the larger version. Check your code if it doesn't appear to work correctly or if it doesn't match Figure 8-10.

Unit 8 Quiz

This short quiz is designed to help you remember things you learned in Unit 8. For each of the following questions, circle the letter of the correct answer or answers.

1. **Text alternatives**

   A. Refer to the lifestyle of your local librarians.

   B. Include things like videos, CDs, and cassettes.

   C. Are used to describe a graphic that your readers may opt not to view.

   D. Are used to alternate between thumbnails and a large graphic.

   E. Both C and D

2. **Thumbnail graphics are**

    A. Photos of those things you chew on when you're nervous.

    B. Bigger than the actual graphic.

    C. Used when the original graphic is particularly large.

    D. Must be included as a text alternative.

    E. None of the above.

3. **You want to include graphics in your HTML page because**

    A. Graphics make your Web pages look spiffier.

    B. Graphics can help express image.

    C. Graphics can make communicating different concepts easier.

    D. Graphics can help you compete with the Joneses.

    E. All of the above.

4. **Why should you include text alternatives in every HTML document?**

    A. Some people cannot decode the meaning of some graphics.

    B. Some people use a browser option that allows them to skip viewing graphics.

    C. Some people don't use graphical browsers.

    D. Both A and B.

    E. Both B and C.

5. **The two possible problems with using alignment options are**

    A. Some browsers don't recognize these attributes.

    B. Some people look under the steering wheel when they drive.

    C. Some browsers don't display alignment attributes correctly.

    D. Some monitors display these attributes as jaggy lines.

    E. Both A and C.

Notes:

Unit 8 Exercise

on the CD

1. Using WebEdit, open up win.htm.

2. Practice inserting winchs.gif and using different alignment options.

3. Make a smaller version of winchs.gif and use it as a thumbnail image. (If you need a review of resizing graphics, refer to Unit 7.)

Using Imagemaps in Your HTML Documents

Prerequisites
▶ Including graphics in your HTML document (Lesson 8-1)
▶ Using text alternatives (Lesson 8-2)
▶ Using graphics as anchors (Lesson 8-4)

Objectives for This Unit

✓ Selecting the imagemap type

✓ Providing alternative navigation

✓ Marking imagemap areas

✓ Defining links in an imagemap

on the CD

▶ imap.htm
▶ menubar.gif
▶ imap2.htm
▶ imap3.htm

No doubt by now you're a regular graphics whiz. Just when you thought things couldn't get any more exciting, we're going to show you one more trick you can do with graphics in your HTML documents — making clickable images (otherwise known as imagemaps or those cool graphics you can click to link to different places).

In the preceding unit, you learned how to use graphics as anchors — that is, you used a graphic to link to other Web pages or other Web sites. In this unit, you learn about *imagemaps* — a single graphic that has more than one link. This unit shows you what you need to know to place imagemaps in your document, including selecting an imagemap type, defining imagemap areas, defining links in an imagemap, and accommodating server-side and client-side imagemaps.

On your mark, get set, go!

Deciding to Use an Imagemap and Selecting Imagemap Type

Lesson 9-1

Imagemaps, also known as *clickable images,* enable readers to click various parts of a single graphic to link to other pages or graphics. For example, a Web site might include a clickable aerial photograph of a city skyline. By

clicking each of the buildings, you link to information about that particular building, tenants, or historical trivia. Clicking an imagemap works differently than clicking a regular graphic that acts as a link — a regular graphic has to link to only one other page or Web address, while different areas on a clickable imagemap can link to all kinds of different documents.

Imagemaps serve two main purposes:

▶ Imagemaps enhance the "shelf appeal" of a Web page by providing a different and potentially more interesting way for your users to navigate to different information. Well-designed imagemaps tend to be more visually appealing than regular text or graphical links.

▶ Imagemaps can help you provide technical information. For example, you could show a picture of a lawnmower that readers can click to view its various parts up-close or click to get more information about the parts they selected. Most readers would find clicking various parts of a lawnmower more interesting than clicking text links, such as "Carburetor," "Blade," or "Engine." Also, the links that imagemaps provide are intuitive to the reader (click the handle to get more information about — you guessed it — the handle).

Deciding to use an imagemap

As the HTML author extraordinaire, you need to decide whether you want to provide an imagemap. Answer the following questions. Your answers should help you determine whether you should do an imagemap at all.

▶ **Does the information lend itself to an imagemap?** A picture of your dog, Sparky, probably doesn't — we can hope — but a picture of canine anatomy with links to more information about various body parts might.

▶ **What kinds of browser software do my readers have?** Sometimes you can determine this if, for example, you're creating imagemaps for use within your company where you know what software everyone has. You also can make educated guesses if you're creating information for the Internet. A Web site for fans of old-and-clunky-but-standards-compliant browsers wouldn't be a good place for client-side imagemaps, while a Web site for hot new Internet stuff would be a great place to include imagemaps.

▶ **Does the added value of enhanced shelf appeal of your Web site justify the time and effort spent in creating an imagemap (particularly if you end up dragging your system administrator into the picture)?** Even if the material lends itself to an imagemap and even if your readers' browsers are new enough to support imagemaps, creating an imagemap will take time. Creating imagemaps — even server-side imagemaps — isn't difficult, but you should consider how much time you want to spend doing enhancements beyond simple graphics.

From these questions, you should be able to determine whether the content, readers' software, and time required are appropriate for including an imagemap in your HTML document. If you answered "no" to the previous questions, consider using other options, like using text links or regular graphical links, to present the information. If you decide that "Yes! Imagemaps are the absolute coolest and my HTML document would just perish without one!" (or even, "Yeah, okay. Including an imagemap looks like fun"), then by all means, include an imagemap!

Selecting an imagemap type

The next step in creating and using imagemaps is to choose the type of imagemap. The type of imagemap you choose determines where the "figuring out what part of the imagemap links to what piece of information" takes place. It's not magic, though it appears to be.

When readers click imagemaps, either their browser or the server has to figure out what to link to. Sometimes the figuring is done by the Web browser (Netscape, for example); these imagemaps are called *client-side imagemaps*. Sometimes the figuring happens back at the Web server that hosts the HTML documents; these are called *server-side imagemaps*.

Client-side imagemaps — ones controlled by readers' browsers — have the advantages of being easy to create and are somewhat faster. The information about where you click doesn't have to go back to the server to make the link work — all the information is handled in the browser.

The pitfall of client-side imagemaps is that not all browsers support them. The newest generations of browser software, like Netscape 2.0 and higher, Internet Explorer 2.0 and higher, and Mosaic 2.1 and higher, support client-side imagemaps. If you create only a client-side imagemap, readers who have browsers that don't support imagemaps can view the image, but the links — the mapping part — won't work.

Server-side maps — ones controlled by the Web server — are the oldest and most widely supported type of imagemap. Creating these maps often requires intervention by your Web administrator before you can use them (which is also why we're only covering the client-side imagemaps in this unit). If it's essential that the widest possible audience be able to use your imagemap, you should discuss setting up a server-side imagemap with your system administrator. (Don't worry, they aren't much different and aren't any more difficult than client-side maps, and you can use them as a supplement to any client-side maps you make.)

Why not just create server-side imagemaps and be safe? Good idea, but you'll have to ask for assistance from your system administrator to put the information on the server. Also, not all Internet service providers support server-side imagemaps, so you may not be able to do server-side maps at all without changing providers.

on the test

In this lesson, we show you how to create client-side imagemaps because you can do that all on your own. We recommend that you consider working with your system administrator to produce a supplemental server-side imagemap, if your imagemap is essential to clearly communicate the information you want to provide.

client-side means figuring is done by readers' browsers

server-side means figuring is done by Web server

☑ Progress Check

If you can do the following, you've mastered this lesson:

❏ Define the term imagemap.

❏ Describe two reasons to use imagemaps.

❏ Discuss the difference between server-side and client-side imagemaps.

❏ Decide whether to use imagemaps and what kind of imagemap to use.

Hello? System administrator? Yes, I'd like to order a server-side imagemap.

If you think your Web site may benefit from a server-side imagemap, you might practice making a client-side imagemap, using the instructions in this unit. More than likely, you'll want to create the client-side imagemap first so that you can have an imagemap in place while you're working with your system administrator. If you only want to use a server-side imagemap, however, you don't actually have to create a client-side imagemap at all, although creating a client-side map would probably be the easiest way to start.

Whether you create a client-side imagemap first or you only create a server-side imagemap, you'll need to contact your system administrator.

1. **Find that itty-bitty scrap of paper you wrote down the administrator's phone number on.**

2. **Call the system administrator.**

3. **Ask the system administrator whether server-side imagemaps are supported (don't forget to say sir or ma'am as applicable).**

   If server-side imagemaps are not supported, you still have the option of creating a client-side imagemap. If you're set on having a server-side imagemap, consider changing Internet service providers to one that does support them.

   If server-side imagemaps are supported, ask the system administrator for specific instructions. You might want to have the instructions in Lessons 9-3 and 9-4 handy — these will probably be similar to what the system administrator provides.

4. **Ask if your service provider has written documentation about creating server-side imagemaps they could mail (or e-mail) to you.**

5. **Find out who you should call if you have problems creating your server-side imagemap (for example, call the system administrator directly or call a technical support number).**

6. **Go for it!**

Lesson 9-2

Providing Alternative Navigation in a Document

In this lesson, you're going to learn how to provide alternative navigation — that is, plain old normal text-only links, just like the ones you've already learned to do. You may recall from Unit 8 that alternative navigation allows readers to still get the information provided in a graphic without having to view the graphic itself.

more info on text alternatives in Lesson 8-2

When you work with imagemaps, including alternative text is *absolutely essential*; the imagemap is the means of navigation, not simply a spiffy graphic. (That's why we're showing you how to include the alternative text before we show you how to create the imagemap.) If you don't include the alternative navigation, readers will not only miss the spiffy graphic, but more importantly, they will not be able to get to other information.

You should include alternative navigation when you create either server-side or client-side imagemaps so that people who opt not to view graphics can still navigate to other information.

Including the alternative navigation is more essential than including the imagemap because the alternative ensures that all readers can link to other information. The imagemap example you're going to build includes links to the previous and next documents, the home page and a page with more information, and a link to a help page. The following steps show you how to provide alternatives to an imagemap in your HTML documents, based on linking to these five pages.

1 **In WebEdit, open imap.htm from your \html101\unit09 folder**

2 **Type the following five lines above the </BODY> tag:**

```
Previous Page
Up a Level
More Information
Help Now!
Next Page
```

3 **Add paragraph tags, <P> above the first line and a </P> below the last one.**

4 **Add links to previous.htm, home.htm, moreinfo.htm, help.htm, and next.htm. You should end up with something like this:**

```
<P>
<A HREF="previous.htm">Previous Page</A>
<A HREF="home.htm">Up a Level</A>
<A HREF="moreinfo.htm">More Information</A>
<A HREF="help.htm">Help Now!</A>
<A HREF="next.htm">Next Page</A>
</P>
```

5 **Add a "|" to the end of the first, second, third, and fourth lines to separate the items:**

```
<A HREF="previous.htm">Previous Page</A> |
<A HREF="home.htm">Up a Level</A> |
<A HREF="moreinfo.htm">More Information</A> |
<A HREF="help.htm">Help Now!</A> |
<A HREF="next.htm">Next Page</A>
```

Look for a vertical line on your keyboard — sometimes it looks like a vertical double-hyphen or a dash doing a headstand.

6 **Save and then test your document in Netscape.**

Your alternative navigation links should look like the example in Figure 9-1. Keep this file open — you'll be using it in Lesson 9-4.

home page is starting point of group of related HTML documents

Notes:

✓ **Progress Check**

If you can do the following, you've mastered this lesson:

❏ List two reasons that you need to include alternative navigation with imagemaps.

❏ Include alternative navigation in your HTML document.

Figure 9-1: Alternatives to imagemaps are essential to a good Web page.

Figure 9-2: The sample imagemap with cursor pointing at coordinate 0,0.

Notes:

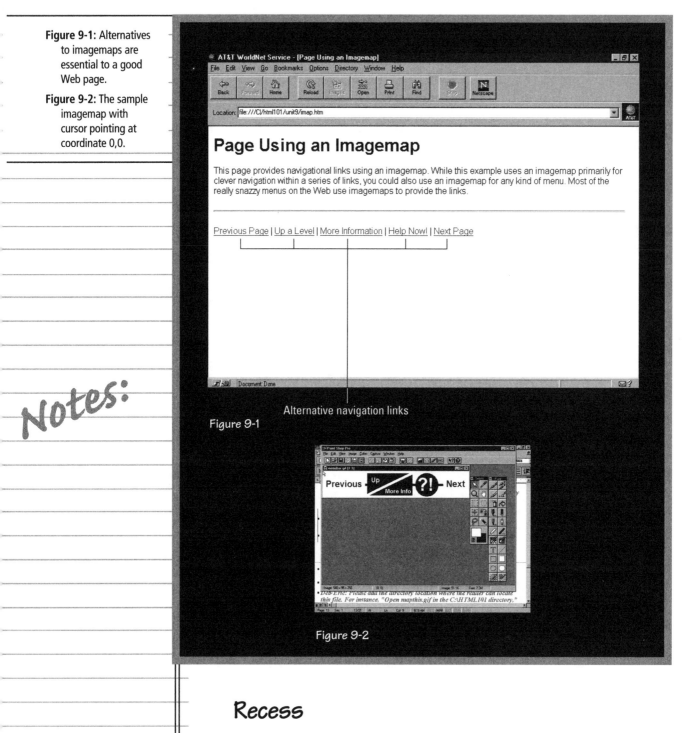

Figure 9-1

Figure 9-2

Recess

You just learned how to determine whether whether an imagemap is right for your HTML document, learned about the two different imagemap types, and even learned how to provide alternative navigation for your imagemaps. Whew! What progress you've made on a fairly difficult topic!

In the next few lessons, you're going to learn how to include the imagemap in your document. This will take some time, so be sure to take all the time you need before diving in.

Marking Clickable Areas in an Imagemap

Lesson 9-3

Before you get started with putting imagemaps into your document, you have to do two things:

- ▶ Define the clickable areas of the imagemap (this lesson).
- ▶ Identify what each clickable area will link to (the next lesson).

Remember that imagemaps have more than one link from a single graphic, so you have to define which areas on the graphic link to what information. In this lesson, you'll be linking to the same documents you linked the alternative navigational links to in the last lesson.

The first thing you have to do is identify or mark the clickable areas within your imagemap. Marking clickable areas is kind of like covering the imagemap with shapes. You have three shapes — rectangles, circles, and polygons — at your disposal. Basically, you can define any area by using these basic shapes and combining them to represent just about anything. For example, you could define, or cover, all the areas of the . . .*For Dummies* Man by using a combination of rectangles, circles, and polygons.

Marking the clickable areas is not really too complicated. All you do is identify various points on the graphic that, if connected, would outline the clickable area (kind of like connecting the dots). To identify points, you'll use *x,y* coordinates — 0,0 is located at the upper-left of the image. Figure 9-2 shows the imagemap you use in this lesson. Notice that the pointer is located at 0,0, which is indicated on the Statusbar at the bottom center of the Paint Shop Pro screen.

The following three sections provide you with instructions on defining a rectangle, circle, and polygon. The example used for this lesson might look familiar to you — it's the menubar you created in Lesson 6-4. Don't worry; if you didn't complete Lesson 6-4, we provide the completed file for you to use. What you're going to do is turn this menubar into an imagemap that links to several different files.

Have a pencil and paper handy to write down the coordinates of the following screen elements. Later in this lesson, you use these coordinates to define the clickable areas on the imagemap. Go ahead and try out each of these exercises.

Marking a rectangle

Rectangular shapes require the coordinates for the upper-left and lower-right corners. The computer figures out the rest.

on the CD

1 **Open menubar.gif in Paint Shop Pro.**

2 **Place the cursor at the top left of the word "Previous".**

You are finding out the coordinates of the rectangle that outlines this word. In the lower center of the screen, you'll see a pair of numbers in parentheses. These are the coordinates of the cursor. If you move the cursor around, you'll see the numbers change. As the cursor goes up and left, the numbers become smaller. At the lower right, they are the highest. With your cursor at the top left corner of the billboard, the coordinates should be approximately 10,30. If your coordinates are within three or four numbers, you're close enough.

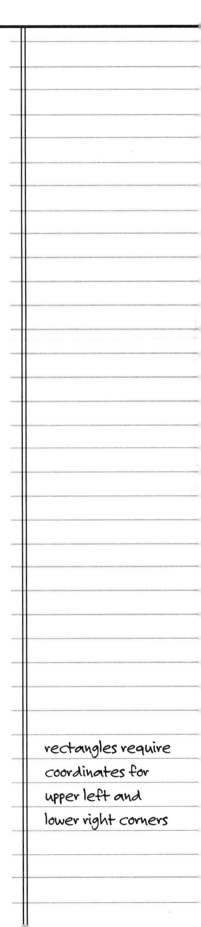

rectangles require
coordinates for
upper left and
lower right corners

3 Write down the upper left coordinates.

4 Point the cursor at the lower right corner of the word and write down those coordinates, too.

You should have something like 145,60. Now, on to the circle.

Marking a circle

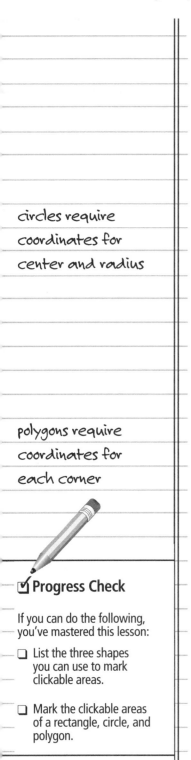

circles require coordinates for center and radius

Circles require the coordinates for the center and the length of the radius. (No panicking. It's not a math test, and you can even use a calculator.)

1 Point the cursor at the center of the circle with ?! in it and record the coordinates.

You should have *x,y* coordinates like 386,45.

2 Move the cursor straight right to the edge of the circle.

The second coordinate shouldn't change (because you're moving horizontally), and you should end up with *x, y* coordinates like 426,45.

3 Subtract the first *x* coordinate from the second *x* coordinate.

We subtracted 426-386 and got 40. How's your math?

Tip: You can use the Windows calculator in Accessories program group.

4 Write down the coordinates of the center point and the length of the radius — 386,45 and 40.

polygons require coordinates for each corner

Marking a polygon

Defining a polygon requires only that you identify each of the corners, and the computer will virtually connect the dots. You're going to mark off the coordinates of the triangle labeled "Up," which will link to the home page eventually.

1 Point the cursor at the top left corner of the Up triangle and write down the coordinates.

We got 165,8.

2 Now do the top right.

We came up with 318,8.

3 Lower left, now.

165,81.

☑ Progress Check

If you can do the following, you've mastered this lesson:

❏ List the three shapes you can use to mark clickable areas.

❏ Mark the clickable areas of a rectangle, circle, and polygon.

Now take this piece of paper with you to the next exercise.

Lesson 9-4   Defining the Links in an Imagemap

After you're done marking the clickable areas, you have to define what each area links to. The following example shows you how to do this with the three areas you just marked. (It looks complicated, but it's not.)

on the CD

1 In WebEdit, open imap2.htm or use the imap.htm file from Lesson 9-2.

2 Above the alternative navigation but below the horizontal rule, put in the image tag for menubar.gif:

```
<IMG SRC="menubar.gif">
```

3 Add the BORDER=0 attribute to make sure that a border doesn't appear on your menu.

We're doing this step primarily because the edges of the graphic are transparent and should blend into the background of the browser.

4 Add the USEMAP= attribute to tell it the name of the map you're getting ready to create:

```
<IMG SRC="menubar.gif" BORDER=0 USEMAP="#menu">
```

This example creates a map called *menu*. (Note that you have to use quotes and a # to identify the map.)

5 Add <MAP> tags so that you can define the imagemap:

```
<MAP>
</MAP>
</BODY>
```

The map tags can go anywhere, but putting them at the end of the file, just above the </BODY> tag, may be easiest.

6 Add the NAME="menu" attribute:

```
<MAP NAME="menu">
</MAP>
```

This allows your browser to associate the USEMAP attribute in step 4 with this map definition. You can have any number of different maps within an HTML document.

7 Now add three <AREA> tags, one for each of the links you're going to make.

```
<MAP NAME="menu">
<AREA>
<AREA>
<AREA>
</MAP>
```

8 You'll use the first area tag for the rectangle, so it gets SHAPE="RECT".

```
<AREA SHAPE="RECT">
```

9 The coordinates for the rectangle are the top left corner followed immediately by the lower right, so add COORDS="10,30,145,60":

```
<AREA SHAPE="RECT" COORDS="10,30,145,60">
```

Remember, you can read all the coordinates you need off that piece of paper on which you took your notes.

Notes:

 # and "" are essential

coordinates for
circle are center
(x,y) followed by
radius

Progress Check

If you can do the following,
you've mastered this lesson:

❏ Define an imagemap in
an HTML document.

❏ Specify rectangle, circle,
and polygon areas in a
map definition.

10 Now add the `HREF="previous.htm"` **attribute for the circle:**

```
<AREA SHAPE="RECT" COORDS="10,30,145,60"
      HREF="previous.htm">
```

What you're doing is creating a link between the area within the coordinates
and the corresponding HTML document.

11 **The next AREA tag is for the circle, so you'll add** `SHAPE="CIRCLE"`
to the next <AREA> tag:

```
<AREA SHAPE="RECT" COORDS="10,30,145,60"
      HREF="previous.htm">
<AREA SHAPE="CIRCLE">
```

12 **The COORDS are the center of the circle, followed by the radius:**

```
<AREA SHAPE="CIRCLE" COORDS="386,45,40">
```

13 **The link for the circle is** `HREF="help.htm"`:

```
<AREA SHAPE="CIRCLE" COORDS="386,45,40"
      HREF="help.htm">
```

14 **The last** `<AREA>` **tag is for the Up link, so it's a triangle. Triangles
(or any other special shapes) are just polygons, so add the
attribute** `SHAPE="POLYGON"` **to the third area tag:**

```
<AREA SHAPE="POLYGON">
```

15 **Now, add the coordinates for the top left corner, then top right,
and then on around clockwise around the shape:**

```
<AREA SHAPE="POLYGON" COORDS="165,8,318,8,165,81">
```

Whether you add coordinates in clockwise or counterclockwise order doesn't
really matter, as long as you start at one spot and work corner by corner
around the shape. Don't skip corners as you work around the shape. In this
example, you're working with a triangle, so you can't really skip a corner. But
if you are working with a different polygon and skip a corner, the resulting
defined area won't be the shape you want.

16 **Add in an** `HREF=` **attribute pointing to the home.htm file.**

```
<AREA SHAPE="POLYGON" COORDS="165,8,318,8,165,81"
      HREF="home.htm">
```

Whew! Finally!

The first shapes defined take priority. If you have overlapping shapes (say a
small circle on a much larger rectangle), define the one on top first. If you
define the bottom one first, it will cover the other shape up so that they won't
work at all.

17 **Save and test your document.**

Be sure and check all the links you've created, both alternative and imagemap
links. Remember that you only defined three links in the imagemap, so don't
panic if the other ones don't work.

Check out Figures 9-3 and 9-4, which show you the HTML code as it should
appear in WebEdit and the imagemap results viewed in Netscape. If your
document didn't turn out as shown in Figure 9-4, compare your code with the
code in imap3.htm. You can use these files for the unit exercise, so you don't
have to close them here if you're moving on to the quiz and exercise now.

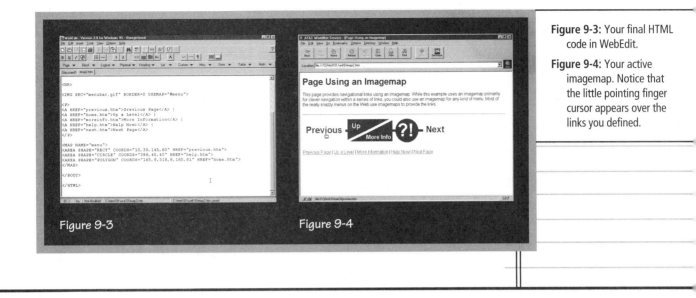

Figure 9-3

Figure 9-4

Figure 9-3: Your final HTML code in WebEdit.

Figure 9-4: Your active imagemap. Notice that the little pointing finger cursor appears over the links you defined.

Unit 9 Quiz

This short quiz is designed to help you remember things you learned in Unit 9. For each of the following questions, circle the letter of the correct answer or answers.

1. **Two reasons that alternative navigation is essential to include with imagemaps are that**

    A. Some browsers can display graphics but do not support imagemaps.

    B. Some people have text-only browsers.

    C. Some people choose not to view graphics — to turn off images in their browser — as they surf the Web.

    D. Some people don't want to see graphics, but want to view them in person.

    E. Graphics are worth a thousand words.

2. **Which definable area requires the upper-left and lower-right coordinates?**

    A. Triangles

    B. Circles

    C. Rectangles

    D. Octagons

    E. All definable areas require these coordinates.

3. **The two steps to making imagemaps are to**

    A. Define the clickable areas of the imagemap.

    B. Define the words rectangle, circle, and polygon so the computer knows what they are.

    C. Define what each area will link to.

    D. Define whatever text is contained in the imagemap.

    E. Define "imagemap" to your cat.

4. **The difference between a server-side imagemap and a client-side imagemap is that**

   A. A client-side imagemap require readers to pay to see the graphic; a server-side imagemap is free.

   B. A client-side imagemap is run by a browser; a server-side imagemap is run by a waiter.

   C. A client-side imagemap is run by a browser; a server-side imagemap is run by a Web server.

   D. A client-side imagemap is run by a Web server; a server-side imagemap is run by a browser.

   E. A client-side imagemap is run by a system administrator; a server-side imagemap is run by an Internet search engine.

5. **You need to consider three things when planning to use an imagemap in your HTML document. They are**

   A. The browser software your readers are using.

   B. Whether the content lends itself to imagemaps.

   C. How fast your readers' Internet connections are.

   D. How much time you want to spend enhancing your Web site beyond using graphics.

   E. Whether your dog, Sparky, can fit his paw on the clickable portion of the graphic.

Unit 9 Exercise

on the CD

1. Open WebEdit and Netscape.

2. In WebEdit, open imap3.htm from your \html101\unit09 folder (or continue with the file you were using in Lesson 9-4).

3. Complete the areas of the imagemap that haven't been mapped yet. You will need to do the More link as well as the Next link.

4. Save and test your imagemap in Netscape.

   Be sure to test all the links!

Part III Review

Unit 6 Summary

▶ **Paint Shop Pro:** Paint Shop Pro is the software you use to create and modify graphics. Using Paint Shop Pro, you can draw and fill objects, use text, and change background and object colors.

Unit 7 Summary

▶ **Suitable graphics:** Graphics suitable for HTML documents load quickly, have a purpose, and are interesting or flashy.

▶ **Resizing graphics:** You can resize graphics — that is, change the physical dimension of the graphic — so that the graphics are better for use in HTML documents. Resizing often is used to reduce overall size.

▶ **Making graphics small:** You can make graphics as small as possible (in terms of disk space) to help graphics load faster in browsers. To make a graphic smaller, you can resize it to decrease the overall dimensions or decrease the color depth of the graphic.

▶ **Pixel:** A pixel is the smallest unit of a graphic on a computer screen.

▶ **Transparent graphic:** A transparent graphic is a graphic with a transparent background so that the background color of the browser shows through. You use a transparent graphic to help the main portion of the graphic stand out.

▶ **Interlaced graphic:** An interlaced graphic is a graphic that comes up in waves in your browser. You use an interlaced graphic to help make your graphic more interesting and to make it *appear* to load more quickly.

Unit 8 Summary

▶ **Graphics (again):** Graphics can be used to make Web pages look spiffier, convey difficult concepts, establish your image, and help you keep up with your competitors.

▶ **Text alternative:** A text alternative is used to describe a graphic. You use a text alternative to allow people who cannot or do not view graphics to understand what the graphic shows.

▶ **Aligning graphics:** Different alignment attributes are available that let you align graphics differently in relation to text. You can use these attributes with most browsers and can use them to improve page design.

▶ **Graphical anchors:** You can use graphics as anchors that link to other information or graphics. Using graphics as anchors is good for enhancing your Web page and for making your page design a bit spiffier.

▶ **Thumbnails:** A thumbnail is a smaller version of a larger graphic. You should use a thumbnail to give your readers an option to view or not to view a large graphic.

Part III Review

Unit 9 Summary

- **Imagemaps:** Imagemaps, also called clickable images, are graphics with more than one link. Imagemaps are useful for enhancing your Web pages and for documentation.

- **Alternative navigation:** Alternative navigation provides readers with a nongraphical way to link to the same information that the imagemap links to. Alternative navigation is essential to use with imagemaps because some people cannot or do not view graphics and will still need access to the linked information.

- **Making imagemaps:** To make an imagemap, you have to do two things: Define the clickable areas and link the areas to other information.

- **Defining areas:** You can define three shapes as clickable areas: rectangles, circles, and polygons. To define these areas, you enter x,y coordinates.

Part III Test

The questions on this test cover all the material from Part III, Units 6 through 9. Good luck!

True   False

Each statement is either true or false.

T   F   1. It is best to save your graphics as GIF files because virtually all Web browsers on all computers can read them.

T   F   2. Interlaced graphics come up on-screen slower than noninterlaced graphics.

T   F   3. Using text alternatives for regular graphics is a good idea, but using them with imagemaps is essential.

T   F   4. A thumbnail in HTML is a link from a really huge graphic to a text alternative.

T   F   5. Graphics viewed in Netscape always look the same as they do in WebEdit.

T   F   6. An alternate graphic file type that can be used for viewing graphics on the Web is PCX.

T   F   7. Transparent graphics cannot be viewed on a browser.

T   F   8. Imagemaps are different from regular graphical links because a single imagemap has more than one link.

T   F   9. Graphics can be effectively used to communicate difficult or complex concepts.

T   F   10. Client-side imagemaps are controlled by the client administrator.

Multiple Choice

For each of the following questions, circle the correct answer or answers. Remember, you may find more than one answer for each question.

11. **When thinking about including an imagemap in your HTML document, you should consider**

   A. The type of information you're trying to convey.

   B. Having a beer . . . or two.

   C. The readers' browser type.

   D. The amount of time you need to spend on enhancements.

12. **Making a graphic transparent is an excellent way of**

   A. Making the main portion of the graphic stand out.

   B. Making the main portion of the graphic disappear.

   C. Making the main portion of the graphic sit up and beg.

   D. Making the main portion of the graphic a part of a larger graphic.

13. **The preferable file subformat for saving graphics is**

   A. 89a, interlaced only.

   B. 87a, either interlaced or noninterlaced.

   C. 89a, noninterlaced only.

   D. 89a, either interlaced or noninterlaced.

14. **It's a good idea to save your documents**

   A. Frequently, in case your computer crashes and you lose changes made since the last change.

   B. Frequently, because you can only put fresh saves on a disk.

   C. Every 30 minutes, which is the maximum your computer will let you save.

   D. You don't have to worry about saving your documents because they originate on the computer's hard drive.

Part III Test

15. **A pixel is**

    A. The long rod that connects your car's tires.

    B. A point on an imagemap indicated by coordinates x,y.

    C. The smallest unit of a graphic on your screen.

    D. The smallest size you can save a graphic.

16. **When the authors took a break in Unit 9, they**

    A. Took a nap.

    B. Took a chill pill.

    C. Had an author quarrel.

    D. Who cares — it's their business.

17. **Server-side imagemaps are**

    A. The oldest and most commonly used type of imagemap.

    B. Younger and more athletic than client-side imagemaps.

    C. For use in restaurants.

    D. Younger and more available than client-side imagemaps.

18. **Imagemaps are different from regular graphics with links because**

    A. Imagemaps can be photographs, and graphics cannot.

    B. Imagemaps have more than one link.

    C. Imagemaps are less dependable than graphics.

    D. Imagemaps have more personality and are generally cuter than regular graphics.

19. **You should be careful about using alignment attributes because**

    A. Alignment attributes often make your graphics have jaggy edges.

    B. Alignment attributes confuse browsers.

    C. Alignment attributes can only be read by text-only browsers.

    D. Alignment attributes are not supported and displayed by all browsers.

20. **Interlaced graphics**

    A. Go poooooooof (rather than wait, wait, wait, poof) when they come up on your computer screen.

    B. Go wait, wait, wait, poof (rather than pooooooof) when they come up on your computer screen.

    C. Go kablooie when you click them.

    D. Often appear grainy on low-resolution monitors.

Part III Lab Assignment

This is the third of your lab assignments. In this assignment, we don't give you too many step-by-step instructions because we want you to be creative and develop the graphics and Web pages as you want. Good luck and have fun!

For this lab assignment, pretend that you're the Web expert at your company and have been asked to incorporate some images on the company's Web site. (This *is* the 90s, you know.) After talking to some of your co-workers, you determine that the Web site really only needs two graphics: a logo that appears somewhere on each page and a picture of your company's primary product, The Wingdinger Multi-purpose Doomaflitchie. Including only these graphics will best suit the company's image without overdoing the Web site.

Here's what to do:

In Paint Shop Pro, develop a simple company logo with text, shapes, and colors. Save this as a graphic.

In Paint Shop Pro, create a picture of the Doomaflitchie. You might consider making a detailed drawing as well as a thumbnail. What do you mean you don't know what it looks like — you work for the company, remember?

Create two Web pages: One with basic company information (and the logo) and the other with information about the Doomaflitchie. Include the logo on both pages, a thumbnail on the Doomaflitchie page, and a link to the larger graphic.

That's all for this part. Better get busy!

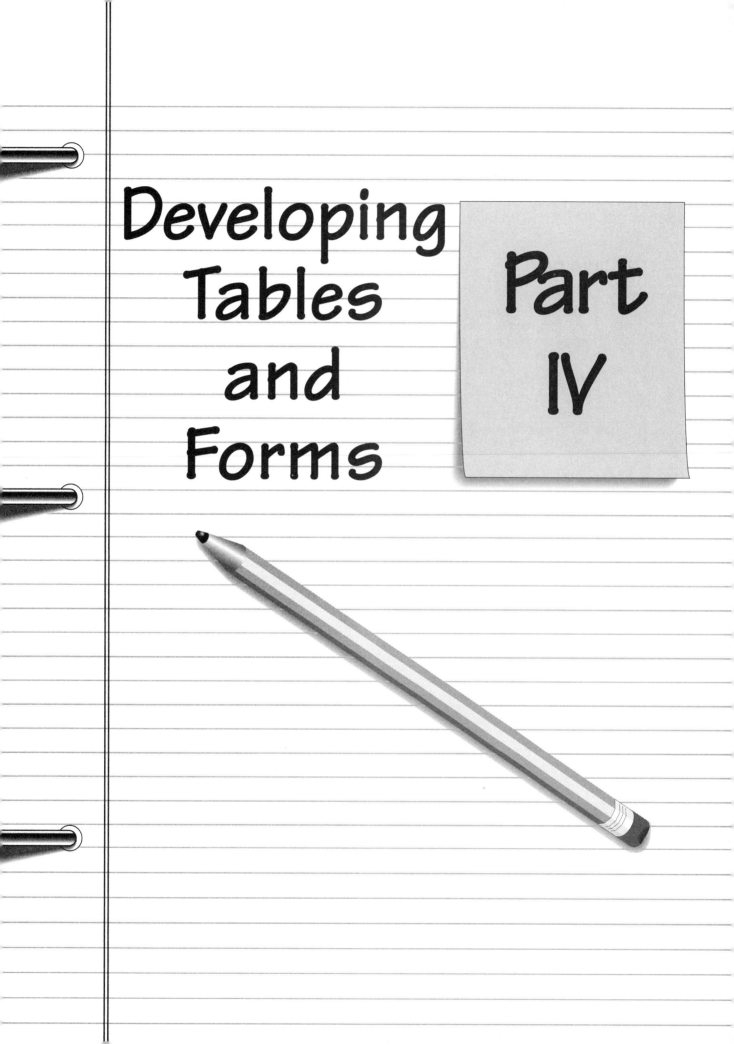

Developing Tables and Forms

Part IV

In this part . . .

In this part, you learn all about tables and forms. This part show how tables are handy for organizing information and how forms are an excellent way to let your readers communicate information back to *you*. These are some of the more fancy HTML effects, but they're really no harder to do than the things you've mastered already.

You may notice that both of the units in this part are fairly long — Okay, they're really long. In the step-by-step instructions, we included many little steps (which is why it seems long) so that you don't get lost in the process. As you become more proficient with tables and forms, you'll probably find yourself combining steps and shortening the process somewhat.

Enjoy!

Developing Tables

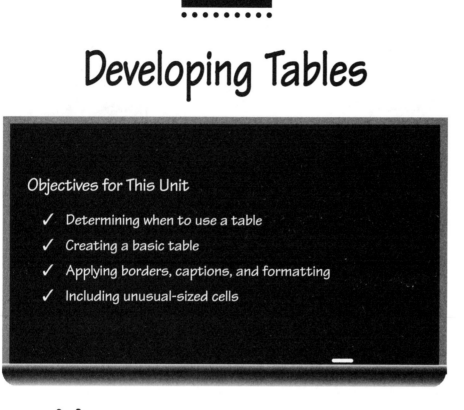

Objectives for This Unit

✓ Determining when to use a table

✓ Creating a basic table

✓ Applying borders, captions, and formatting

✓ Including unusual-sized cells

Prerequisites:

▶ Understanding the fundamentals of HTML (Part I)

▶ Building basic HTML documents (Part II)

on the CD

▶ samptabl.htm
▶ table.htm
▶ table2.htm
▶ table3.htm
▶ table4.htm
▶ table5.htm
▶ table6.htm

No doubt that you absorbed a great deal of information in the last few parts, learning all that stuff about graphics and imagemaps. (By the way, congratulations!) But now, we're switching gears.

This unit explains all you need to know about tables — when to use them, how to create them, and how to enhance them. Tables enable you to present tabular information so that you, the writer, can control layout and design more effectively. You don't have to use tables, but you'll probably find that you need them for some of the designs or information you choose to present.

The following lessons show you how to determine whether you should use a table, how to create a basic table, and how to add nifty effects to tables.

Deciding to Use a Table

Lesson 10-1

In this lesson, you learn when and why to use tables in your HTML documents. A *table,* in this instance, is a grid of rows and columns that you can put information in.

rows go across; columns go down

You use tables in your HTML documents for the following reasons:

▶ **To help readers find information quickly:** Providing information in tables often helps readers find information faster than if the information is in paragraphs.

Figure 10-1: A couple of sample tables.

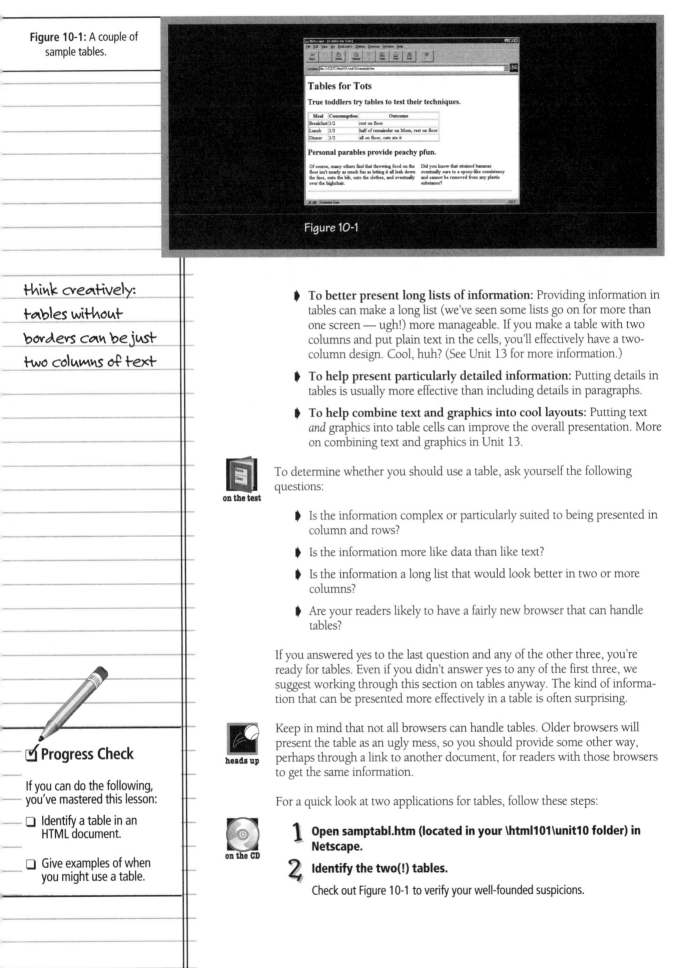

Figure 10-1

think creatively:
tables without
borders can be just
two columns of text

▶ **To better present long lists of information:** Providing information in tables can make a long list (we've seen some lists go on for more than one screen — ugh!) more manageable. If you make a table with two columns and put plain text in the cells, you'll effectively have a two-column design. Cool, huh? (See Unit 13 for more information.)

▶ **To help present particularly detailed information:** Putting details in tables is usually more effective than including details in paragraphs.

▶ **To help combine text and graphics into cool layouts:** Putting text *and* graphics into table cells can improve the overall presentation. More on combining text and graphics in Unit 13.

on the test

To determine whether you should use a table, ask yourself the following questions:

▶ Is the information complex or particularly suited to being presented in column and rows?

▶ Is the information more like data than like text?

▶ Is the information a long list that would look better in two or more columns?

▶ Are your readers likely to have a fairly new browser that can handle tables?

If you answered yes to the last question and any of the other three, you're ready for tables. Even if you didn't answer yes to any of the first three, we suggest working through this section on tables anyway. The kind of information that can be presented more effectively in a table is often surprising.

heads up

Keep in mind that not all browsers can handle tables. Older browsers will present the table as an ugly mess, so you should provide some other way, perhaps through a link to another document, for readers with those browsers to get the same information.

For a quick look at two applications for tables, follow these steps:

on the CD

1 **Open samptabl.htm (located in your \html101\unit10 folder) in Netscape.**

2 **Identify the two(!) tables.**

Check out Figure 10-1 to verify your well-founded suspicions.

☑ **Progress Check**

If you can do the following, you've mastered this lesson:

❑ Identify a table in an HTML document.

❑ Give examples of when you might use a table.

Creating a Basic Table

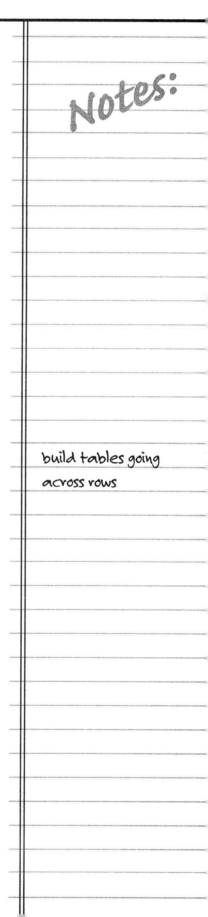

In this lesson, you create a basic table by using the basic tags and attributes:

- `<TABLE>...</TABLE>` indicates table format.
- `<TD>...</TD>` indicates table data cell.
- `<TR>...<TR>` indicates table row items.

The remaining lessons in this unit help you customize and format the table to be more useful to you.

Creating a basic table is fairly easy. For the following examples, suppose that your company has a fairly complex matrix of services you offer, different types of customers, and different prices depending on the customer. Your matrix might look something like Table 10-1.

Table 10-1	Pricing Schedule for 1997		
Products	**Wholesale**	**Retail**	**Direct**
Basic Whatzit	250.00	500.00	750.00
Enhanced Whatzit	350.00	600.00	850.00
Advanced Whatzit	450.00	700.00	1000.00

In the following exercises, you build this table by going across each row in turn. You're ready to get started:

on the CD

1 **In WebEdit, open the document table.htm in your \html101\unit10 folder.**

2 **Put your cursor on the line immediately below the** `</P>` **tag (the closing paragraph tag).**

3 **Enter a** `<TABLE>` **and** `</TABLE>` **tag, preferably with a few blank lines in between:**

```
<TABLE>



</TABLE>
```

This step just marks where the table will go; it won't make anything appear on-screen.

4 **Insert a** `<TR>` **and** `</TR>` **tag on the first blank line between the** `<TABLE>` **tags:**

```
<TABLE>
<TR></TR>
</TABLE>
```

The `<TR>...</TR>` tags mark a table row.

build tables going
across rows

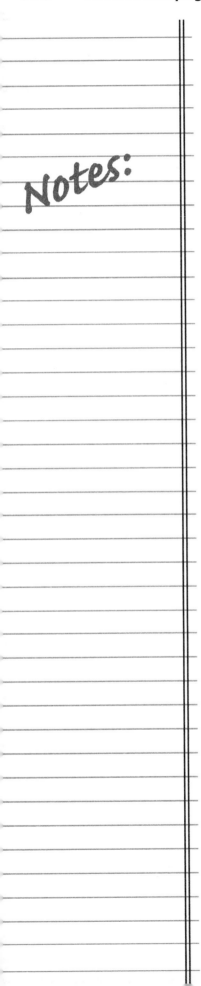

5 **Add a** `<TD>` **and** `</TD>` **tag between the** `<TR>` **tags:**

```
<TABLE>
<TR><TD></TD></TR>
</TABLE>
```

The `<TD>` tags mark each separate cell in the table. Think of the TD as representing Table Data, if that helps you remember what it does. We're building our table across the first row right now.

6 **Add the words "Basic Whatzit" between the** `<TD>` **tags.**

Basic Whatzit is at the left end of the second line of our sample table. We didn't just make it up. We're skipping the header row of this table, but we'll come back to it in the next lesson.

```
<TABLE>
<TR><TD>Basic Whatzit</TD></TR>
</TABLE>
```

7 **Add another set of** `<TD>...</TD>` **tags immediately after the first one:**

```
<TABLE>
<TR><TD>Basic Whatzit</TD><TD></TD></TR>
</TABLE>
```

This set of table data tags is for the second item in the first row.

8 **Add the number** 250.00 **between the second set of Table Data tags:**

```
<TABLE>
<TR><TD>Basic Whatzit</TD><TD>250.00</TD></TR>
</TABLE>
```

9 **Add another set of table data tags with** 500.00 **between them:**

```
<TABLE>
<TR><TD>Basic
      Whatzit</TD><TD>250.00</TD>
      <TD>500.00</TD></TR>
</TABLE>
```

10 **And add one more set of table data tags with** 750.00 **between them:**

```
<TABLE>
<TR><TD>Basic
      Whatzit</TD><TD>250.00</TD>
      <TD>500.00</TD><TD>750.00</TD></TR>
</TABLE>
```

11 **Save and then test your document in Netscape.**

The document won't be particularly pretty yet, but it's a start. Notice that the table — actually the first row of your table — is just below the paragraph of text. If you don't see familiar text under the existing paragraph, make sure that you entered the tags correctly. Figure 10-2 shows how the table should look.

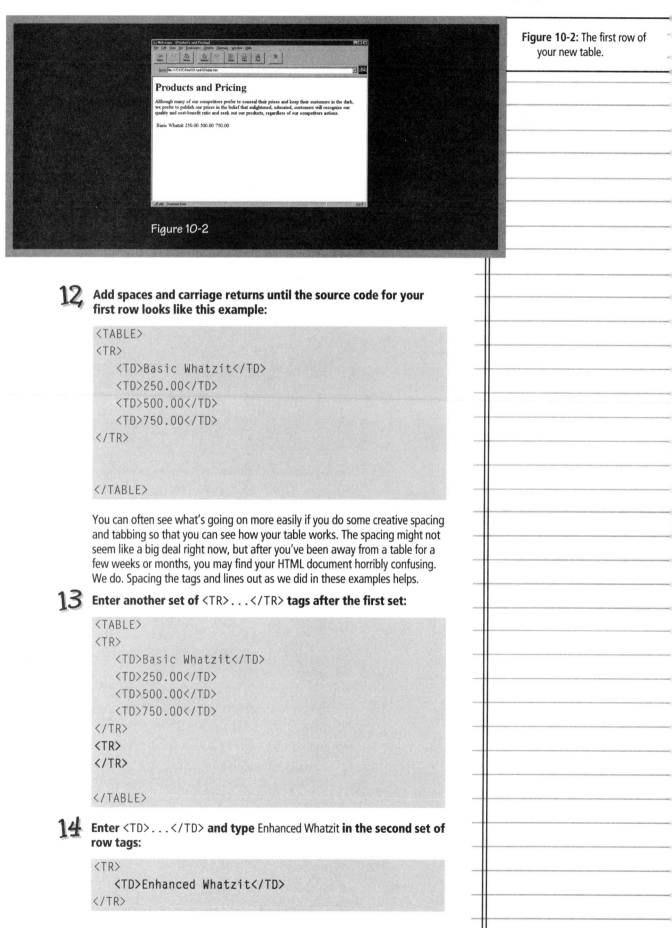

Figure 10-2: The first row of
your new table.

Figure 10-2

12 **Add spaces and carriage returns until the source code for your
first row looks like this example:**

```
<TABLE>
<TR>
   <TD>Basic Whatzit</TD>
   <TD>250.00</TD>
   <TD>500.00</TD>
   <TD>750.00</TD>
</TR>


</TABLE>
```

You can often see what's going on more easily if you do some creative spacing
and tabbing so that you can see how your table works. The spacing might not
seem like a big deal right now, but after you've been away from a table for a
few weeks or months, you may find your HTML document horribly confusing.
We do. Spacing the tags and lines out as we did in these examples helps.

13 **Enter another set of** `<TR>...</TR>` **tags after the first set:**

```
<TABLE>
<TR>
   <TD>Basic Whatzit</TD>
   <TD>250.00</TD>
   <TD>500.00</TD>
   <TD>750.00</TD>
</TR>
<TR>
</TR>

</TABLE>
```

14 **Enter** `<TD>...</TD>` **and type** Enhanced Whatzit **in the second set of
row tags:**

```
<TR>
   <TD>Enhanced Whatzit</TD>
</TR>
```

Figure 10-3: Your first table takes shape.

Figure 10-4: Your first HTML table should look like this figure.

Notes:

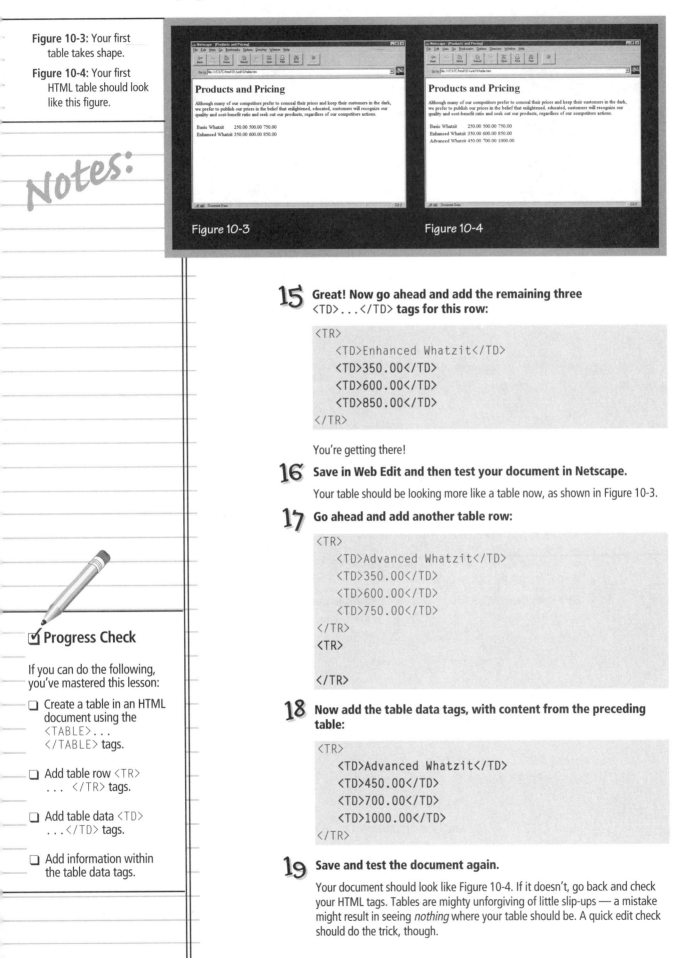

Figure 10-3

Figure 10-4

15 **Great! Now go ahead and add the remaining three `<TD>...</TD>` tags for this row:**

```
<TR>
    <TD>Enhanced Whatzit</TD>
    <TD>350.00</TD>
    <TD>600.00</TD>
    <TD>850.00</TD>
</TR>
```

You're getting there!

16 **Save in Web Edit and then test your document in Netscape.**

Your table should be looking more like a table now, as shown in Figure 10-3.

17 **Go ahead and add another table row:**

```
<TR>
    <TD>Advanced Whatzit</TD>
    <TD>350.00</TD>
    <TD>600.00</TD>
    <TD>750.00</TD>
</TR>
<TR>

</TR>
```

18 **Now add the table data tags, with content from the preceding table:**

```
<TR>
    <TD>Advanced Whatzit</TD>
    <TD>450.00</TD>
    <TD>700.00</TD>
    <TD>1000.00</TD>
</TR>
```

19 **Save and test the document again.**

Your document should look like Figure 10-4. If it doesn't, go back and check your HTML tags. Tables are mighty unforgiving of little slip-ups — a mistake might result in seeing *nothing* where your table should be. A quick edit check should do the trick, though.

☑ **Progress Check**

If you can do the following, you've mastered this lesson:

❏ Create a table in an HTML document using the `<TABLE>...</TABLE>` tags.

❏ Add table row `<TR>...</TR>` tags.

❏ Add table data `<TD>...</TD>` tags.

❏ Add information within the table data tags.

Recess

See, that wasn't too hard — and that was the worst part of the whole unit! So far, you've learned to make a basic HTML table. In the rest of the unit, you learn how to format tables, how to set up a table header, and how to use different-sized cells in your table. Right now it's chow time in our household, so we're taking a break before starting the next lesson.

save final changes in WebEdit before leaving computer

Applying Additional Features

Lesson 10-3

Now that you have a table in your document, you're ready to spiff it up a little with borders, captions, headers, and formatting.

Each of the following sections provides instructions for including these things in your table. Each section has a list of instructions in which you'll be building the table with the following tags and attributes:

- BORDER= draws a border around the cells.
- <CAPTION>...</CAPTION> identifies the caption for a table.
- ALIGN=TOP (or BOTTOM) controls whether the caption appears above or below the table.
- ALIGN=LEFT (or CENTER or RIGHT) controls the alignment of the table on the page.
- CELLPADDING= adds space around cells.
- CELLSPACING= inserts specified space between cells.
- WIDTH=n changes the width of the table based on *n*.

Applying borders

Using borders on tables helps your readers more clearly see where cells are. If your text is truly tabular, as in our example, you'll probably want to use borders.

However, you don't have to use borders at all (and of course, in that case, you just wouldn't add the border attribute). For example, tables with many rows and many columns may look too busy if you apply a border. Also, if you have several tables on a page, borders might actually make the tables less readable. You have to decide for yourself whether the border helps — try the table with and without the border to help you decide.

view table with and without border before deciding which way is best

To apply borders to your table, follow these steps:

on the CD

1 **In WebEdit, open table2.htm in your \html101\unit10 folder (or keep working with your file from the last lesson).**

2 **Add a BORDER=3 attribute to your opening <TABLE> tag.**

```
<TABLE BORDER=3>
```

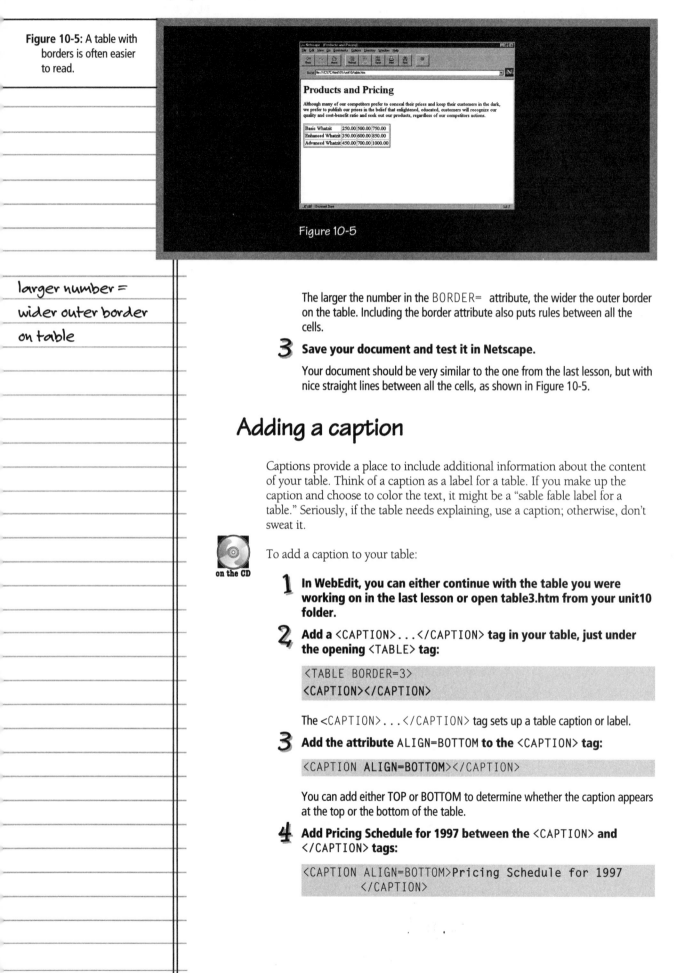

Figure 10-5

larger number =
wider outer border
on table

The larger the number in the BORDER= attribute, the wider the outer border on the table. Including the border attribute also puts rules between all the cells.

3 Save your document and test it in Netscape.

Your document should be very similar to the one from the last lesson, but with nice straight lines between all the cells, as shown in Figure 10-5.

Adding a caption

Captions provide a place to include additional information about the content of your table. Think of a caption as a label for a table. If you make up the caption and choose to color the text, it might be a "sable fable label for a table." Seriously, if the table needs explaining, use a caption; otherwise, don't sweat it.

on the CD

To add a caption to your table:

1 In WebEdit, you can either continue with the table you were working on in the last lesson or open table3.htm from your unit10 folder.

2 Add a `<CAPTION>...</CAPTION>` **tag in your table, just under the opening** `<TABLE>` **tag:**

```
<TABLE BORDER=3>
<CAPTION></CAPTION>
```

The `<CAPTION>...</CAPTION>` tag sets up a table caption or label.

3 Add the attribute `ALIGN=BOTTOM` **to the** `<CAPTION>` **tag:**

```
<CAPTION ALIGN=BOTTOM></CAPTION>
```

You can add either TOP or BOTTOM to determine whether the caption appears at the top or the bottom of the table.

4 Add Pricing Schedule for 1997 between the `<CAPTION>` **and** `</CAPTION>` **tags:**

```
<CAPTION ALIGN=BOTTOM>Pricing Schedule for 1997
        </CAPTION>
```

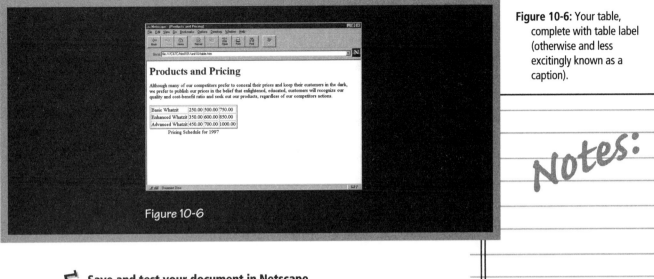

Figure 10-6

Figure 10-6: Your table,
complete with table label
(otherwise and less
excitingly known as a
caption).

Notes:

5 **Save and test your document in Netscape.**

Your page should look like Figure 10-6, complete with the fable table label at
the bottom. If your table doesn't look like Figure 10-6, go back to WebEdit and
make sure that you entered the tags correctly by comparing them to the tags
in the instructions.

Adding table headers

The next step in developing your table is to add the table headers. *Table
headers* are simply headers at the top of each column that describe the content
of the column.

When should you use table headers? There's not really a tried-and-true
formula for when you should or when you shouldn't use them. If the information in each column of the table won't be completely clear from the context,
however, you should probably use a table header.

*use table headers
if information in
columns isn't self-
describing*

on the CD

1 **In WebEdit, you can either continue with the table you were
working on in the last lesson or open table4.htm in your \html101\
unit10 folder.**

2 **Add an additional table row <TR> tag in your table, just under the
<CAPTION>...</CAPTION> tags and above the first real row of
data in the table:**

```
<CAPTION ALIGN=BOTTOM>Pricing Schedule for 1997
            </CAPTION>
<TR>
</TR>
```

3 **Add a <TH> </TH> tag between the <TR> tags:**

```
<TR>
   <TH></TH>
</TR>
```

Notice that the <TH> tags are very similar to the <TD> tags in the way they're
used — in pairs and around each word or words that should appear as a
single table cell.

4 **Type Products between the <TH> tags:**

```
<TH>Products</TH>
```

*<TH> tags are very
similar to <TD> tags
in the way they're
used*

Figure 10-7: Your table is now equipped with a header.

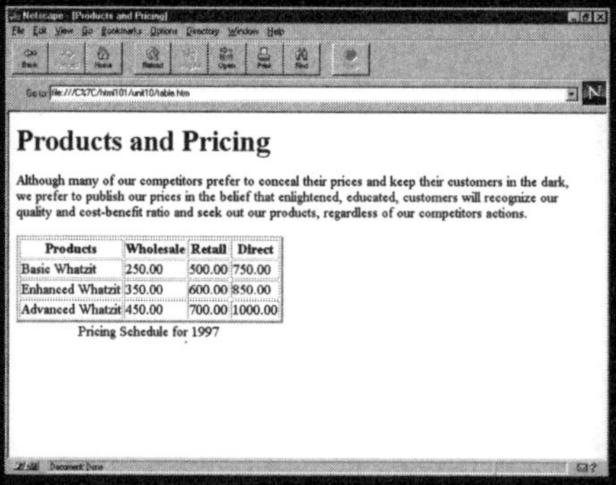

Figure 10-7

Notes:

5   **Add another set of** `<TH>` **tags with the word Wholesale between them:**

```
<TH>Wholesale</TH>
```

6   **Add the last two sets of** `<TH>` **tags with the words Retail and Direct between them:**

```
<TR>
<TH>Products</TH>
<TH>Wholesale</TH>
<TH>Retail</TH>
<TH>Direct</TH>
</TR>
```

You just finished adding four table header tags, one for each column in your table.

7   **Save and test your document in Netscape.**

Your table should now have an additional row at the top. The header is generally formatted by browsers with both boldface and italic, so the text stands out from the text. Compare your table with Figure 10-7 to make sure that you're on the right track. If your table doesn't show headers, make sure that you entered the tags correctly.

Adding table formatting

Next, you'll apply a couple of attributes — `CELLPADDING` and `CELLSPACING` — to make the table look better and less compressed:

1   **In WebEdit, you can either continue with the table you were working on in the last lesson or open table5.htm from the \html101\unit10 folder.**

on the CD

2   **Add the attribute** `CELLPADDING=2` **to your opening** `<TABLE>` **tag.**

```
<TABLE CELLPADDING=2 BORDER=3>
```

Cellpadding adds space above and below the text, to make the table look a little better. The space is measured in *pixels,* which are the smallest dots the computer can draw on-screen. When someone is pointing at your monitor and smudging it up, you might suggest that they move their finger several

CELLPADDING =
inserts space around
cells

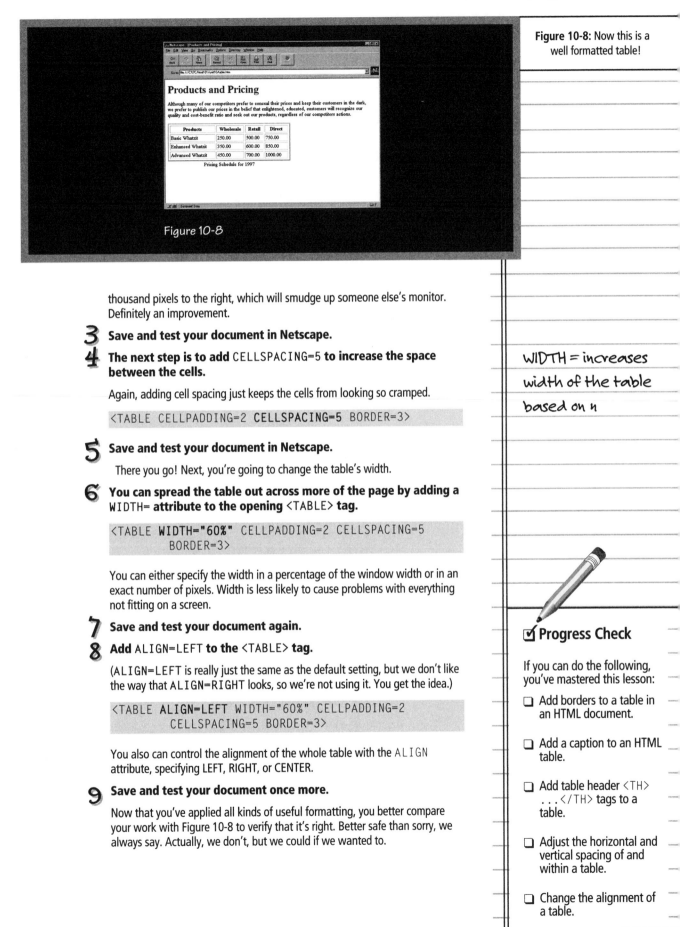

Figure 10-8: Now this is a well formatted table!

Figure 10-8

thousand pixels to the right, which will smudge up someone else's monitor. Definitely an improvement.

3 **Save and test your document in Netscape.**

4 **The next step is to add** CELLSPACING=5 **to increase the space between the cells.**

Again, adding cell spacing just keeps the cells from looking so cramped.

```
<TABLE CELLPADDING=2 CELLSPACING=5 BORDER=3>
```

5 **Save and test your document in Netscape.**

There you go! Next, you're going to change the table's width.

6 **You can spread the table out across more of the page by adding a** WIDTH= **attribute to the opening** <TABLE> **tag.**

```
<TABLE WIDTH="60%" CELLPADDING=2 CELLSPACING=5
        BORDER=3>
```

You can either specify the width in a percentage of the window width or in an exact number of pixels. Width is less likely to cause problems with everything not fitting on a screen.

7 **Save and test your document again.**

8 **Add** ALIGN=LEFT **to the** <TABLE> **tag.**

(ALIGN=LEFT is really just the same as the default setting, but we don't like the way that ALIGN=RIGHT looks, so we're not using it. You get the idea.)

```
<TABLE ALIGN=LEFT WIDTH="60%" CELLPADDING=2
        CELLSPACING=5 BORDER=3>
```

You also can control the alignment of the whole table with the ALIGN attribute, specifying LEFT, RIGHT, or CENTER.

9 **Save and test your document once more.**

Now that you've applied all kinds of useful formatting, you better compare your work with Figure 10-8 to verify that it's right. Better safe than sorry, we always say. Actually, we don't, but we could if we wanted to.

WIDTH = increases width of the table based on *n*

☑ **Progress Check**

If you can do the following, you've mastered this lesson:

❏ Add borders to a table in an HTML document.

❏ Add a caption to an HTML table.

❏ Add table header <TH> ...</TH> tags to a table.

❏ Adjust the horizontal and vertical spacing of and within a table.

❏ Change the alignment of a table.

Lesson 10-4

Adding Unusual-Sized Cells

Well, now that you have a pretty doggone good table, you may want to add a couple more cells to provide some additional information.

Say that you want to add a second table header with additional information about the pricing — full or discounted. You can do that with the <TH> tags as well as the COLSPAN attribute.

- <TH>...</TH> indicates table header
- COLSPAN indicates column span

1 In WebEdit, you can either continue with the table you were working on in the last lesson, or open table6.htm from your unit10 folder.

on the CD

2 Add an additional <TR>...</TR> immediately below the "Products and Pricing" caption.

```
<TR>
</TR>
```

3 Add three <TH>...</TH> tags between the <TR>...</TR> tags.

```
<TR>
<TH></TH>
<TH></TH>
<TH></TH>
</TR>
```

4 Leave the first <TH>...</TH> blank, add Discounted to the second, and add Full Price to the third.

```
<TH></TH>
<TH>Discounted</TH>
<TH>Full Price</TH>
```

Now you've added all the headers you need. We take care of lining them up properly after you see the results of your handiwork. Notice that you don't have as many cells as you do columns, so you will not end up with one header per column.

5 Save and test your document.

Now you have to make sure that the Discounted header clearly applied to both the second and third column.

6 Add COLSPAN=2 to the second <TH>...</TH> tag.

```
<TH></TH>
<TH COLSPAN=2>Discounted</TH>
<TH>Full Price</TH>
```

7 Save and test your document in Netscape.

These cell-spanning dealies are pretty cool! Check with Figure 10-9 to make sure that you've got it right. Again, if your table column widths don't look like those in Figure 10-8, double-check your tags in WebEdit or check out table 7.htm, which shows the WebEdit file as it should look at this point.

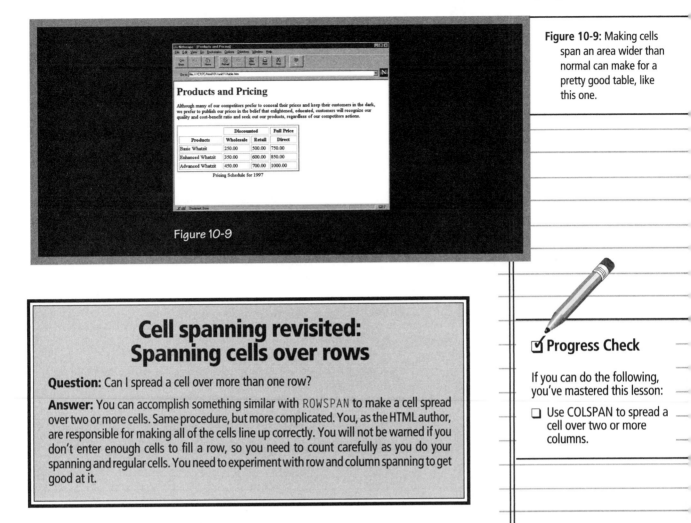

Figure 10-9

Figure 10-9: Making cells span an area wider than normal can make for a pretty good table, like this one.

Cell spanning revisited: Spanning cells over rows

Question: Can I spread a cell over more than one row?

Answer: You can accomplish something similar with ROWSPAN to make a cell spread over two or more cells. Same procedure, but more complicated. You, as the HTML author, are responsible for making all of the cells line up correctly. You will not be warned if you don't enter enough cells to fill a row, so you need to count carefully as you do your spanning and regular cells. You need to experiment with row and column spanning to get good at it.

☑ **Progress Check**

If you can do the following, you've mastered this lesson:

❏ Use COLSPAN to spread a cell over two or more columns.

Unit 10 Quiz

It's quiz time again. Circle the correct answer or answers for each of the following questions.

1. A <TABLE> tag is

    A. Used to identify the beginning of a table.

    B. Paired.

    C. Acceptable for all browsers.

    D. What lawyers do with a motion.

    E. Only used in combination with the </TABLE> tag.

2. **You list the individual cells of the table**

    A. Row by row and cell by cell.

    B. Column by column and then cell by cell.

    C. In any order — the browser can figure it out.

    D. In combination with a matrix to show which contents go where.

    E. In a form.

3. **Which of the following attributes are allowed for `<TABLE>` tags?**

    A. `BORDER=`

    B. `ALIGN=`

    C. `ACTION=`

    D. All of the above

    E. None of the above

4. **Which one of the following statements is true?**

    A. Table headers `<TH>...</TH>` are required in all tables.

    B. Applying `<TH>...</TH>` attributes is done cell by cell.

    C. Captions are optional in tables.

    D. `<TH>...</TH>` only affects tables without borders.

    E. None of the above

5. `COLSPAN`

    A. Lets you spread a cell across two or more columns.

    B. Lets you spread a cell over two or more rows.

    C. Both A and B

    D. Specifies the total number of cells in a column.

    E. Is only used in documents that do not contain tables as a table substitute.

Unit 10 Exercise

1. Create a new document in WebEdit.

2. Make a table to record the names of your nearest and dearest, their birthdays, and what you do to observe their birthdays — ignore, send card, send present, take to dinner, or hire a skywriter to humiliate.

3. Add appropriate formatting, such as a big fat border, a header row, and a caption.

4. Save your document as dutiful.htm and test it. Keep revising until you get the results you expect (and want).

Unit 11
• • • • • • • • • •

Developing Forms

Objectives for This Unit

✓ Determining when to use a form

✓ Creating a form

✓ Adding submit and reset buttons to a form

✓ Adding input areas to a form

✓ Adding checkboxes to a form

✓ Adding radio buttons to a form

Unit 10 showed how to use tables as a useful means of presenting information to your readers. Forms, on the other hand, are the only way you can use HTML to get information back from your readers. For example, you can use a form to survey people right from your Web site. You ask the questions, and then people fill in their answers and send the information back to you. So if you want feedback on your products or services or if you just want opinions on the best way to keep your kitty cats from eating your favorite plant, include a form in your HTML document.

Using forms is sort of like sending out a questionnaire and including an address for people to return the information, or like including a self-addressed, stamped envelope, making it *easy* to send the information back. If you don't provide a way (such as a mailing address) for the people to return the information, you won't receive responses; likewise, with a form, you not only have to send out the questionnaire, but you also have to get that information back.

That's what this unit is all about — providing forms for people to fill out and making sure that you get that information back. The good news is that you are really only responsible for the "providing forms" part. For the "getting information back" part, you need to work with your system administrator. He or she will take care of the program or special arrangements that are necessary to get the information back to you. Exactly what they do is way-techie and extremely variable — let them worry about the specifics; that's what they're paid to do. For information on contacting your system administrator, see the "System administrators" sidebar in this section.

For this unit, you should start with Lesson 11-1 and move through each of the lessons in the order provided. If you want to pick and choose which form options you want to include, you should at least complete Lesson 11-2, in which you create a basic form, before moving on to the other lessons.

This unit contains several figures against which you can check your progress. If your form doesn't look like the figure, return to WebEdit and verify that you entered the text, tags, and attributes correctly.

Lesson 11-1

Deciding to Use a Form

Notes:

What exactly is a form, anyway? A *form* is part of a Web page with places for readers to input information and send it back to the Web server (and then, if you want, back to you). Forms are interactive, allowing you to gather information from your readers. In this lesson, you learn the process for creating a form, the various parts of a form, and how to identify information for the form.

Creating a form

Creating forms is a little different from creating the HTML documents you've learned about so far in this book. With the HTML documents you've created so far, you simply put your HTML documents "out there" on a Web server so that your readers can access them. With forms, however, you not only need to put them on a Web server, but you also need to provide a way for that information to get back to you. It'll probably find you through e-mail, but only your system administrator knows for sure.

Getting help from your system administrator

Just who is this system administrator person? That propeller-head neighbor kid? That aloof person who lurks in the basement of your office building? That person in plaid pants you see standing in line at the doughnut shop every morning?

Hmmm. Could be.

System administrators are often perceived as mysterious, nerdy types, but more often than not, they're just normal people who are glad to help with your Web page needs. Whoever they are, you're going to need their help when you create a form.

If your Internet service provider or your employer lets you put pages on the Web, they will also have a system administrator, or Webmaster, who can help you set up your form. If you don't know who that is, try rooting through all that paperwork you got when you set up your account and looking for a name or phone number. Or you could look for a link on the system home page for the Webmaster.

After you figure out who to contact, ask questions:

- What's my URL?

- I'm developing a form and need to know the `ACTION=` and `POST=` attributes to put in it so I get the results back.

- What other neat stuff do you have that I should know about?

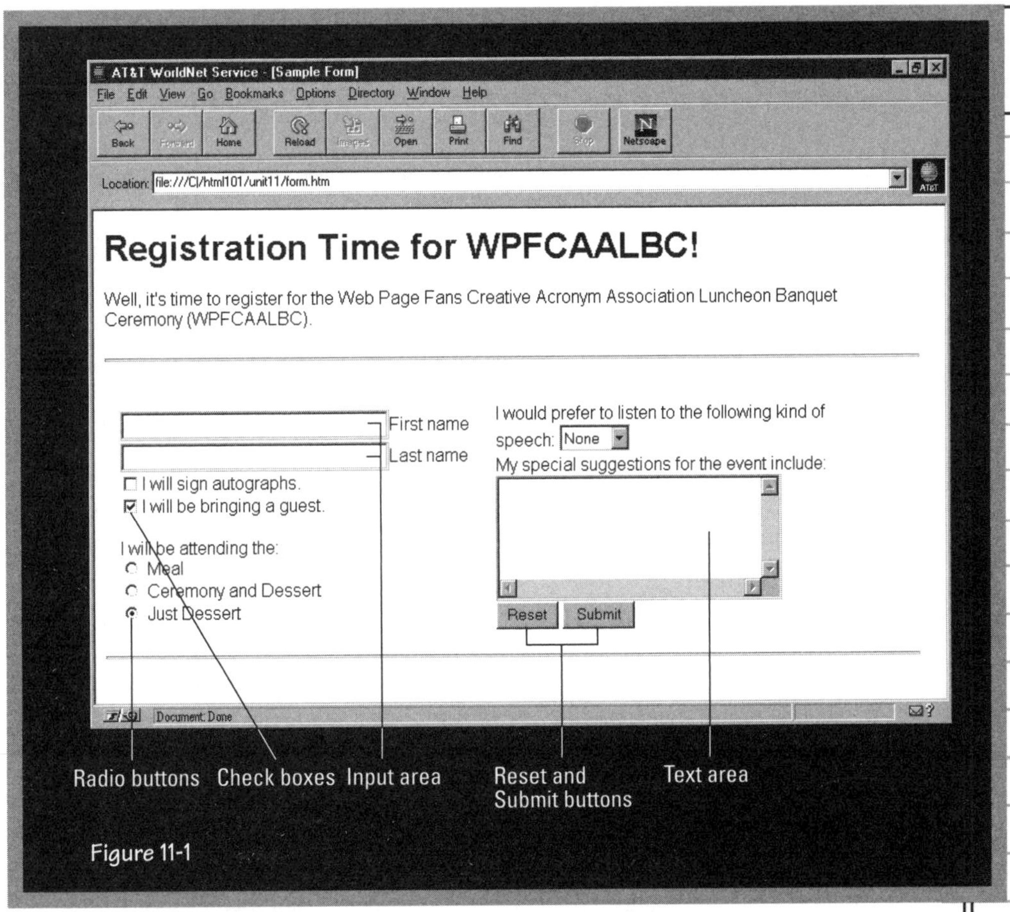

Figure 11-1: A sample form with all the major pieces.

Creating forms isn't difficult, but the process is fairly involved. Before you start putting fingers to keyboard to develop the form, you have to do some planning. You should ask yourself two questions:

▶ **Do you know what information you want to collect from your readers?**

If you're just looking for your readers' names and addresses or a quick response to a yes or no question, you're probably set to start developing a form. If you are still at the early stages of development and only know that you want to collect information about a certain topic, however, you need to structure your thinking somewhat.

If you find that the information you want cannot be structured effectively — that is, cannot be reduced to yes/no and multiple-choice–type questions — consider adding a link to allow your readers to easily send you an e-mail message and forego the form altogether.

▶ **Will you be putting your HTML documents on a server, and is the system administrator willing to help a little?**

Huh? Remember that you have to put the documents on the server and work with the system administrator in order to allow people to submit information back to you.

When you've answered these questions — either on paper or in your head — you're ready to move on to the next section.

Identifying functions of form parts

In this section, you learn about the different form parts as well as what each of the parts do. Forms have two parts:

- **The visible part of the form that people fill out.** This part can contain input areas, checkboxes, and radio buttons. The basic tag for the form is `<FORM>...</FORM>`. Figure 11-1 shows these parts.

- **The part that controls what happens with the data people enter into the form.** This part designates which program on the Web server will process the results of your form; it also specifies how the program will process the information.

What can you do with the data people submit? Basically, you can have the information returned to you in two ways — both of which involve your system administrator.

- **You can have the information sent back to the server and then have it sent to you.** That is, have the results e-mailed to you. You have to contact your server administrator and find out exactly what that program is and what command you have to use to get that information mailed to you. Additionally, your server administrator may need to do some setup on the server end as well.

- **You can have the information sent to the server where it can be dealt with however you and the administrator determine.** If you're working on a more specific project and will be collecting lots of data, for example, you may want to have the results of the form go directly into a database. You need to contact your system administrator (and probably also your favorite programming geek) to get this to happen.

heads up

Using forms won't cause security problems for you — the system administrator's job is to ensure that your information is *your* information.

Identifying information for the form

This section focuses on determining what to include in the form so you'll be better prepared to move ahead in the next lesson. The following example probably doesn't identify *exactly* the same information that you'll want to include, but it should serve more as an example of the type of information you need to identify each time you develop a form.

Go ahead and grab a pencil, answer the questions, and start making notes about your form.

- **Why do you want to create a form?**

  Collecting basic demographics, as well as soliciting a couple of opinions about business services, are fairly standard uses of forms. The examples in this unit develop a form to collect this information.

- **What types of information, specifically, do you want to collect?**

  Make sure that you list the data in the smallest possible chunks. Having smaller pieces and reassembling them into a larger block is easier than having one big blob and wishing that it were in smaller chunks.

If the zip code is a separate bit of data, for example, you could eventually use the same form to feed a mailing list. If the zip is combined with other information, however, you'd have to manually edit each and every address before you could use them in a mailing list. Go for the smaller chunk of information.

- First name
- Last name
- E-mail address
- Type of computer
- Primary use of computer
- Preferred way of learning about computers
- Additional comments about computer use

▶ **What command do you have to include in your form to get the results mailed back to you?**

We asked our Webmaster and found that our command is `ACTION="http://www.server.com/cgi-bin/email?ourid" METHOD="POST"`. The information your Webmaster provides also will come in two parts, a METHOD and an ACTION.

What's your command? _____

☑ Progress Check

If you can do the following, you've mastered this lesson:

❏ Explain what kind of information you'd use a form to collect.

❏ Know what information you need from your Webmaster to do a form.

❏ Make a list of data that you plan to collect.

Creating a Form

Lesson 11-2

The basics of creating a form aren't exciting at all. In fact, you can't even see the results of your work for a couple more lessons. However, this part is essential.

In this lesson, you use the form tag, `<FORM>...</FORM>`, and the `ACTION` and `METHOD` attributes.

- ▶ The `<FORM>...</FORM>` tag identifies the information within the tags as belonging to a form.
- ▶ The `ACTION` attribute identifies the program that the server will use to collect your data.
- ▶ The `METHOD` attribute identifies what the program will *do* with your data.

Use the following instructions to start your form. If you haven't contacted your system administrator or if you're still waiting for a response (these things happen), you can still complete these steps.

on the CD

1 **In WebEdit, open newform.htm from the \html101\unit11 folder.**

2 **The form will go under the `<HR>` in the document, so go ahead and start by putting in `<FORM>` and `</FORM>` tags:**

```
<HR>
<FORM>
</FORM>
```

<FORM>...</FORM>
= basic form tag

ACTION = identifies
program that
collects your data
METHOD =
identifies what
program will do with
your data

quotes are
necessary!

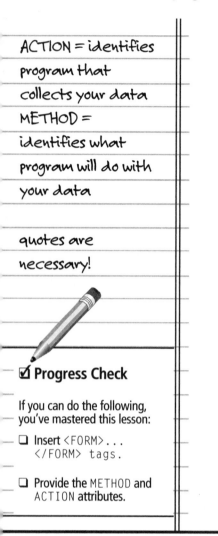

☑ Progress Check

If you can do the following,
you've mastered this lesson:

❑ Insert `<FORM>`...
  `</FORM>` tags.

❑ Provide the `METHOD` and
  `ACTION` attributes.

3 **Add the** `ACTION` **and** `METHOD` **attributes by using the information your Webmaster provided.**

If you don't have this information yet, you can still complete your form by using the following steps. You will need to get this information before the "getting information back to you" part of the form will work, however. See the "System administrators" sidebar at the beginning of this unit for information on contacting your system administrator.

Remember that attributes just go in the initial tag. The command we were given by the Webmaster is `ACTION="http://www.server.com/cgi-bin/email?ourid" METHOD="POST"`, so our `<FORM>` tags look like the following:

```
<FORM ACTION="http://www.server.com/cgi-bin/
              email?ourid" METHOD="POST">
</FORM>
```

4 **Save your document as newform.htm.**

You can use the same document throughout the rest of this unit, so leave it open if you're continuing on to the next lesson.

If you test your document at this point, you won't see anything different. The tags you've entered so far don't include information that will show up in the form itself. (These tags are kind of like the structure tags you learned about in Unit 3 — they're necessary, but most of them don't actually show up in your HTML document.)

Lesson 11-3

Adding Submit and Reset Buttons

The next step in developing your form is to add buttons that allow your readers to actually send the information to you. In this lesson, you add a few new tags and attributes to the document:

▶ The `<INPUT>`...`</INPUT>` tags make a place in your document in which your readers can provide information.

▶ The `VALUE=` attribute indicates the information that the field contains.

▶ The `SUBMIT` value allows your readers to submit the information they enter.

▶ The `RESET` value allows your readers to clear the form if they goofed up.

Use the following instructions to add Submit and Reset buttons. We strongly recommend that you work through Lesson 11-2, which shows you how to create a basic form, before completing this exercise.

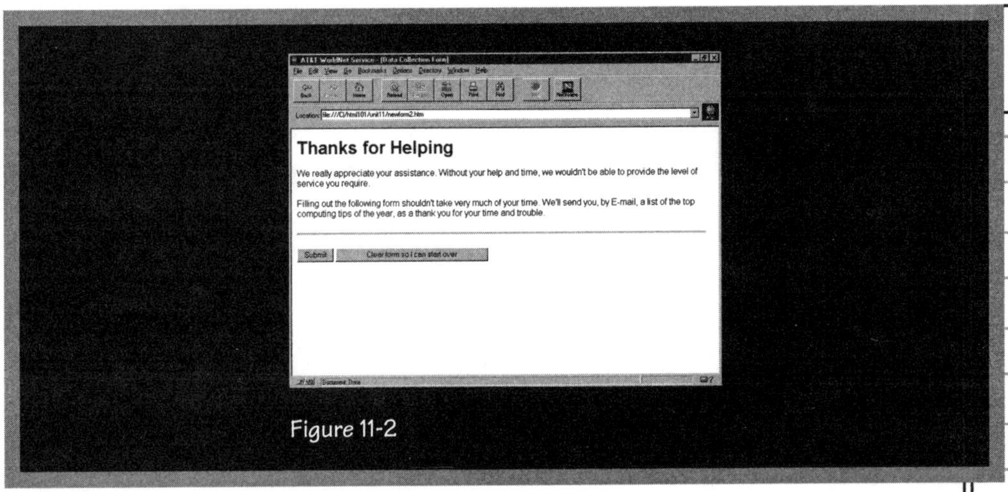

Figure 11-2: A form in excellent "form."

Figure 11-2

1 In WebEdit, make sure that newform.htm is still open.

If you're just jumping in here (or want to verify that you're on track), you can open newform2.htm.

2 Add an `<INPUT>` tag between the `<FORM>` and `</FORM>` tags:

```
<FORM ACTION="http://www.server.com/cgi-bin/
              email?ourid" METHOD="POST">

<INPUT>
</FORM>
```

The `<INPUT>` tag is one of the ways that readers can provide information.

<INPUT> place in which your readers can provide information

3 Add a `TYPE="SUBMIT"` attribute to the `<INPUT>` tag:

```
<INPUT TYPE="SUBMIT">
```

The `TYPE=` attribute specifies what this input tag will do. The submit type produces a special button to submit the information. You have to use the submit information, or the readers won't be able to return — or "submit" — the information back to you.

SUBMIT= allows readers to submit information

4 Add a `VALUE="Submit"` attribute to the `<INPUT>` tag:

```
<INPUT TYPE="SUBMIT" VALUE="Submit">
```

The `VALUE` attribute determines what text is present on the button. We're sticking with Submit on the button for now, but you can put anything you want on the button.

That's it for the first button, so now you're ready for the Reset button.

VALUE= determines the information that field contains

5 Add another `<INPUT>` tag under the first one.

6 Add a `TYPE="RESET"` attribute:

```
<INPUT TYPE="RESET">
```

This attribute also cannot be changed without breaking the form.

7 Add a `VALUE="Reset"` attribute to the `<INPUT>` tag:

```
<INPUT TYPE="RESET" VALUE="Reset">
```

The value attribute for the Reset button determines the text on the button, just as it did for the Submit button.

RESET allows readers to clear form

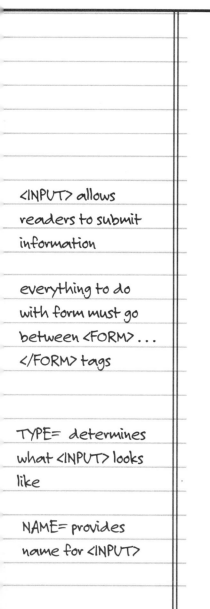

✓ **Progress Check**

If you can do the following, you've mastered this lesson:

❑ Create Submit and Reset buttons.

❑ Change the text on the buttons.

8 **Save and test your document.**

See, you have some buttons there (see Figure 11-2). Cool, huh?

9 **Change the** VALUE **of the reset button to "Clear form so I can start over":**

```
<INPUT TYPE="RESET" VALUE="Clear form so I can
          start over">
```

We didn't think that Reset made much sense (nor would our readers understand it), so something more explanatory was called for.

10 **Save and test your work again.**

Neato!

Leave your document open if you're going to work on the next lesson

---

Lesson 11-4 Adding Input Fields

Now that you have the basics of the form done, you're ready for the fun part. This lesson shows you how to add a different kind of <INPUT> field. You added input fields in the last lesson, too, but they were kind of special cases. Those input fields resulted in nifty little Submit and Reset buttons that readers click to get the information to you.

In this lesson, you use <INPUT> tags to create "fill-in-the-blank" fields. These fields allow readers to fill in specific information, such as their name, street address, or e-mail address.

<INPUT> allows readers to submit information

▶ The <INPUT> field identifies a place for readers to provide information.

▶ The TYPE= attribute determines what the <INPUT> field will look like.

▶ The NAME= attribute provides a unique name for the <INPUT> field.

everything to do with form must go between <FORM>... </FORM> tags

Use the following instructions to add an input field to your document. We strongly recommend that you work through Lesson 11-2, which shows you how to create a basic form, before completing this exercise.

on the CD

1 **Make sure newform.htm is open in WebEdit.**

If you're just catching up here, open newform3.htm.

2 **Place the cursor in front of the beginning of the** <INPUT> **tag you used for the Submit button and press Enter several times.**

This step just opens up a little space so you can see what you're doing.

3 **Enter an** <INPUT> **tag.**

TYPE= determines what <INPUT> looks like

4 **Add a** TYPE="TEXT" **attribute to the tag:**

```
<INPUT TYPE="TEXT">
```

5 **Add the attribute** NAME="firstname"**:**

```
<INPUT TYPE="TEXT" NAME="firstname">
```

NAME= provides name for <INPUT>

You do this step to give the field a logical name so you can reference it later.

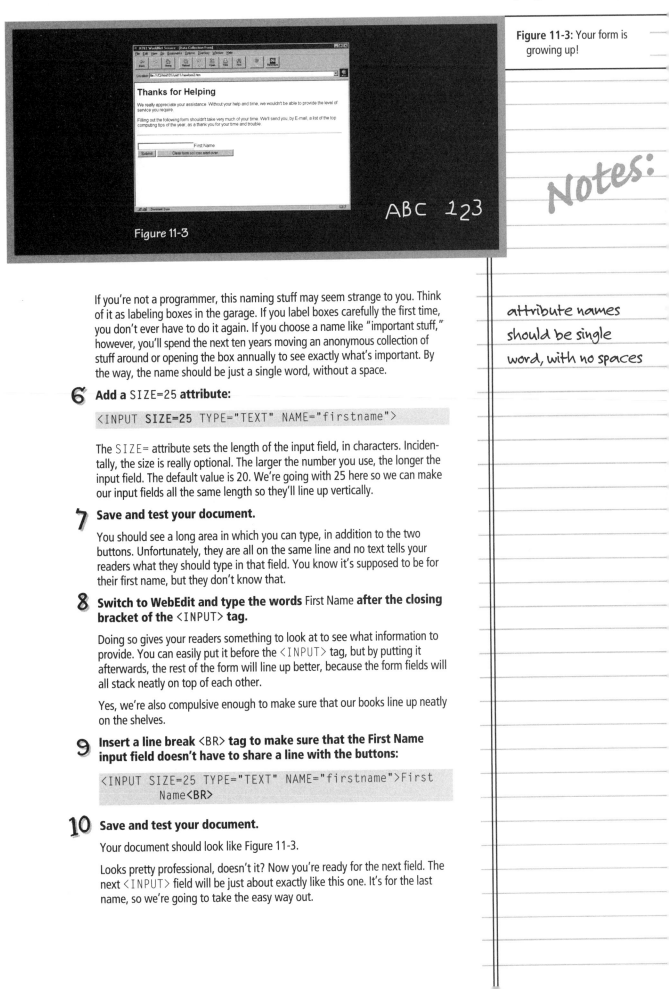

Figure 11-3: Your form is growing up!

Figure 11-3

ABC 123

Notes:

attribute names
should be single
word, with no spaces

If you're not a programmer, this naming stuff may seem strange to you. Think of it as labeling boxes in the garage. If you label boxes carefully the first time, you don't ever have to do it again. If you choose a name like "important stuff," however, you'll spend the next ten years moving an anonymous collection of stuff around or opening the box annually to see exactly what's important. By the way, the name should be just a single word, without a space.

6 **Add a** `SIZE=25` **attribute:**

```
<INPUT SIZE=25 TYPE="TEXT" NAME="firstname">
```

The `SIZE=` attribute sets the length of the input field, in characters. Incidentally, the size is really optional. The larger the number you use, the longer the input field. The default value is 20. We're going with 25 here so we can make our input fields all the same length so they'll line up vertically.

7 **Save and test your document.**

You should see a long area in which you can type, in addition to the two buttons. Unfortunately, they are all on the same line and no text tells your readers what they should type in that field. You know it's supposed to be for their first name, but they don't know that.

8 **Switch to WebEdit and type the words** First Name **after the closing bracket of the** `<INPUT>` **tag.**

Doing so gives your readers something to look at to see what information to provide. You can easily put it before the `<INPUT>` tag, but by putting it afterwards, the rest of the form will line up better, because the form fields will all stack neatly on top of each other.

Yes, we're also compulsive enough to make sure that our books line up neatly on the shelves.

9 **Insert a line break** `<BR>` **tag to make sure that the First Name input field doesn't have to share a line with the buttons:**

```
<INPUT SIZE=25 TYPE="TEXT" NAME="firstname">First
    Name<BR>
```

10 **Save and test your document.**

Your document should look like Figure 11-3.

Looks pretty professional, doesn't it? Now you're ready for the next field. The next `<INPUT>` field will be just about exactly like this one. It's for the last name, so we're going to take the easy way out.

Figure 11-4: Your form with set of input fields.

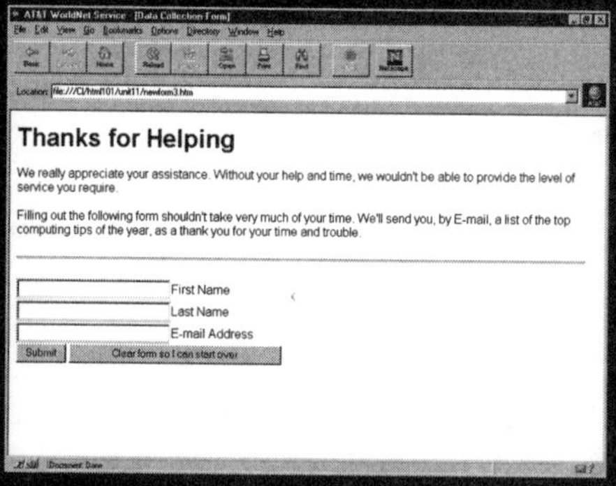

Figure 11-4

Edit→Paste

11 Select that whole <INPUT> tag line, all the way down to and including the <BR> tag, and copy it.

12 Paste the line immediately below the first one.

There. You just copied and pasted the line of text and tags so that you don't have to retype a bunch of tags.

13 Save and test.

You should have two identical lines. We're just going to make the minimal changes to make this line work here.

14 Switch to WebEdit and in the second <INPUT> line, change NAME="firstname" to NAME="lastname":

```
<INPUT SIZE=25 TYPE="TEXT" NAME="firstname">First
        Name<BR>
<INPUT SIZE=25 TYPE="TEXT" NAME="lastname">First
        Name<BR>
```

15 Change the "First" in the second line to Last, like this:

```
<INPUT SIZE=25 TYPE="TEXT" NAME="lastname">Last
        Name<BR>
```

There. Now you've done two of the input tags. One more of these to go!

16 Do that copy and paste thing again to duplicate one of the input lines.

17 Add NAME="email":

```
<INPUT SIZE=25 TYPE="TEXT" NAME="email">Last
        Name<BR>
```

18 Change the visible text at the end to read E-mail Address, like this:

```
<INPUT SIZE=25 TYPE="TEXT" NAME="email">E-mail
        Address<BR>
```

19 Save and test your document.

Your form should look like Figure 11-4. If you're continuing on to the next lesson, you can keep this document open.

You've got it! By the way, if you don't really like this HTML stuff, don't let your boss see this form. Doing good forms tends to get you appointed "Guru of HTML."

☑ **Progress Check**

If you can do the following, you've mastered this lesson:

❑ Create an <INPUT> tag with a TYPE="TEXT" attribute.

❑ Be able to create a NAME= attribute.

❑ Add text with your <INPUT> tag for your readers to see.

Recess

You've been at this for a while and have accomplished a great deal — you've created a basic form and added buttons and input fields. In the next part of this unit, you learn how to add checkboxes, radio buttons, and select buttons to your forms. This stuff is cool, so stay tuned!

We're doing the root beer and chips thing here — and we highly recommend it, by the way.

Adding Checkboxes to Your Form Lesson 11-5

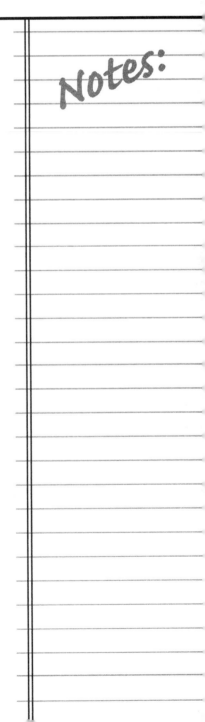

Notes:

A checkbox is an object on a form that allows users to select more than one choice from a list. Checkboxes are handy when you want to provide readers with a way to select more than one answer to a question. For example, if you asked us what our cats like to eat — dry food, canned food, people food, or trash-can food — we'd have to say "yes" to all four.

In this lesson, you continue to work with the form from the last lesson and use checkboxes to get information about what kind of computer people have. You set everything up to allow people to choose from a list of four computers: 486, Pentium, Macintosh, and Other. Because they may have more than one computer, you also need to provide a way for them to choose multiple items from the list. Sounds like a job for checkboxes. You use the attribute `TYPE="CHECKBOX"` to create a checkbox.

In this lesson, you're going to be using the same tags and attributes as you used in the last few lessons, but you'll be using new values and getting different results. We strongly recommend that you work through Lesson 11-2, which shows you how to create a basic form, before completing this exercise.

on the CD

1 **Make sure that newform.htm is open in WebEdit.**

If you're just picking back up here, open newform4.htm and keep right on swinging.

2 **Put your cursor on the line immediately under the e-mail address** `<INPUT>` **tag.**

3 **Type instructions for your readers:**

```
<P>Please select the type or types of computer you
        have.</P>
```

Technically, the instructions aren't essential for the form, but telling people how to fill out the form generally helps responses.

4 **On the next line, type an** `<INPUT>` **tag.**

Yes, another one. This one is somewhat different though.

```
<P>Please select the type or types of computer you
            have.</P>
<INPUT>
```

5 **Add a** `TYPE="CHECKBOX"` **attribute to it:**

```
<INPUT TYPE="CHECKBOX">
```

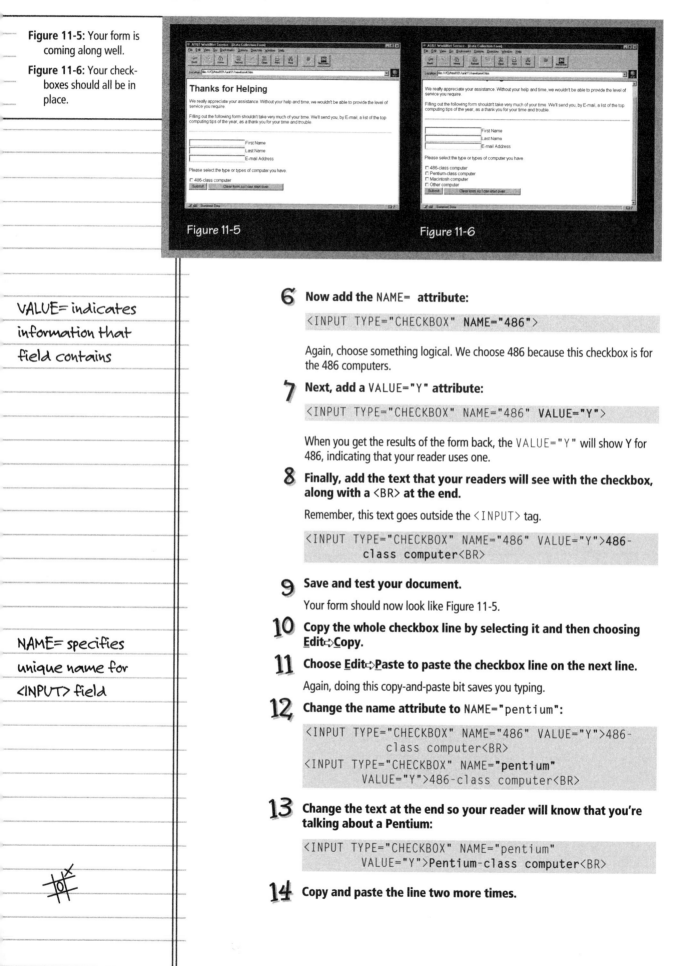

Figure 11-5: Your form is coming along well.

Figure 11-6: Your checkboxes should all be in place.

Figure 11-5

Figure 11-6

VALUE= indicates information that field contains

6 Now add the NAME= **attribute:**

```
<INPUT TYPE="CHECKBOX" NAME="486">
```

Again, choose something logical. We choose 486 because this checkbox is for the 486 computers.

7 Next, add a VALUE="Y" **attribute:**

```
<INPUT TYPE="CHECKBOX" NAME="486" VALUE="Y">
```

When you get the results of the form back, the VALUE="Y" will show Y for 486, indicating that your reader uses one.

8 Finally, add the text that your readers will see with the checkbox, along with a
 at the end.

Remember, this text goes outside the <INPUT> tag.

```
<INPUT TYPE="CHECKBOX" NAME="486" VALUE="Y">486-
        class computer<BR>
```

9 Save and test your document.

Your form should now look like Figure 11-5.

10 Copy the whole checkbox line by selecting it and then choosing Edit⇨Copy.

11 Choose Edit⇨Paste to paste the checkbox line on the next line.

Again, doing this copy-and-paste bit saves you typing.

NAME= specifies unique name for <INPUT> field

12 Change the name attribute to NAME="pentium"**:**

```
<INPUT TYPE="CHECKBOX" NAME="486" VALUE="Y">486-
        class computer<BR>
<INPUT TYPE="CHECKBOX" NAME="pentium"
        VALUE="Y">486-class computer<BR>
```

13 Change the text at the end so your reader will know that you're talking about a Pentium:

```
<INPUT TYPE="CHECKBOX" NAME="pentium"
        VALUE="Y">Pentium-class computer<BR>
```

14 Copy and paste the line two more times.

15 **Change one of the lines to** `NAME="mac"` **with text reading Macintosh computer:**

```
<INPUT TYPE="CHECKBOX" NAME="mac"
       VALUE="Y">Macintosh computer<BR>
```

16 **Change the last line to** `NAME="other"` **with text reading Other computer:**

```
<INPUT TYPE="CHECKBOX" NAME="other" VALUE="Y">Other
       computer<BR>
```

17 **Save and test your document.**

Your form should look like the one shown in Figure 11-6. You're cooking now!

18 **Suggest a value for your readers to select by adding a checked attribute to one of the** <INPUT> **tags:**

```
<INPUT TYPE="CHECKBOX" NAME="pentium" VALUE="Y"
       CHECKED>Pentium-class computer<BR>
```

We can assume that many or most of the readers will be using Pentium computers, so we'll make that one checked by default:

19 **Save and test your document.**

You may have to click the Reset (that is, Clear form so I can start over) button to see the results of the last step. Leave this document open if you're going on to the next lesson.

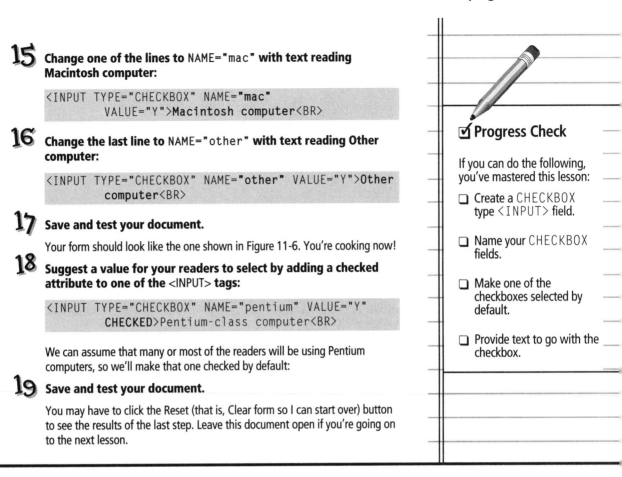

☑ **Progress Check**

If you can do the following, you've mastered this lesson:

❏ Create a `CHECKBOX` type `<INPUT>` field.

❏ Name your `CHECKBOX` fields.

❏ Make one of the checkboxes selected by default.

❏ Provide text to go with the checkbox.

Adding Radio Buttons to Your Form   Lesson 11-6

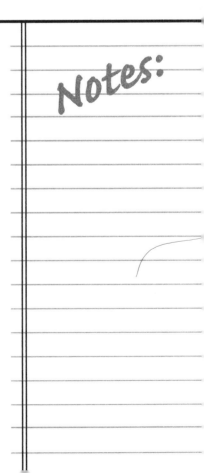

Notes:

Radio buttons are included in forms to allow readers to select only one choice from a list. For example, you could use radio buttons when you ask readers to select the age group they're in, such as 20–25, 26–35, 36–50, or 50+. In this case, readers would only need to select one item from the list (unless something *really* strange is going on).

Continuing from the example in the last lesson, you're going to find out what the readers' primary computer use is. You'll prepare for a list of three: Surfing the Internet, Working, or Playing Games. (See, we're even realistic about it.) Because you're looking for their primary use, you want only one response. That means you want to use radio buttons. You create a radio button by using the `TYPE="RADIO"` attribute.

In this lesson, you're going to be using the same tags and attributes you've been using, but you'll be using new values and getting different results. We strongly recommend that you work through Lesson 11-2, which shows you how to create a basic form, before completing this exercise.

on the CD

1 **Make sure that newform.htm is open in WebEdit, or open up newform5.htm and keep going.**

2 **Put your cursor on the line immediately below the last of the checkbox tags.**

3 **Type in instructions for your readers:**

```
<P>Please select your primary use of computers.</P>
```

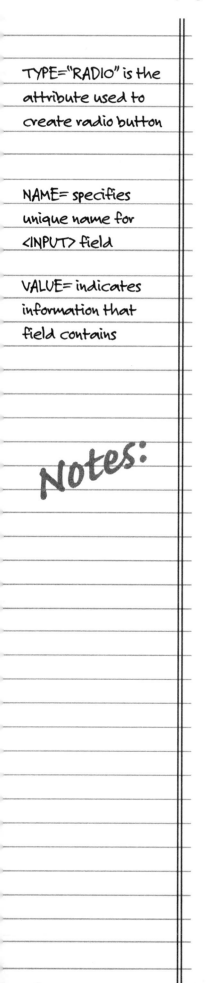

Notes:

TYPE="RADIO" is the attribute used to create radio button

NAME= specifies unique name for <INPUT> field

VALUE= indicates information that field contains

4 **On the next line, enter an** <INPUT> **tag.**

Again, this one is very similar to the checkboxes.

5 **Add a** TYPE="RADIO" **attribute to it:**

```
<INPUT TYPE="RADIO">
```

The radio tag will require that only one item of any name be selected.

6 **Add a** NAME="computeruse" **to the tag:**

```
<INPUT TYPE="RADIO" NAME="computeruse">
```

The set of radio buttons you're creating in this lesson will all have the NAME="computeruse". Giving each of the buttons the same name allows the browser to require that one and only one of the radio buttons in a set be selected.

7 **Add a** VALUE="netsurfing" **to correspond with the first value in our list:**

```
<INPUT TYPE="RADIO" NAME="computeruse"
        VALUE="netsurfing">
```

8 **Next, after the closing bracket, add the text that your readers will see, followed by a**
:

```
<INPUT TYPE="RADIO" NAME="computeruse"
        VALUE="netsurfing">Surfing the
        Internet<BR>
```

9 **Copy and paste that line two times:**

```
<INPUT TYPE="RADIO" NAME="computeruse"
          VALUE="netsurfing">Surfing the
          Internet<BR>
<INPUT TYPE="RADIO" NAME="computeruse"
          VALUE="netsurfing">Surfing the
          Internet<BR>
<INPUT TYPE="RADIO" NAME="computeruse"
          VALUE="netsurfing">Surfing the
          Internet<BR>
```

You're doing exactly what you did in the previous lessons and keeping your typing fingers from getting tired.

10 **On the second line of this set, change the value to** VALUE="working":

```
<INPUT TYPE="RADIO" NAME="computeruse"
        VALUE="working">Surfing the Internet<BR>
```

11 **Change the text your reader will see to Working. Be sure to leave the**
 at the end.

```
<INPUT TYPE="RADIO" NAME="computeruse"
        VALUE="working">Working<BR>
```

12 **Change the third line to have** VALUE="games":

```
<INPUT TYPE="RADIO" NAME="computeruse"
        VALUE="games">Surfing the Internet<BR>
```

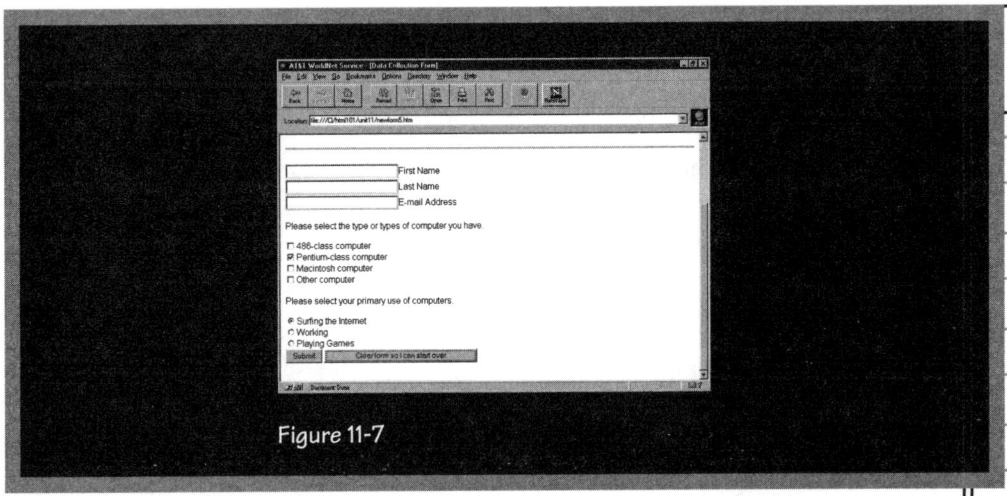

Figure 11-7

Figure 11-7: Turn on that radio button!

13 Change the text your reader sees in the third line to Playing Games:

```
<INPUT TYPE="RADIO" NAME="computeruse"
       VALUE="games">Playing Games<BR>
```

14 Save and test your document.

Remember that you may have to press the Reset button (Clear...) to get rid of anything you might have typed.

15 Because radio buttons also allow you to preselect an option, select the Surfing the Internet one by adding the CHECKED attribute to the <INPUT> tag:

```
<INPUT TYPE="RADIO" NAME="computeruse"
       VALUE="netsurfing" CHECKED>Surfing the
       Internet<BR>
```

16 Save and test your document.

Congratulations! You're zipping right along now! Your form should look like Figure 11-7. Leave your document open if you're moving on to the next lesson.

☑ Progress Check

If you can do the following, you've mastered this lesson:

❏ Create a radio button <INPUT> field.

❏ Name your set of radio button input fields.

❏ Make one of the buttons selected by default.

❏ Provide text to go with the radio button.

Adding Select Boxes to Your Form　　Lesson 11-7

So far, so good. You've got most of this form licked. The next step is to collect your readers opinions about how they prefer to learn about computers. The choices they'll get include: Using . . .*For Dummies* Books, Trial and Error, and Training Classes.

In this lesson, you use a few new tags and attributes:

- The <SELECT>...</SELECT> tag identifies a set of tags from which readers can select information.
- The <OPTION> tag identifies one of the select options.
- The SELECTED attribute indicates which <OPTION> will be selected by default.
- The SIZE= attribute indicates how many options will be visible at once.

<SELECT>...
</SELECT> specifies
set of information

NAME= indicates
unique name for
<INPUT> field

<OPTION> specifies
item within select
list

☑ Progress Check

If you can do the following,
you've mastered this lesson:

❏ Create a <SELECT> field.

❏ Name your <SELECT>
fields.

❏ Specify the <OPTION> for
the select field.

❏ Determine the size of the
<SELECT> field.

❏ Force one of the options
to be selected by default.

We strongly recommend that you work through Lesson 11-2, which shows
you how to create a basic form, before completing this exercise.

1 **Make sure that newform.htm is open in WebEdit.**

If you're just joining us now, open newform6.htm and continue.

2 **Put your cursor on the line immediately below the last of the
radio button tags.**

3 **Type instructions for your readers:**

```
<P>Please select your preferred method of learning
        ab  out computers.</P>
```

4 **On the next line, put in a <SELECT> tag:**

```
<SELECT>
```

5 **A couple of lines below the <SELECT> tag (but still within the
form), add a </SELECT> and a <BR> tag:**

```
<SELECT>
</SELECT><BR>
```

6 **Add the NAME="learning" attribute to the <SELECT> tag.**

```
<SELECT NAME="learning">
```

The name attribute just names the set of information, as it did for the radio
buttons.

7 **Add an <OPTION> tag and closing </OPTION> tag on the line
immediately under the <SELECT> tag:**

```
<SELECT NAME="learning">
<SELECT>
<OPTION></OPTION>
<SELECT>
```

8 **Add Using . . .For Dummies books, of course between the opening
and closing <OPTION> tags:**

```
<OPTION>Using . . .For Dummies books, of course
        </OPTION>
```

9 **Add another <OPTION>...</OPTION> line with Trial and Error in
between the tags:**

```
<OPTION>Trial and Error</OPTION>
```

10 **And add another one with Training Classes:**

```
<OPTION>Training Classes</OPTION>
```

At this point, you have the SELECT box completed. Good for you!

11 **Save and test your document.**

Your form should now look like Figure 11-8. Getting more and more impres-
sive, isn't it?

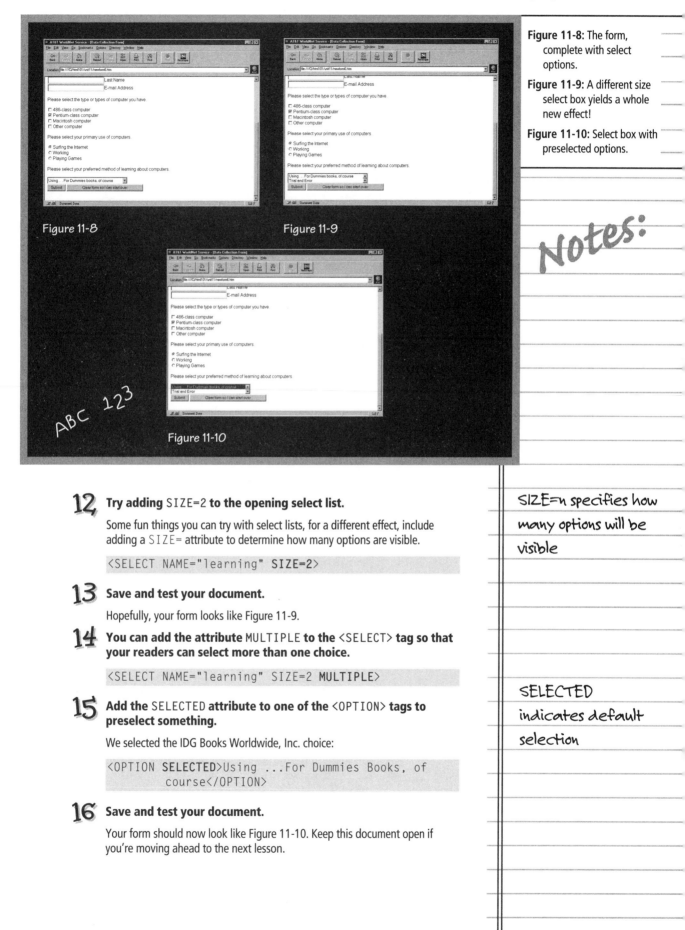

Figure 11-8

Figure 11-9

Figure 11-10

Figure 11-8: The form, complete with select options.

Figure 11-9: A different size select box yields a whole new effect!

Figure 11-10: Select box with preselected options.

Notes:

12 **Try adding** `SIZE=2` **to the opening select list.**

Some fun things you can try with select lists, for a different effect, include adding a `SIZE=` attribute to determine how many options are visible.

```
<SELECT NAME="learning" SIZE=2>
```

13 **Save and test your document.**

Hopefully, your form looks like Figure 11-9.

14 **You can add the attribute** `MULTIPLE` **to the** `<SELECT>` **tag so that your readers can select more than one choice.**

```
<SELECT NAME="learning" SIZE=2 MULTIPLE>
```

15 **Add the** `SELECTED` **attribute to one of the** `<OPTION>` **tags to preselect something.**

We selected the IDG Books Worldwide, Inc. choice:

```
<OPTION SELECTED>Using ...For Dummies Books, of
          course</OPTION>
```

16 **Save and test your document.**

Your form should now look like Figure 11-10. Keep this document open if you're moving ahead to the next lesson.

`SIZE=n` specifies how many options will be visible

`SELECTED` indicates default selection

Lesson 11-8   Adding TEXTAREA to Your Form

Notes:

One last detail, and you're done with your form. Tired yet? Us, too!

Continuing with the example, one final option you might want to add to your form is to give your readers a place to type in their own comments about computer use. The textarea tag, `<TEXTAREA>...</TEXTAREA>`, provides this capability. Hang in there! You're almost done.

In this lesson, you're going to use one new tag and two new attributes:

▶ The `<TEXTAREA>...</TEXTAREA>` tag marks an area in which your readers can type.

▶ The ROWS attribute indicates how many rows high the textarea will be.

▶ The COL attribute indicates how many columns wide the textarea is.

We strongly recommend that you work through Lesson 11-2, which shows you how to create a basic form, before completing this exercise.

1 **Make sure that newform.htm is open in WebEdit, or pick up newform7.htm and go from here.**

2 **Put your cursor on the line immediately below the closing `<SELECT>` tag.**

3 **Type instructions for your readers:**

```
<P>Please add any other comments you'd like to
        volunteer:</P>
```

4 **Insert `<TEXTAREA>` and `</TEXTAREA>` below the instructions:**

```
<TEXTAREA>
</TEXTAREA>
```

5 **Add a `<BR>` tag right after the closing `</TEXTAREA>` tag:**

```
<TEXTAREA>
</TEXTAREA><BR>
```

6 **Add NAME= attribute.**

Because these are comments, you'll use NAME="comment":

```
<TEXTAREA NAME="comment">
</TEXTAREA><BR>
```

7 **You need to designate the size of the area by using ROWS= and COLS= attributes. Start with the TEXTAREA attributes ROWS=5 and COLS=60:**

```
<TEXTAREA ROWS=5 COLS=60 NAME="comment">
</TEXTAREA><BR>
```

`<TEXTAREA>...`
`</TEXTAREA>`
specifies area for
readers to type
information.

ROWS= determines
number of rows high
the area is

COL= determines
number of columns
wide area is

on the CD

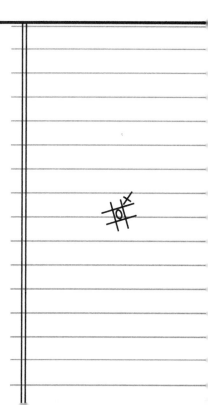

Figure 11-11: Now your readers can express their own thoughts!

Figure 11-11

8 **If you want to help get your readers started, put sample text between the** TEXTAREA **tags:**

```
<TEXTAREA ROWS=5 COLS=60 NAME="comment">
Please type your comments here.
</TEXTAREA><BR>
```

9 **Save and test your document.**

You may have to click the Reset button to see the results of the last step. Your form should look like the one shown in Figure 11-11.

Close your document. If you want, you can check your work with newform8.hmt

---

☑ **Progress Check**

If you can do the following, you've mastered this lesson:

❑ Create a <TEXTAREA> ...</TEXTAREA> field.

❑ Name your <TEXTAREA> ...</TEXTAREA> fields.

❑ Provide default text to go in the field.

Unit 11 Quiz

You're now ready for the inevitable end-of-the-unit quiz. Circle the correct answer or answers for each question.

1. **The** <FORM> **tag is used**

   A. To identify the beginning of the form.

   B. In the head of the document to tell the browser it's a form.

   C. As a British synonym for class or grade.

   D. In the body tag of the document to tell the browser it's a form.

   E. Only in combination with the </FORM> tag.

2. **Checkboxes are used to**

   A. Allow readers to select more than one item from a list.

   B. Require readers to select more than one item from a list.

   C. Allow readers to type in the information they want to select.

   D. Limit readers to selecting two items from a list.

   E. Allow readers to have a drop-down list with items to check.

3. **Which of the following attributes are required by all `<INPUT>` tags?**

   A. `TYPE=`

   B. `VALUE=`

   C. `NAME=`

   D. All of the above

   E. None of the above

4. **Which one of the following statements is true?**

   A. `<TEXTAREA>` tags do not require a `NAME=` attribute.

   B. Using `<OPTION>` with `<SELECT>` tags is unnecessary.

   C. Sets of radio buttons must have the same `NAME=` attribute.

   D. `<INPUT>` tags are only for typing in short bits of text.

   E. All of the above

5. **`<SELECT>` lists are great if**

   A. Your readers have lots of text to type in.

   B. You need to have a long list of selections that takes little space on the page.

   C. You want your readers to be able to type in their own selections.

   D. Your readers are indecisive.

   E. You've always thought drop-down lists were cool!

Unit 11 Exercise

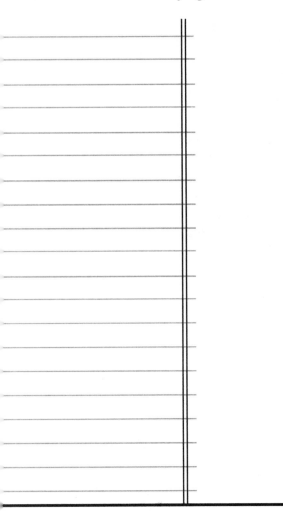

1. Create a new document in WebEdit.

2. Make a form to record the full name, e-mail address, credit card number, type of card and expiration date, and the amount of the donation to your company. (If you collect anything, you have to share it with the authors of this book!)

3. Save and test your document.

Part IV Review

Unit 10 Summary

- **Tables:** A table is a grid of rows and columns that you can put information in.
- **Table purpose:** Use tables to help readers find information quickly, to better present long lists of information, to help present detailed information, and to help design cool layouts.
- **Table tags:** To create tables, you need to use several tags and attributes:
  - `<TABLE>...</TABLE>` indicates table format
  - `BORDER` controls a table's border
  - `<TD>...</TD>` indicates table data cell
  - `<TH>...</TH>` indicates table headings
  - `<TR>...<TR>` indicates table row items

Unit 11 Summary

- **Forms:** A form is part of an HTML document that has places for readers to input information and then send it back to the server, so it can then be sent back to you.
- **Form parts:** Forms have two parts: the part that readers enter and submit information, and the part that sends the information back to the server.
- **Form tags and attributes:** To make a basic form, you use the following tags and attributes:
  - `<FORM>...</FORM>` is the basic form tag.
  - `ACTION` identifies the program that collects your data.
  - `METHOD` identifies what the program will do with your data.
  - `SUBMIT` submits the information.
- **Other tags:** Depending on what you want to include in your form, you can add various tags and attributes:
  - `<INPUT>` allows readers to submit information.
  - `SUBMIT` allows readers to submit information.
  - `RESET` allows readers to clear the form.
  - `TYPE` indicates what kind of `<INPUT>...</INPUT>` tag you are creating, including `CHECKBOX`, `TEXT`, and `RADIO` buttons.
  - `NAME=` specifies a name for the information from `<INPUT>`, `<SELECT>...</SELECT>`, and `<TEXTAREA>...</TEXTAREA>` tags.
  - `CHECKED` indicates which radio button or check box will be checked by default.
  - `<SELECT>...</SELECT>` creates an area in which readers can choose among options.
  - `<OPTION>...</OPTION>` specifies the items within a select list.
  - `SELECTED` indicates which option will be selected by default.
  - `SIZE=` determines how many options are visible at one time in a select list.
  - `<TEXTAREA>...</TEXTAREA>` provides an area in which readers can type information.
  - `ROWS` indicates how many rows high the `<TEXTAREA>...</TEXTAREA>` is.
  - `COLS` indicates how many columns wide the `<TEXTAREA>...</TEXTAREA>` is.

Part IV Test

The questions on this test cover all the material from Part IV, Units 10 and 11. Good luck!

True   False

Each statement is either true or false.

T   F   1. A table is a dancing surface made of columns and rows.

T   F   2. You can use tables to help readers find information more quickly and to better format long lists of information.

T   F   3. You can use tables to format text and graphics into cool layouts and use tables to present particularly detailed information.

T   F   4. The `CHECKBOX` attribute allows readers to select only one item in the list; the `RADIO` attribute allows readers to select more than one item in a list.

T   F   5. Input fields are where readers enter information on a form.

T   F   6. An HTML table always has to have borders.

T   F   7. If you want to put a usable form in your HTML document, you have to work with your system administrator.

T   F   8. When planning a form, you have to consider what information you want to collect from your readers, whether you want to put your document on a server, and whether the server administrator is willing to help.

T   F   9. When planning a table, you have to consider whether the information is suited for the table format as well as the browser software your readers will be using.

T   F   10. By the time you finished Unit 11, you had aged considerably.

Multiple Choice

Circle the correct answer or answers for each of the following questions.

11. **When you create tables, you**

   A. Indicate the beginning and end with `<TABLE>...</TABLE>` tags.

   B. Add each cell of information using `<TR>...</TR>` tags.

   C. Must use at least two sets of `<CAPTION> ...</CAPTION>` tags or it won't work.

   D. All of the above

12. **Tables can be aligned**

   A. Top, middle, and bottom.

   B. Left, right, and center.

   C. Both A and B

   D. Only cells within tables can be aligned.

13. **In addition to `<FORM>...</FORM>` tags, you must include in all forms**

   A. `<TEXTAREA>...<TEXTAREA>`

   B. `<INPUT TYPE="Submit" VALUE="SUBMIT">`

   C. `<SELECT>...</SELECT>`

   D. `TYPE=CHECKBOX`

14. **Radio buttons allow you to**

   A. Select several items.

   B. Select only one item.

   C. Select either one or many items, depending on the attributes you use.

   D. All of the above

Part IV Test

15. **If you use an attribute of SIZE=2 in a <SELECT> ...</SELECT> tag, you will**

    A. Allow your readers to see two choices at once.

    B. Allow your readers to choose two items at once.

    C. Force the select options to be no more than two characters wide.

    D. Not do anything because that isn't a valid attribute for a select tag.

16. **<TEXTAREA>...</TEXTAREA> tags**

    A. Must be at least four rows high.

    B. Only work in forms with more than six choices.

    C. Allow readers to type longer bits of information than input tags do.

    D. Do not need a NAME= attribute.

17. **Forms will not work if**

    A. Your readers use very old browsers.

    B. You don't include a SUBMIT button.

    C. You don't put a correct ACTION= attribute in the opening <HTML> tag.

    D. You don't put a correct ACTION= and METHOD= attribute in the opening <FORM> tag.

    E. All of the above

18. **You can change the text that appears on the**

    A. Submit button.

    B. Reset button.

    C. Neither

    D. Both

Matching

For each of the following questions, match the tags and attributes in the left column to the appropriate effect in the right column.

19. **Match the following table tags and attributes:**

A. <TABLE>...</TABLE>	1. Indicates table data cell
B. BORDER	2. Indicates table row items
C. <TD>...</TD>	3. Indicates table format
D. <TH>...</TH>	4. Indicates table headings
E. <TR>...</TR>	5. Controls table border

20. **Match the following forms tags and attributes:**

A. <FORM>...</FORM>	1. Identifies what the program will do with your data
B. ACTION	2. Submits the information
C. METHOD	3. Is the basic form tag
D. SUBMIT	4. Identifies the program that collects your data

Part IV Lab Assignment

This is the fourth of your lab assignments. For this lab assignment, you're going to continue creating HTML pages for your own Web site.

Step 1: Create two new documents

Create a new HTML document, complete with the structure tags. In this document, you're going to use to create a form for collecting data from your readers.

Step 2: Develop a form

In the first document, determine what information you can get from your readers regarding the topic of your Web site. Develop an appropriate form and include some of the more nifty features like check boxes and radio buttons.

Step 3: Save and test

Save. Test. Again.

Step 4: Take a break

Take a very well-deserved break. This part of the book has been some part, hasn't it? We thought about subtitling this one "Learn HTML in only 2,572 Steps" but decided that might be a little discouraging. It gets easier from here.

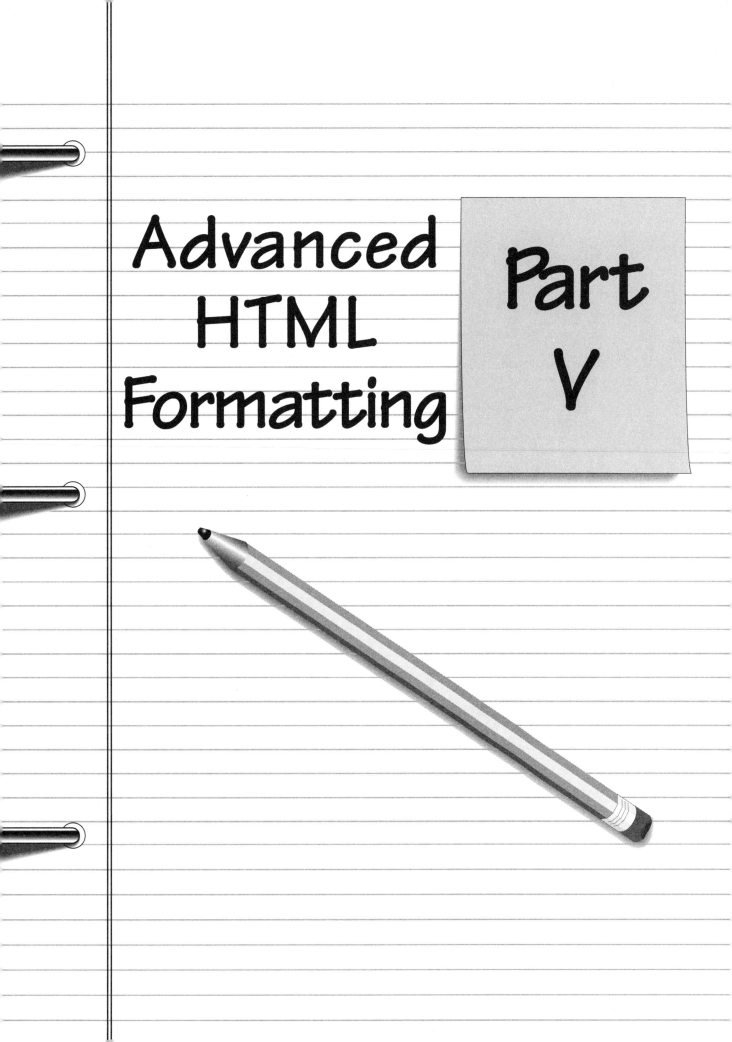

In this part . . .

Whew! You survived the last part and came back for more. We hope you didn't find the last unit too overwhelming, although we know it was a little intense. This HTML stuff gets much easier from here on out. Really. Trust us. The check's in the mail.

In this part, you learn some of the tips and tricks of advanced HTML formatting, including using colors in Unit 12, getting creative within HTML limitations with formatting and stuff in Unit 13, and doing some special fine-tuning to your Web pages (the little things) in Unit 14. All these units are fairly easy — well, compared to the last several units — and they will help you achieve neat effects and produce much more striking Web pages.

Unfortunately, many topics covered in this part are rather nonstandard HTML. That is, although most newer browsers, including Microsoft's Internet Explorer, Netscape Navigator, and many versions of Mosaic, can easily handle these features, many other browsers cannot. If you're trying to create a completely one-size fits all Web page, just as chocolate chip cookies are a one-size fits all present, you should steer clear of many of these tags. That said, *most* (85 percent) of the browsers out there can handle these tags, and those that cannot will probably soon be able to, so don't worry much about it.

Using Colors and Backgrounds to Jazz Up Your Documents

Objectives for This Unit

✓ Providing background color

✓ Coloring text

✓ Coloring links

✓ Using a background graphic

Prerequisites

▸ Understanding HTML basics (Part I, Getting Started)

▸ Creating basic HTML tags (Unit 3 and Unit 4)

▸ Making links (Unit 5)

▸ Understanding how and when to put graphics in your HTML documents (Unit 7 and Unit 8)

on the CD

▸ color.htm
▸ swipe.htm
▸ bkg-col.htm
▸ allcolor.htm
▸ catlett.htm
▸ personlt.htm

This unit brings color to your HTML documents — kind of like the *Wizard of Oz* when Dorothy left black-and-white Kansas and arrived in colorful Oz. Adding color is an excellent way to bring excitement and appeal to your Web pages. Just as colorful Oz is more interesting and exciting than hum-drum ol' black-and-white Kansas, your HTML documents can be more exciting if you use color.

Using and enjoying color can be great, but you need to remember that not all your readers will have new enough browsers to view all colors. Readers with older browsers will see only the traditional colors (black text with a gray background), just as people with black-and-white televisions don't have as much fun with the Oz scenes.

In this unit, you learn several ways you can transform your "Kansas" document into an "Oz" document:

▸ Adding colors to the background

▸ Adding colors to text and links

▸ Using graphics as backgrounds

Lesson 12-1   # Using Background Color

on the test

Background colors can spice up your Web pages. Just as many people prefer to watch a color TV rather than a black-and-white TV, people also like to see a little color when they're browsing through Web pages. Most browsers display a gray or white background color by default. When you add a background color, you change the gray or white background to whatever color you specify.

You should consider changing background colors for two reasons:

- Changing background colors is fun and easy and makes your Web pages look cool.

- Changing background colors is one way that you can keep up with developments in Web page design. (Many individuals and companies are using colors in their Web page backgrounds these days.)

Choosing a background color is up to you. As you select a background color, keep in mind that the color you choose helps set the tone of your Web pages:

- Bright background colors (like the *primary* colors — you know those crayon-type colors) provide a cheery or fast-paced tone.

- Dark background colors (such as ocean blue and forest green) provide a sober or mysterious tone.

- Earthy background colors (such as khaki, tan, taupe, or terra-cotta) offer a serious or subdued tone.

- Pastel background colors (such as seaweed green, light pink, or baby blue) offer a warm or creative tone.

on the test

Be sure that your background colors significantly contrast with your text colors so that the text is easy to read. By *contrast,* we mean that you should use light background colors with dark text colors and dark background colors with light text colors. (You learn how to change the text color in this unit, too.) If the background and text colors don't contrast, nobody can read your Web pages.

If you aren't sure that the contrast is sufficient, it probably isn't. Take the cover of this book, for example — black on yellow is great contrast and would also be good online. Yellow on white, however, probably wouldn't catch on because the contrast is not significant enough. Remember that the greater the contrast between your background and text colors, the easier your Web page is to read.

greater contrast means easier reading

If you change only your document's background color, make sure that you keep the background light so that the reader can see the default black lettering. If you change both the background and text color, you don't need to worry as much about keeping the background light. Simply make sure that one color is very dark and the other is very light.

heads up

Remember, older browsers and text-only browsers such as Lynx cannot display colors; your colors will revert to the default background colors (usually gray or white) when viewed through those browsers.

extra credit

Colors, colors everywhere

Anytime you specify colors in HTML documents, you use something called an *RGB color*. RGB stands for Red Green Blue and refers to the way that monitors combine those three colors to make all other colors, such as yellow and purple. Red, green, and blue are the primary colors of the video world.

The combinations of letters and numerals are fancy computer numbers called *hexadecimal numbers*. Hexadecimal numbers look like #222222 or #FF00EE. They always start with a number sign (#) and have six numbers and/or letters following, depending on the color. The six digits of an RGB number show the proportions of red, green, and blue — the first two digits are for red, the next two for green, and the final two for blue. You count from 1 to 9 and then continue with A (10), B (11), and so on to F (15). So, for example, a number like #000000 indicates that no color is used (#000000 is black). #FFFFFF is the maximum (15) of red, green, and blue, (#FFFFFF makes white). Finally, #FF0000 uses only red, and a lot of it.

The most common way to find background colors to use is to borrow them from existing Web sites. Borrowing colors is not the same as borrowing graphics, text, or ideas because you're borrowing an RGB number, which is a standard, universal number that matches a color. Nobody holds a copyright on these numbers, although people hold copyrights to text, graphics, or other elements you might see in Web sites.

To borrow a color from an existing Web site, follow these instructions:

1. **Make sure that WebEdit and Netscape are open.**

2. **In WebEdit, open the document called swipe.htm from your \html101\unit12 folder.**

3. **Switch to Netscape, enter the following address in the Location line, and press Enter.**

   `http://www.idgbooks.com/`
   The IDG Books Worldwide, Inc. home page should appear.

4. **Choose View⇨Document Source.**

   The HTML code the author used to create the Web page appears.

5. **Look at the opening <BODY> tag.**

   You should see the attribute BGCOLOR="#000000" (the number might be different, but the BGCOLOR= will be the same.

6. **Copy the RGB number by highlighting it with your mouse and then choose Edit⇨Copy.**

7. **Switch to WebEdit, where swipe.htm should be open.**

8. **Paste the RGB number into the <BODY> tag, like this:**

   <BODY BGCOLOR="#000000">

9. **Save the document and then test it in Netscape.**

   Your document should now have the same background color as that of the IDG Books Worldwide, Inc. site.

If you don't want to search for colors you like in existing Web sites, check out the document \html101\unit12\backgrnd\color.htm, which provides samples of colors and the corresponding RGB numbers. As with the preceding exercise, you can copy the RGB number from the file and paste it into the <BODY> tag of your document in WebEdit. Specific instructions for copying and pasting RGB numbers are provided in Lesson 12-1.

You can use the same process to copy any formatting from a Web site into a document of your own. Simply choose View⇨Document Source and browse around in the HTML code. You may be surprised at how much you learn by looking at how other people achieved cool effects.

BGCOLOR="#RRGGBB"
changes
background color

don't forget # and " "

Progress Check

If you can do the following,
you've mastered this lesson:

❑ Explain how using
background colors
enhances your Web
pages.

❑ Select a background color
from color.htm.

❑ Add a background color
to an HTML document.

Adding a background color

Adding a background color to a document requires adding the
BGCOLOR="#RRGGBB" attribute to the <BODY>...</BODY> tag. You simply
replace the RRGGBB in the preceding code with the RGB values you choose,
as in the following exercise:

on the CD

**1   In Netscape, open color.htm (located in the \html101\unit12\
backgrnd folder).**

You see 100 sample color squares with the corresponding RGB number below
each square. The colors in color.htm are not all possible combinations, but they
are some of the most common. Each number for RRGGBB gives you a slightly
different color.

on the CD

**2   In WebEdit, open bkg-col.htm (located in the \html101\unit12
folder).**

You use this sample document to practice changing the background color.

**3   Switch to Netscape, where color.htm should be open; in the
second column, find the second color's number.**

It's a light blue square with the number #00FFFF.

**4   Write the RGB number on a piece of paper. Or in this case, you can
highlight the number and choose Edit⇨Copy.**

**5   Switch to WebEdit and add the BGCOLOR="#00FFFF" attribute to
the <BODY> tag.**

If you wrote down the RGB number, type the RGB number in the initial tag. If
you copied the number, put your cursor where the number should go and
choose Edit⇨Paste.

Your code should look like the following:

```
<BODY BGCOLOR="#00FFFF">
```

6   Save your document in WebEdit and then test it in Netscape.

Your document should now have a light blue background. If it doesn't, make
sure that you entered the background attribute and the RGB number correctly.

For your future documents (you *are* going to keep having all this fun, aren't
you?), you can continue using the RGB numbers provided in the color.htm
document. Or you can find a wider variety to choose from by borrowing
colors from existing Web sites. For more information on borrowing colors
from Web sites, take a look at the sidebar in this lesson called "Colors, colors
everywhere."

You can close this file now; you use a different one for the next lesson.

Recess

Pretty nifty stuff, eh? You have turned a plain background into a nice light
blue background. In the next lesson, you learn how to change text color,
which will let your text contrast any background color you choose.

For now, though, take a break! We're going out for a Banana Nut Fudge
Sundae with caramel, whipped cream, and a big ol' cherry.

Coloring Text and Links

Lesson 12-2

In the last lesson, you applied a background color to an HTML document. In this lesson, you learn how to change the text and link colors. You need to be able to change text and link colors because if you color only the background, you have only restricted choices for color combinations. For example, if you love a dark blue (#400080) background, but your text is still black, you won't have a very readable page (understatement warning here). You need to pick a good background color and then select text and link colors that provide good contrast.

on the test

Erring on the conservative side is much better than going wild when dealing with colors. Remember that your readers are going to have to sit and look at the background, text, and link colors you choose, so consider choosing colors that are pleasant (non-offensive) to look at. If you're really into fuchsia and bright orange color combinations, consider that your readers might not be.

When you choose a color for text and links, you're choosing a color for all the text within the `<BODY>...</BODY>` tags (although you only insert the attribute in the initial `<BODY>` tag). In addition to changing normal text — that is, text that's used for things like headings and paragraphs — you also can change the color of link text. Three different kinds of links are available:

- **Unvisited links:** The reader has not ever selected that link on the page.
- **Visited links:** The reader has used that link to visit somewhere else.
- **Active links:** The link that someone is actually selecting at that time.

You color text and links by adding the following attributes to the `<BODY>` tag:

- `TEXT="#RRGGBB"` changes text color.
- `LINK="#RRGGBB"` changes link text color.
- `VLINK="#RRGGBB"` changes visited link color.
- `ALINK="#RRGGBB"` changes active link color.

In this first exercise, you learn how to change the color of text. (You learn to color links in the next exercise in this lesson.) Follow these steps to color your text:

on the CD

1 In WebEdit, open allcolor.htm.

2 Set the document's background color to #400080:

```
<BODY BGCOLOR="#400080">
```

3 Add the `TEXT="#FFFFFF"` attribute to the `<BODY>` tag:

```
<BODY BGCOLOR="#400080" TEXT="#FFFFFF">
```

4 Save and test your document.

Your document should have new background and text colors. If you don't see new colors, check to see that you entered the tags and attributes correctly.

At this point, the links are kind of hard to see, but in the next series of steps, you can fix that problem by changing the link colors to ones that contrast the background.

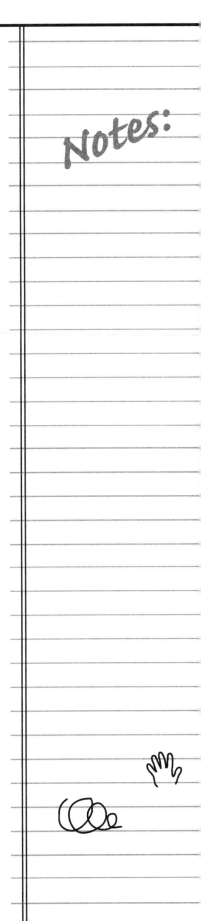

Notes:

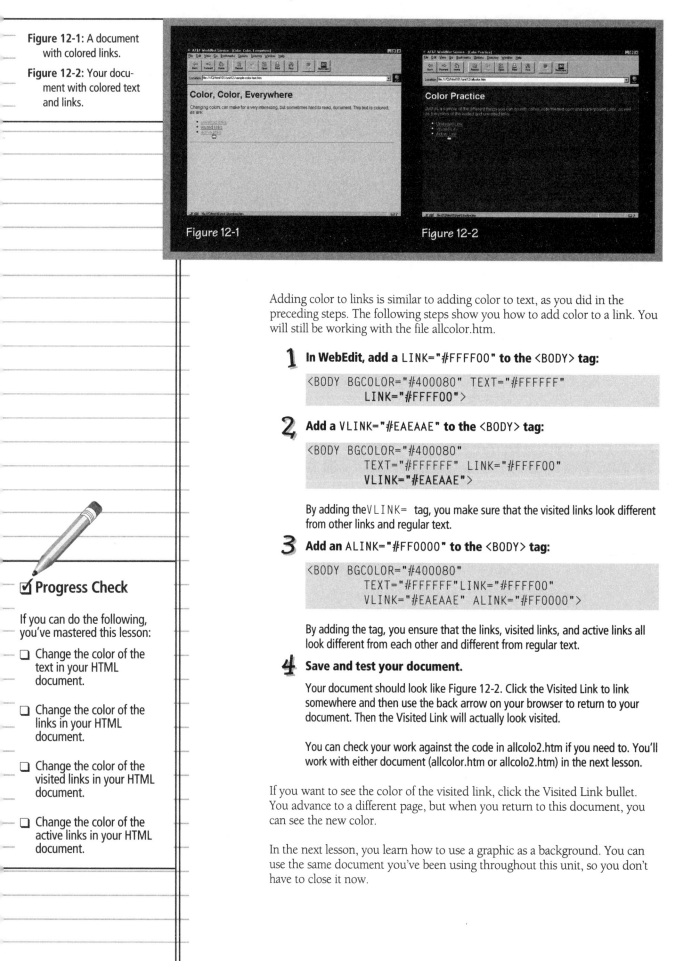

Figure 12-1   Figure 12-2

Adding color to links is similar to adding color to text, as you did in the preceding steps. The following steps show you how to add color to a link. You will still be working with the file allcolor.htm.

1 **In WebEdit, add a** LINK="#FFFF00" **to the** <BODY> **tag:**

```
<BODY BGCOLOR="#400080" TEXT="#FFFFFF"
        LINK="#FFFF00">
```

2 **Add a** VLINK="#EAEAAE" **to the** <BODY> **tag:**

```
<BODY BGCOLOR="#400080"
        TEXT="#FFFFFF" LINK="#FFFF00"
        VLINK="#EAEAAE">
```

By adding the VLINK= tag, you make sure that the visited links look different from other links and regular text.

3 **Add an** ALINK="#FF0000" **to the** <BODY> **tag:**

```
<BODY BGCOLOR="#400080"
        TEXT="#FFFFFF"LINK="#FFFF00"
        VLINK="#EAEAAE" ALINK="#FF0000">
```

By adding the tag, you ensure that the links, visited links, and active links all look different from each other and different from regular text.

4 **Save and test your document.**

Your document should look like Figure 12-2. Click the Visited Link to link somewhere and then use the back arrow on your browser to return to your document. Then the Visited Link will actually look visited.

You can check your work against the code in allcolo2.htm if you need to. You'll work with either document (allcolor.htm or allcolo2.htm) in the next lesson.

If you want to see the color of the visited link, click the Visited Link bullet. You advance to a different page, but when you return to this document, you can see the new color.

In the next lesson, you learn how to use a graphic as a background. You can use the same document you've been using throughout this unit, so you don't have to close it now.

☑ Progress Check

If you can do the following, you've mastered this lesson:

❑ Change the color of the text in your HTML document.

❑ Change the color of the links in your HTML document.

❑ Change the color of the visited links in your HTML document.

❑ Change the color of the active links in your HTML document.

Using Graphics for Backgrounds

Lesson 12-3

So far in this unit, you've learned about adding color to your document's background, text, and links. In this lesson, you learn how to use graphics as backgrounds. Using graphics as backgrounds, you can include you're company's logo, a cool pattern, or even an array of colors.

The process is basically the same as the processes you used in Lessons 12-1, but you add a graphic in addition to a color. Regardless of the size of the image you choose to use, the graphic will be *tiled* (multiple copies will be placed side by side to fill all the available space) across the background of your document.

If you do decide to use a graphic as a background, you should continue to provide colored backgrounds as an alternative to the graphic. If, for example, you make all the text white on a dark graphic background and for some reason the graphic doesn't load into your reader's browser, your reader will be stuck looking at white text on a light background. Yuck — not to mention nearly impossible to read. By using both a colored background and a graphic, you can ensure that the text is easy to read.

heads up

Be careful when you use a graphic as a background. The graphic can make reading your text extremely difficult. For example, if a graphic has a lot of colors, overlapping shapes, or busy patterns, the text tends to get lost in the boldness of the graphic. Try to stick to few colors, shapes, and patterns to help the text show up well against the background.

As with the colors, most newer browsers can successfully load backgrounds, but older browsers will not be able to. Plan accordingly.

Adding background images involves adding the `BACKGROUND="..."` attribute to the `<BODY>` tag:

on the CD

1 **Make sure that allcolor.htm is open in WebEdit and Netscape.**

If you just finished the preceding lesson, you're right where you need to be. If you're jumping back in here, open allcolo2.htm, which includes the changes made in the last lesson.

2 **Add the `BACKGROUND=` attribute to the body tag and use the graphic tree.gif (located in your unit12 folder) for the background image:**

```
<BODY BACKGROUND="tree.gif" BGCOLOR="#400080"
      TEXT="#FFFFFF" LINK="#FFFF00"
      VLINK="#EAEAAE" ALINK="#FF0000">
```

3 **Save and test your document.**

Your document should look like Figure 12-4. If your document doesn't look like this figure, go back to WebEdit and check to see that you entered the text and tags correctly.

If you want to play with some really ugly backgrounds, look in the \html101\unit12 folder. Person.gif is cute, but horrible as a background. Win-bck1.gif is just strange.

Figure 12-3: A document with a tiled background image.

Figure 12-4: Using a graphic as a background is cool!

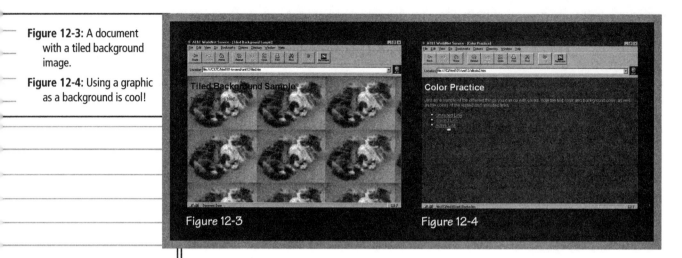

Figure 12-3   Figure 12-4

Unit 12 Quiz

Quiz time! And no peeking at the lessons! (Okay, peek if you have to.) Circle the correct answer or answers for each of the following questions.

1. **Adding color to your HTML documents is similar to**

    A. Dorothy arriving to Oz and things turning from black and white to color.

    B. Watching a color TV show on a black-and-white TV set.

    C. Installing plaid carpeting over your solid-colored carpeting.

    D. Using markers instead of crayons.

    E. Both C and D

2. **You add the various color attributes to which tag?**

    A. `<H1>...</H1>`

    B. `<P>...</P>`

    C. `<BODY>...</BODY>`

    D. `<LI>...</BR>`

    E. None of the above

3. **Tiled means that**

    A. The graphic appears on top of a black-and-white tile pattern.

    B. Multiple copies are placed side by side to fill all the available space.

    C. Only a single tile appears to fill the entire screen.

    D. You have to wash the screen with tile floor cleaner.

    E. None of the above

4. **RGB refers to**

   A. Red, Green, and Blue tiles.

   B. The Really Good Backgrounds that you can use in an HTML document.

   C. Ripe Green Beans.

   D. The way that monitors combine Red, Green, and Blue.

   E. None of the above

5. **When changing colors in your HTML document, you need to consider your readers' browsers because**

   A. Newer browsers make colors look brighter.

   B. Older browsers make colors blend better.

   C. Older browsers cannot successfully load colors.

   D. Newer browsers cannot successfully load colors.

   E. Both C and D

Unit 12 Exercise

1. Using WebEdit, open catlett.htm and personlt.htm from your \html101\unit12 folder.

2. In the first document (catlett.htm), add a color for the background and add an appropriately contrasting color to the text. Be sure that the background color contrasts with all text and link colors.

3. In the second document (personlt.htm), add a graphic for the background — you can use one of the backgrounds we provided if you need to. Color all the text on this page so that it contrasts with the graphic background.

4. Save and test both these documents. You should see the new colors and background in the documents.

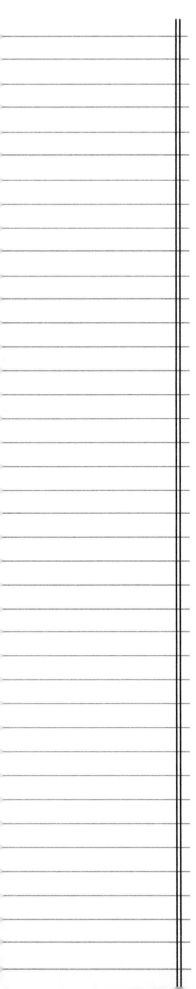

Creativity within HTML Limitations

Prerequisites
- ◗ Understanding how to create basic HTML documents (Part II)
- ◗ Using Graphics in Your HTML Documents (Part III)
- ◗ Developing Tables (Unit 10)

Objectives for This Unit

✓ Using tables to create columns of text

✓ Using tables to create sideheads

✓ Aligning stuff on the left, in the middle, or on the right

on the CD
- ◗ column.htm
- ◗ sidehead.htm
- ◗ align.htm

N ow that you know how to brighten up your documents with color, you're ready for more fun. In this unit, you learn how to use tables to create columns and use alignment options to build creative page designs.

The lessons in Unit 13 help you overcome some of the formatting limitations of HTML. For example, so far all the text, headings, and graphics you've included in your documents have been aligned with the left margin. Left alignment is the HTML default, but you can change the alignment of these things to align either to the center or right. Doing so allows you to be creative with page design and put headings and graphics in more effective places on the page.

Check out Figure 13-1, which shows an example of a Web page that uses right and center alignment options.

Also, all the paragraphs of text you've included so far appear in one fat column. Although one fat column may be adequate in many cases, sometimes you may want to put text into two or more columns. Putting text in, say, two columns, can help break up long sections of text so that they're not so dense. (Remember, breaking long sections of text into smaller pieces is important to help readers wade through the information.) Using two columns helps break the text into smaller pieces — only instead of breaking the information itself into smaller pieces, you break the information visually. Kind of sneaky, we think.

Figure 13-1: Alignment options or columns can help make your page design more interesting.

Figure 13-2: A one-column format, which is the HTML default.

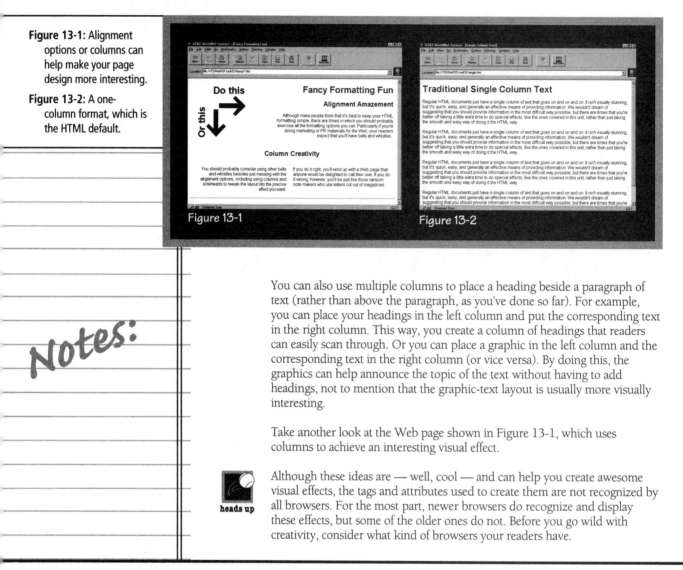

Figure 13-1

Figure 13-2

Notes:

You can also use multiple columns to place a heading beside a paragraph of text (rather than above the paragraph, as you've done so far). For example, you can place your headings in the left column and put the corresponding text in the right column. This way, you create a column of headings that readers can easily scan through. Or you can place a graphic in the left column and the corresponding text in the right column (or vice versa). By doing this, the graphics can help announce the topic of the text without having to add headings, not to mention that the graphic-text layout is usually more visually interesting.

Take another look at the Web page shown in Figure 13-1, which uses columns to achieve an interesting visual effect.

Although these ideas are — well, cool — and can help you create awesome visual effects, the tags and attributes used to create them are not recognized by all browsers. For the most part, newer browsers do recognize and display these effects, but some of the older ones do not. Before you go wild with creativity, consider what kind of browsers your readers have.

heads up

Lesson 13-1 Using Tables for Columns

In this lesson, you put information into columns by using tables, which is the only way you can put information into columns. Normally, your text appears in one fat column that stretches from the left margin to the right margin. Using tables, you can put information into multiple, thinner columns to help ease reading or to better present the information.

Take a look at Figures 13-2 and 13-3. Figure 13-2 shows a page that has one fat column of text; Figure 13-3 shows the same information presented in two columns.

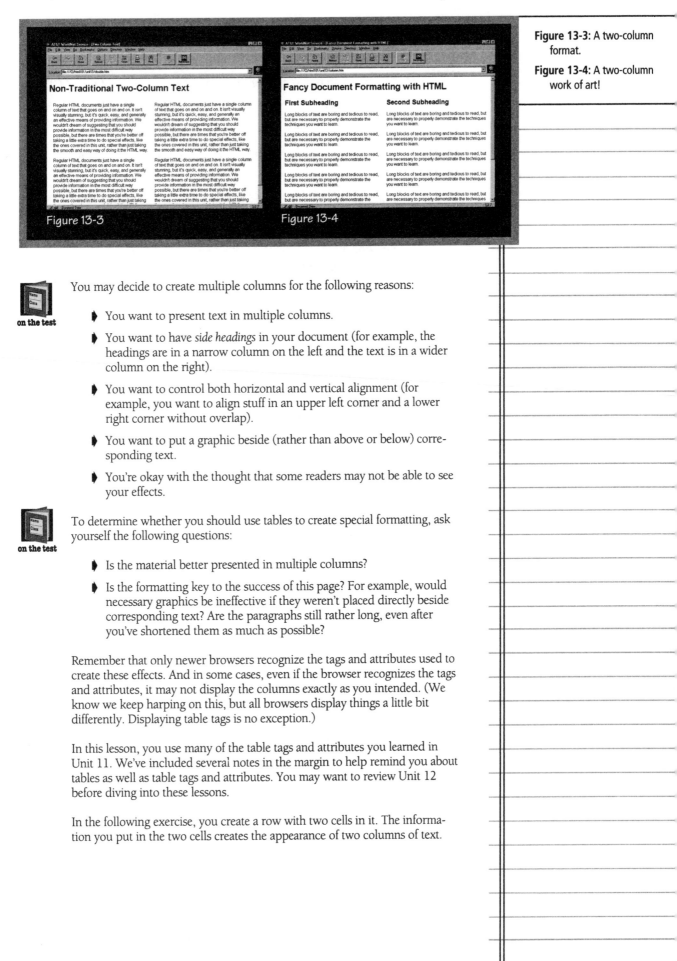

You may decide to create multiple columns for the following reasons:

on the test

▶ You want to present text in multiple columns.

▶ You want to have *side headings* in your document (for example, the headings are in a narrow column on the left and the text is in a wider column on the right).

▶ You want to control both horizontal and vertical alignment (for example, you want to align stuff in an upper left corner and a lower right corner without overlap).

▶ You want to put a graphic beside (rather than above or below) corresponding text.

▶ You're okay with the thought that some readers may not be able to see your effects.

on the test

To determine whether you should use tables to create special formatting, ask yourself the following questions:

▶ Is the material better presented in multiple columns?

▶ Is the formatting key to the success of this page? For example, would necessary graphics be ineffective if they weren't placed directly beside corresponding text? Are the paragraphs still rather long, even after you've shortened them as much as possible?

Remember that only newer browsers recognize the tags and attributes used to create these effects. And in some cases, even if the browser recognizes the tags and attributes, it may not display the columns exactly as you intended. (We know we keep harping on this, but all browsers display things a little bit differently. Displaying table tags is no exception.)

In this lesson, you use many of the table tags and attributes you learned in Unit 11. We've included several notes in the margin to help remind you about tables as well as table tags and attributes. You may want to review Unit 12 before diving into these lessons.

In the following exercise, you create a row with two cells in it. The information you put in the two cells creates the appearance of two columns of text.

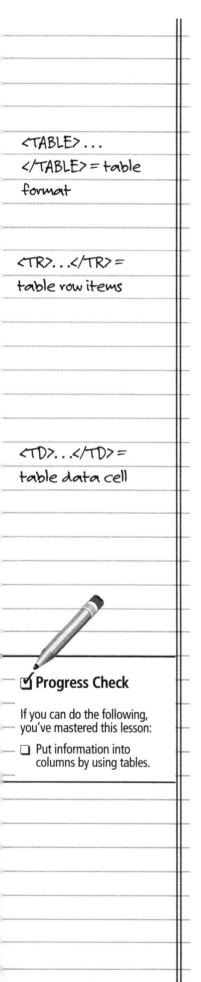

<TABLE> . . .
</TABLE> = table
format

<TR> . . .</TR> =
table row items

<TD> . . .</TD> =
table data cell

Progress Check

If you can do the following,
you've mastered this lesson:

❏ Put information into
columns by using tables.

1 **Open the document column.htm in WebEdit.**

2 **Insert an opening <TABLE> tag above the first <H2>...</H2>:**

```
<TABLE>
<H2>First Subheading</H2>
```

3 **Insert a closing </TABLE> tag below the last </P> in the document:**

```
want to learn.</P>
</TABLE>
```

4 **Add a <TR>...</TR> inside the <TABLE>... </TABLE> tags:**

```
<TABLE><TR>
<H2>First Subheading</H2>
```

and

```
want to learn.</P>
</TR></TABLE>
```

5 **Add a <TD> after the opening <TR> tag:**

```
<TABLE><TR><TD>
```

6 **Add a </TD>...<TD> just before the second <H2> in the document:**

```
</TD><TD>
<H2>Second Subheading</H2>
```

What you just did is added a closing table </TD> tag (to close the <TD> tag you entered in Step 6) and added an opening <TD> tag for the next set of table data.

7 **Add a </TD> just before the </TR>:**

```
want to learn.</P>
</TD></TR></TABLE>
```

Here, you just closed the <TD> tag you started in Step 7.

8 **Save your document in WebEdit and then test it in Netscape.**

You just added table, table row, and table data tags to make a one row, two column table. Cool, huh? Take a look at Figure 13-4, which shows what your two-column document should look like. If you don't see two columns, go back to WebEdit and make sure that you entered the tags correctly.

You use this document in the next lesson, so don't worry about closing it.

extra credit

Placing a graphic next to text

Another neato design trick is to place a graphic next to a paragraph of text. Check out Figure 13-1, which was created by using a table to place the graphic on the left and the text on the right.

You may remember that you can use ALIGN= attributes to place text next to a graphic. Using the ALIGN= attribute with your image tags just wraps text around the graphics and forces the image to the side. The downside is that the text or graphic on the right might get wrapped around to the next line, so your text-graphic combo would appear with one stacked partially on top of the other.

However, tables provide a slightly more reliable means of making different elements line up horizontally. Tables sort of act as a cage — all the information in the table stays in the table and won't wrap onto the next line. So the text-graphic package will remain complete (in any browser that supports tables, that is).

Using tables to place a graphic next to corresponding text is useful for several reasons:

▶ Readers can quickly associate the graphic with the text. Many times, placing graphics above or below text forces readers to scroll up or down to get the full effect of the text-graphic combination. Side-by-side text and graphics are much more effective.

▶ You can squeeze more information on-screen because you make better use of horizontal space. If you plop a graphic in your document, chances are that you'll have a great deal of wasted space right next to it. Placing the text beside the graphic is more space-efficient.

▶ You can ensure that the side-by-side layout stays — well — side-by-side. Because the text and graphic is contained within the <TABLE>... </TABLE> tags, browsers treat them as one object.

To create a text-graphic (or graphic-text) combination, create a one-row, two-cell table. Then for example, put the <P>...</P> tags with text included in the left cell and the <IMG> tag with the graphic's URL in the right cell.

Your HTML code might look something like this:

```
<TABLE><TR>
<TD><IMG SRC="animage.gif" ALT="An Image"></TD>
<TD><P>All kinds of cool text can line up
        with an image.</P></TD>
</TR></TABLE>
```

You can also use tables to make text-graphic combinations align vertically. Just create a two-row, one cell table. Try it!

For a review of including graphics in your HTML documents, see Unit 8; for a review of making tables, check out Unit 10.

Notes:

Figure 13-5: Way too close for comfort.

Figure 13-6: Comfy columns.

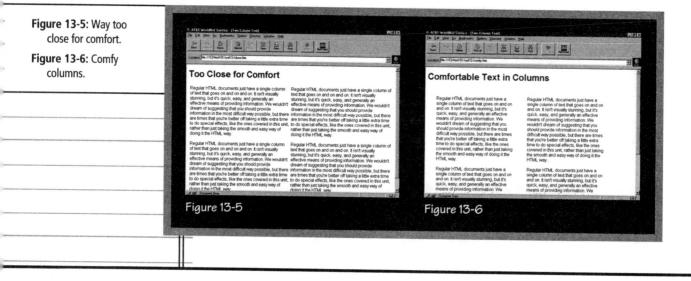

Figure 13-5   Figure 13-6

Lesson 13-2   Customizing Your Columns

In this lesson, you add a couple of attributes that help customize the columns, such as changing the cell width and cell spacing. Changing the cell width and cell spacing is particularly important when you use tables to create columns. If your columns are too wide, for example, they appear very close together, which can be just as difficult to read as one fat column. Similarly, if you don't have enough space between the individual cells, the information within the cells tends to *blend* together and appear like one fat cell with too much information in it.

Check out Figures 13-5 and 13-6. Figure 13-5 shows you an example of two columns that are too close together; Figure 13-6 shows those same columns spaced farther apart. The information in Figure 13-6 is much easier to read.

The following steps show you how to change the cell width and cell spacing.

1 **In WebEdit, make sure that column.htm is open. If you're just joining in now, open column2.htm.**

2 **Add a** WIDTH=580 **attribute to the** <TABLE> **tag:**

```
<TABLE WIDTH=580>
```

This step established the table width at 580 pixels — slightly smaller than the narrowest screen you can anticipate your readers having.

3 **Add a** CELLSPACING=20 **attribute to the** <TABLE> **tag to keep the columns from running into each other:**

```
<TABLE WIDTH=580 CELLSPACING=20>
```

4 **Save and test your document.**

Your document should look like Figure 13-7. If your columns don't look like the ones in Figure 13-7, verify that you entered the attributes and numbers correctly. You can also check out column3.htm if you want to see what the full code should look like.

Go ahead and close this document because you work with a different document in the next lesson.

WIDTH=n sets width of the table based on n

CELLSPACING= sets space between cells

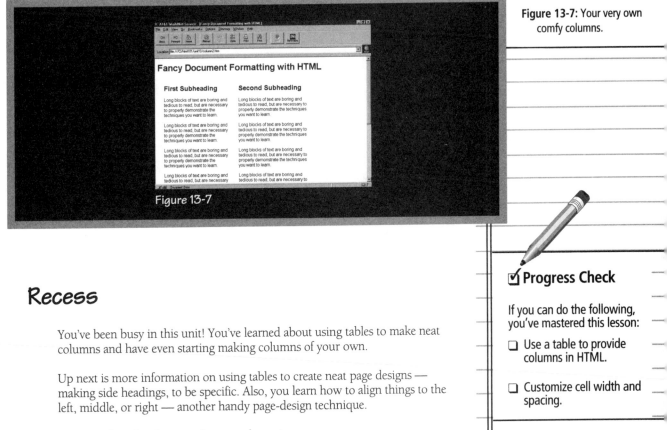

Figure 13-7

Figure 13-7: Your very own comfy columns.

Recess

You've been busy in this unit! You've learned about using tables to make neat columns and have even starting making columns of your own.

Up next is more information on using tables to create neat page designs — making side headings, to be specific. Also, you learn how to align things to the left, middle, or right — another handy page-design technique.

For now, though, it's recess time, so take ten!

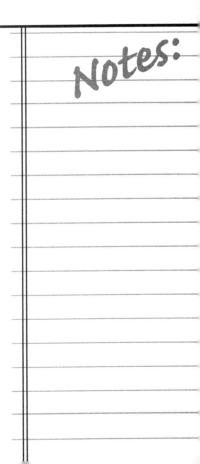

☑ Progress Check

If you can do the following, you've mastered this lesson:

❑ Use a table to provide columns in HTML.

❑ Customize cell width and spacing.

Using a Table for Sideheads

Lesson 13-3

Notes:

In this lesson, you use a table to create sideheads. *Sideheads* are headings that appear to the side of the text, not above it. Most commonly, sideheads appear in a narrow column on the left, and the text appears in a wider column on the right.

Using sideheads offers a few advantages over using regular headings that appear above paragraphs of text. Using sideheads can help you create a more interesting page design — more interesting because this type of page design is less commonly used. Also, sideheads are easier to read because they appear as a column of headings that stand out from the text better than regular headings do.

Figures 13-8 and 13-9 show you how sideheads stand out better than regular headings that appear above text.

In this lesson, you use the table tags you learned in Unit 10. You also use a new attribute that affects vertical alignment: VALIGN=.

For the following exercise, you start by creating a basic table. This table has two rows, and each row has two cells. When you make a sidehead, what you're actually doing is putting the heading in the left cell; when you add the text, you're putting the heading in the right cell. The VALIGN= attribute makes the two cells align beside each other. (If you don't use the VALIGN= attribute, the cells will be aligned in the center of the cells, rather than at the top. It looks goofy that way.)

Figure 13-8: Regular headings are — well — adequate.

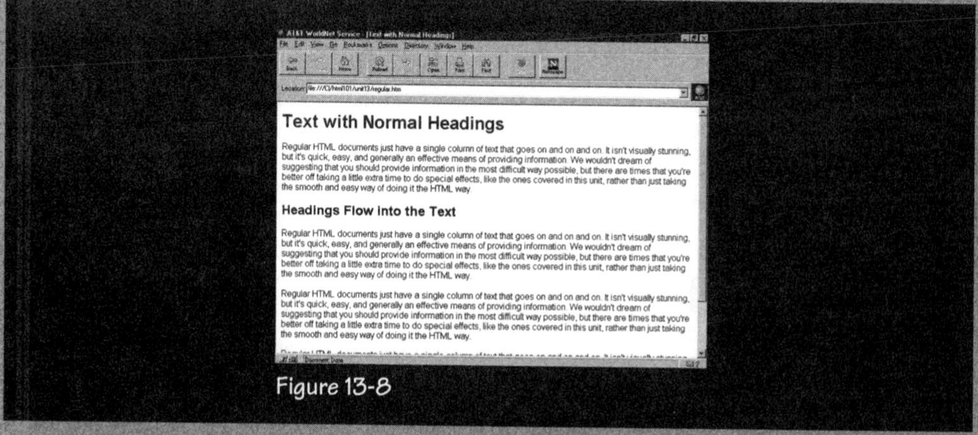

Text with Normal Headings

Regular HTML documents just have a single column of text that goes on and on and on. It isn't visually stunning, but it's quick, easy, and generally an effective means of providing information. We wouldn't dream of suggesting that you should provide information in the most difficult way possible, but there are times that you're better off taking a little extra time to do special effects, like the ones covered in this unit, rather than just taking the smooth and easy way of doing it the HTML way.

Headings Flow into the Text

Regular HTML documents just have a single column of text that goes on and on and on. It isn't visually stunning, but it's quick, easy, and generally an effective means of providing information. We wouldn't dream of suggesting that you should provide information in the most difficult way possible, but there are times that you're better off taking a little extra time to do special effects, like the ones covered in this unit, rather than just taking the smooth and easy way of doing it the HTML way.

Regular HTML documents just have a single column of text that goes on and on and on. It isn't visually stunning, but it's quick, easy, and generally an effective means of providing information. We wouldn't dream of suggesting that you should provide information in the most difficult way possible, but there are times that you're better off taking a little extra time to do special effects, like the ones covered in this unit, rather than just taking the smooth and easy way of doing it the HTML way.

Figure 13-8

Notes:

1 In WebEdit, open sidehead.htm.

2 Insert an opening `<TABLE>` tag just above the first `<H2>`...`</H2>`:

```
<TABLE>
<H2>First Subheading</H2>
```

You will use this table to achieve a sidehead effect.

3 Insert a closing `</TABLE>` tag below the last `</P>` in the document:

```
want to learn.</P>
</TABLE>
```

4 Add a `<TR>` before the first `<H2>` tag:

```
<TABLE><TR>
<H2>First Subheading</H2>
```

5 Add a `</TR><TR>` before the second `<H2>` tag:

```
</TR><TR>
<H2>Second Subheading</H2>
```

In this step, you're closing the `<TR>` tag you entered in Step 4 and starting a new table row with `<TR>`.

6 Add a `</TR>` after the last `</P>` in the document:

```
want to learn.</P>
</TR></TABLE>
```

7 Add `<TD></TD>` around the first subheading `<H2>` in the document:

```
<TD><H2>First Subheading</H2></TD>
```

8 Add a `<TD>` before the first `<P>` in the document:

```
<TD><H2>First Subheading</H2></TD>
<TD>
<P>Long blocks of text are boring and
```

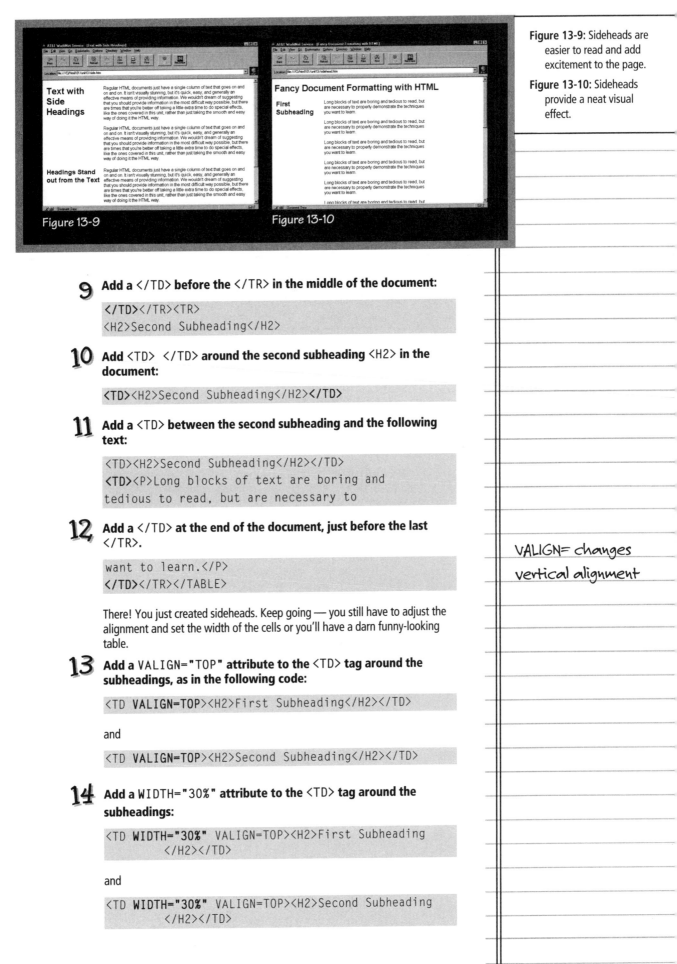

Figure 13-9

Figure 13-10

Figure 13-9: Sideheads are easier to read and add excitement to the page.

Figure 13-10: Sideheads provide a neat visual effect.

9 Add a `</TD>` before the `</TR>` in the middle of the document:

```
</TD></TR><TR>
<H2>Second Subheading</H2>
```

10 Add `<TD>  </TD>` around the second subheading `<H2>` in the document:

```
<TD><H2>Second Subheading</H2></TD>
```

11 Add a `<TD>` between the second subheading and the following text:

```
<TD><H2>Second Subheading</H2></TD>
<TD><P>Long blocks of text are boring and
tedious to read, but are necessary to
```

12 Add a `</TD>` at the end of the document, just before the last `</TR>`.

```
want to learn.</P>
</TD></TR></TABLE>
```

There! You just created sideheads. Keep going — you still have to adjust the alignment and set the width of the cells or you'll have a darn funny-looking table.

13 Add a `VALIGN="TOP"` attribute to the `<TD>` tag around the subheadings, as in the following code:

```
<TD VALIGN=TOP><H2>First Subheading</H2></TD>
```

and

```
<TD VALIGN=TOP><H2>Second Subheading</H2></TD>
```

14 Add a `WIDTH="30%"` attribute to the `<TD>` tag around the subheadings:

```
<TD WIDTH="30%" VALIGN=TOP><H2>First Subheading
     </H2></TD>
```

and

```
<TD WIDTH="30%" VALIGN=TOP><H2>Second Subheading
     </H2></TD>
```

VALIGN= changes vertical alignment

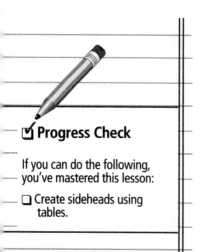

Progress Check

If you can do the following, you've mastered this lesson:

❑ Create sideheads using tables.

15 Add a `WIDTH=580` **attribute to the opening** `<TABLE>` **tag:**

`<TABLE WIDTH=580>`

16 **Save and test your document.**

Check your results with Figure 13-8. If your table doesn't look like the one in Figure 13-8, check to see that you entered the tags and attributes correctly. Keeping track of all the opening tags, closing tags, and attributes is pretty tricky. If your columns don't look right, check your work against sidehed2.htm

Close your document when you're done — you use a different document in the next lesson.

Lesson 13-4   Using Alignment Options

on the test

Just as you can change the alignment within table cells, you also can align regular text either left, center, or right. Changing alignment of tables (as well as other page elements, such as paragraphs, headings, and graphics) is another option you have to develop creative layouts. Although all browsers do not support all of these options, most support most of the options reasonably well. (How's that for hedging! Seriously, this goes back to the "all browsers display things differently" concept that we were on the soapbox about earlier.)

You can use the following attributes with paragraph tags, heading tags, and many others. (You may notice that you've already seen these tags and attributes in the context of images, but not in the context of text, paragraphs, and headings.)

▶ `ALIGN=RIGHT` Aligns text, headings, paragraphs, graphics, or tables to the right.

▶ `ALIGN=LEFT` (This one is usually the default.) Aligns text, headings, paragraphs, graphics, or tables to the left.

▶ `ALIGN=CENTER` Aligns text, headings, paragraphs, graphics, or tables in the center.

`ALIGN=LEFT` generally isn't used, because it's the default value for align.

Additionally, you can use the following vertical alignment attributes with graphics and table cells:

▶ `VALIGN=TOP` Vertically aligns text, paragraphs, and headings with the top of graphics or tables.

▶ `VALIGN=BOTTOM` Vertically aligns text, paragraphs, and headings with the bottom of graphics or tables.

▶ `VALIGN=MIDDLE` Vertically aligns text, paragraphs, and headings within the middle of graphics or tables.

heads up

As with some of the other tags and attributes you've worked with, these alignment tags are not supported by all browsers — most of the newer browsers do support them. If a browser does not support the alignment tags and attributes, anything marked with alignment attributes appears with default alignment (left).

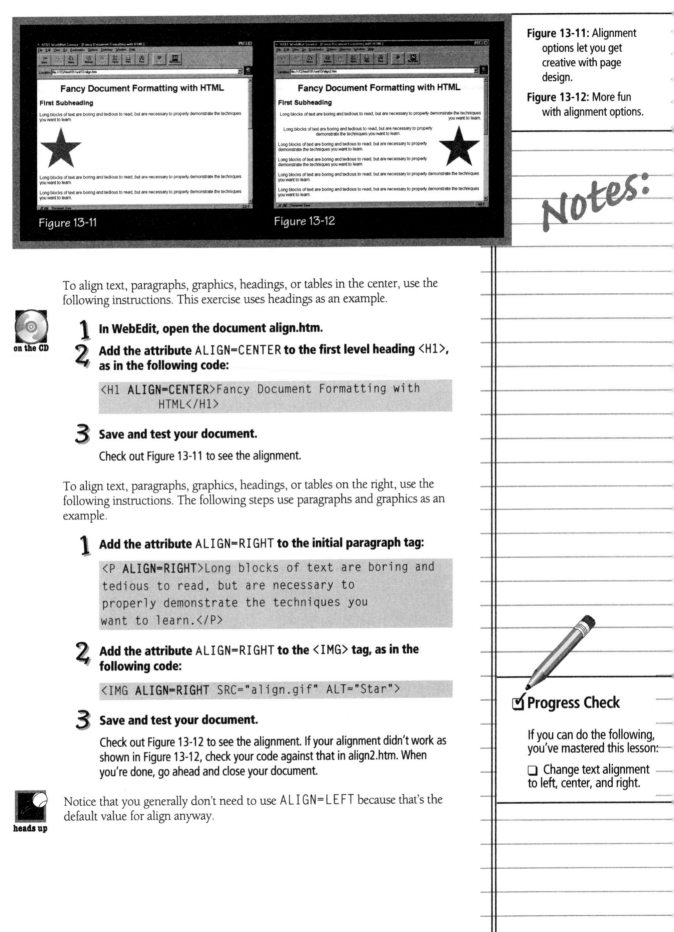

Figure 13-11

Figure 13-12

Figure 13-11: Alignment
options let you get
creative with page
design.

Figure 13-12: More fun
with alignment options.

Notes:

To align text, paragraphs, graphics, headings, or tables in the center, use the
following instructions. This exercise uses headings as an example.

on the CD

1 **In WebEdit, open the document align.htm.**

2 **Add the attribute** ALIGN=CENTER **to the first level heading** <H1>,
as in the following code:

```
<H1 ALIGN=CENTER>Fancy Document Formatting with
        HTML</H1>
```

3 **Save and test your document.**

Check out Figure 13-11 to see the alignment.

To align text, paragraphs, graphics, headings, or tables on the right, use the
following instructions. The following steps use paragraphs and graphics as an
example.

1 **Add the attribute** ALIGN=RIGHT **to the initial paragraph tag:**

```
<P ALIGN=RIGHT>Long blocks of text are boring and
tedious to read, but are necessary to
properly demonstrate the techniques you
want to learn.</P>
```

2 **Add the attribute** ALIGN=RIGHT **to the** <IMG> **tag, as in the
following code:**

```
<IMG ALIGN=RIGHT SRC="align.gif" ALT="Star">
```

3 **Save and test your document.**

Check out Figure 13-12 to see the alignment. If your alignment didn't work as
shown in Figure 13-12, check your code against that in align2.htm. When
you're done, go ahead and close your document.

heads up

Notice that you generally don't need to use ALIGN=LEFT because that's the
default value for align anyway.

☑ Progress Check

If you can do the following,
you've mastered this lesson:

❏ Change text alignment
to left, center, and right.

Unit 13 Quiz

Yes, another quiz — time to see what you've learned! The quiz isn't that hard, we promise. All you have to do is circle the correct answer or answers and be done with it.

1. **You use a table to**

    A. Put text in multiple columns.

    B. Make sideheads.

    C. View text sideways.

    D. Control vertical and horizontal alignment.

    E. A, B, and D

2. **Using tables to make special formatting effects**

    A. Will work in everyone's browsers.

    B. Will work in older, text-only browsers.

    C. Will work in newer browsers.

    D. Will work with most alignment options.

    E. Will work in a form.

3. **Which of the following attributes is a default alignment tag?**

    A. `ALIGN=RIGHT`

    B. `ALIGN=LEFT`

    C. `ALIGN=ABOVE`

    D. `ALIGN=BELOW`

    E. None of the above

4. **You can use the alignment options with what tags?**

    A. Paragraph tags

    B. Heading tags

    C. Table tags

    D. List tags

    E. A, B, and C

5. **Sideheads are**

    A. Headings that appear in a column to the side of text.

    B. Headings that appear instead of text.

    C. Headings that appear inside of text.

    D. Headings that disappear when you click on them.

    E. None of the above

Unit 13 Exercise

1. Open alignmnt.htm in WebEdit.

2. Set up a two-column table with each column having sideheads. Use the text that's available in the file.

3. Have fun!

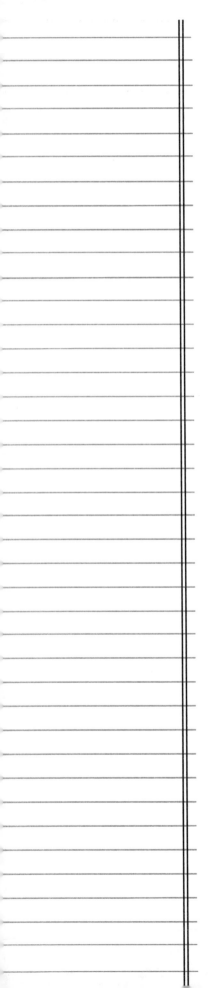

Including Special Stuff

Prerequisites

▶ Understanding HTML basics (Part I)

▶ Understanding the basics of making links (Unit 6)

▶ Understanding the basics of including graphics (Part III)

Objectives for This Unit

✓ Adding special characters

✓ Soliciting e-mail feedback

✓ Using addresses and line breaks

▶ special.htm

on the CD

If you've read the entire book up to this point, you should have the basics of HTML well in hand. This unit gives information about special characters and tags that you haven't needed until now but will probably want to use in your own HTML documents.

Many of the special characters — such as characters with umlauts or accents — are ones you use to help polish your documents, which is something you do after you develop the content and organization (and why you really haven't needed them until now). Other special characters, such as the registered trademark and copyright symbols, are essential.

heads up

Publishing HTML documents on the Web is just like publishing a book, an article, or any other paper publication. If you include copyright or trademark information, you should cite it as such.

This unit is divided into two parts:

▶ The first part of this unit covers *special characters,* which you cannot enter by using single keys on your keyboard. Special characters include things like copyright and trademark symbols, as well as characters with umlauts and accents.

▶ The second part of this unit covers special HTML tags that let you do neat tricks like provide an e-mail link from your Web page right to your mailbox. One of the most significant uses for some of these special tags is to provide a footer for your document. Each of your HTML documents, particularly main pages, should have a footer with basic contact information, including a name and e-mail address.

Using special characters and tags adds a finishing touch to your documents and shows others that you have paid attention to the details.

Keep in mind that you can use gobs more HTML tags, attributes, and special symbols in your documents — the ones presented in the first 13 units of this book are not all that are available, just the ones that will likely be most useful to you. For a comprehensive list of HTML tags, attributes, and special symbols, check out the *HTML For Dummies Quick Reference,* written by yours truly (published by IDG Books Worldwide, Inc.).

Lesson 14-1   Adding Special Characters

In this lesson, you learn to add special characters, such as the copyright symbol (©) and registered trademark (®). Special characters come in two varieties:

- **Ones that you can but shouldn't enter by using single keys on your keyboard.** For example, you can enter an angle bracket (such as < or >) by using your keyboard — right? Consider, though, that angle brackets are part of HTML tags. If you type the angle bracket, the browser will mistake the "<" or ">" as an error in HTML code. To prevent this mistake, you need to use a series of characters (< or >) for special characters.

- **Ones that you can't enter at all using single keys on your keyboard.** These are things like an umlaut (a horizontal colon over a letter), cent sign, or fraction, which are not provided for on your keyboard.

on the test

Special characters are characters that you cannot enter in an HTML document by using single characters on your keyboard. You must enter them by using a series of characters, such as <.

Table 14-1 lists special characters that although you normally could enter by using single keys on your keyboard, you need to use the character combinations (such as) when using them in an HTML document. Table 14-2 lists other special characters that you cannot enter by using your keyboard to type them (such as a cent sign). You can include any of these symbols by using the instructions provided in this lesson.

You can type some characters and symbols in more than one way. To type the character Æ, for example, you can type **Æ** (which is shown in the center column) or **Æ** (which is shown in parentheses in the description column). The way with letters is easier to remember, but the way with numbers is more generally recognized by browsers.

heads up

You must substitute " (") for a double-quote character inside an attribute.

Table 14-1   Special Characters That Look Like Regular Characters

Special Character	What You Type	Description
"	&#34;	Quotation mark (&quot)
#	&#35;	Number sign
%	&#37;	Percent sign
<	&#60;	Less than (&lt)
>	&#62;	Greater than (&gt)
\	&#92;	Reverse solidus (backslash)

Table 14-2	Special Characters That You Can't Just Type	
Appear As	**Characters**	**Description**
¡	&#161;	Inverted exclamation
¢	&#162;	Cent sign
£	&#163;	Pound sterling
¤	&#164;	General currency sign
¥	&#165;	Yen sign
§	&#167;	Section sign
©	&#169;	Copyright
ª	&#170;	Feminine ordinal
«	&#171;	Left angle quote, guillemet
¬	&#172;	Not sign
®	&#174;	Registered trademark
°	&#176;	Degree sign
±	&#177;	Plus or minus sign
²	&#178;	Superscript two
³	&#179;	Superscript three
µ	&#181;	Micro sign
¶	&#182;	Paragraph sign
¹	&#185;	Superscript one
º	&#186;	Masculine ordinal
»	&#187;	Right angle quote, guillemet
¼	&#188;	Fraction one-fourth
½	&#189;	Fraction one-half
¾	&#190;	Fraction three-fourths
¿	&#191;	Inverted question mark
×	&#215;	Multiplication sign
Ø	&#216;	Capital O, slash (Ø)
ß	&#223;	Small sharp s, German (sz ligature) (ß)
æ	&#230;	Small ae dipthong (ligature) (æ)
ç	&#231;	Small c, cedilla (ç)
ñ	&#241;	Small n, tilde (ñ)
÷	&#247;	Division sign
ø	&#248;	Small o, slash (ø)

Notes:

Figure 14-1: Including copyright and trademark symbols can help show that you've paid attention to details.

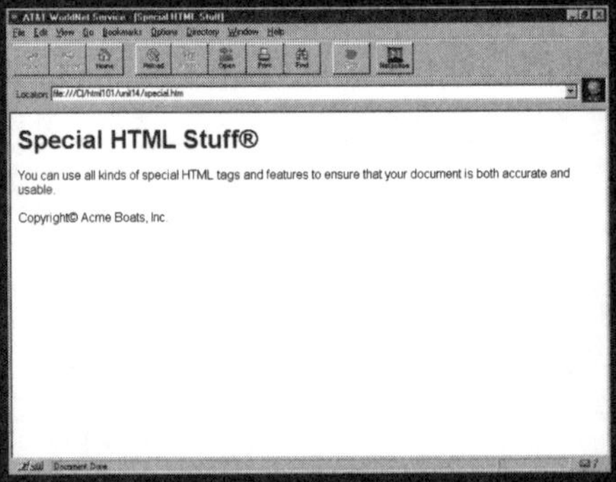

Figure 14-1

Notes:

The following exercise shows you how to include special characters in HTML documents. This exercise uses the copyright and trademark characters as examples, but you use the same process for most any of the special characters.

on the CD

1 **Open the document special.htm in WebEdit.**

2 **Add a new paragraph, <P>...</P>, after the first one.**

3 **Type** Copyright Acme Boats, Inc. **between the paragraph tags:**

```
<P>Copyright Acme Boats, Inc.</P>
```

Include all the parts of the special symbol code

4 **Put your cursor between the words** Copyright **and** Acme.

5 **Type** ©:

```
<P>Copyright &#169; Acme Boats Inc.</P>
```

The & tells the browser it's a special character, the # shows that it's a number, and the 169 tells which special character to insert. The closing ; indicates the end of the number.

6 **Save your document in WebEdit, and then test it in Netscape.**

You should see © in the copyright line you just entered. Next you add a trademark symbol to the document.

7 **Position your cursor at the end of the <H1>...</H1> text (just inside the </H1>).**

8 **Type** ®:

```
<H1>Special HTML Stuff&#174;</H1>
```

You don't want space between the word and the trademark symbol, so make sure that you don't leave a space before the special character code.

9 **Save and test your document.**

You should see ® at the end of the first level heading, as shown in Figure 14-1. If you don't see the special symbols, double-check your HTML code.

If you're moving on to the next lesson now, you can keep your document open and use it in the next lesson.

heads up

copyright symbols normally appear as superscript

Normally, copyright symbols appear as a *superscript* — that is, slightly above the baseline. You learn how to do superscripts in the next lesson.

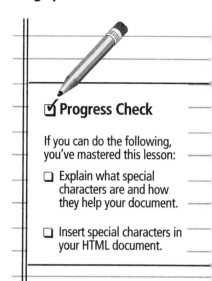

Recess

Hooray! You just learned how to use special characters, which by the way have nothing in common with your Uncle Louie, an *odd* character. Coming up next is a lesson on special HTML tags — ones that let you add those last-minute perks to your documents, like including superscript characters and making an e-mail link. Before you move on, though, take a break.

Using Special HTML Tags

Lesson 14-2

In this lesson, you add special HTML tags to your repertoire. Special HTML tags include all kinds of non-essential but nice-to-have tags. These tags are like having a golf club to play golf with — you could use a baseball bat or tree branch to swat the ball across the course, but having the golf club sure improves the focus of your efforts. Just as the golf club helps smooth out and improve your game, special HTML tags help smooth out and improve your document. (And in either case, you might look like a yahoo if you use the wrong tool.)

In this lesson, you meet the ^{superscript} and _{subscript} tags, as well as one to label the address in an HTML document. Other specialized tags exist — check out *HTML For Dummies,* by Ed Tittel and Steve James (published by IDG Books Worldwide, Inc.), for details — but these are some of the most common ones you use.

heads up

Not all browsers recognize these tags, so only use them when you think the benefits of using them outweigh the risk of someone not being able to view them.

The tags in Table 14-3 allow you to use superscript and subscript characters, as well as indicate addresses.

Table 14-3   Special HTML Tags and their Functions

Tag	Function
`<SUP>...</SUP>`	Makes text superscript
`<SUB>...</SUB>`	Makes text subscript
`<ADDRESS>...</ADDRESS>`	Labels text as an address
`<A HREF="...">...</A>`	Allows people to send e-mail; used with `<ADDRESS>...</ADDRESS>` tag

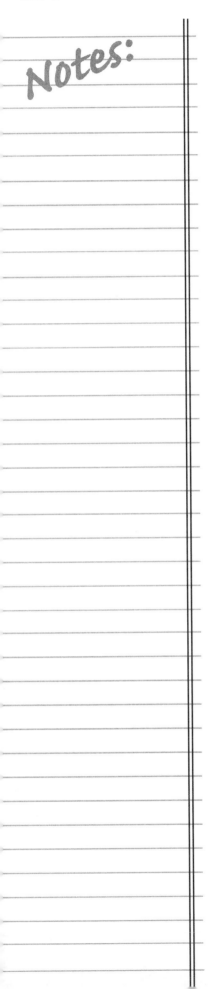

Of special interest in Table 14-3 is the `<ADDRESS>...</ADDRESS>` tag. The address tag is what you use if you want your readers to be able to e-mail you directly from your Web site. It also allows your contact information to be recognized and displayed by Internet search services. People use these services to search the Web for information on topics of their choice. If you use the address tag in your document, people can easily contact you by using the information provided by the search service. You learn more about Internet search services in Unit 16.

heads up

Note that the `<ADDRESS>...</ADDRESS>` tag is not formatted in any definite way — many browsers present this tag in italic, but not always.

This lesson builds on the last to introduce several new tags, so make sure that you're using the same document that you modified in the last lesson.

on the CD

1 **You can use the special.htm document you used in Lesson 14-1, or if you're just joining us now, open special2.htm from your \html101\unit14 folder.**

2 **Put your cursor just before the & in the `<H1>...</H1>` tag.**

3 **Add a `<SUP>` tag where the cursor is.**

```
<H1>Special HTML Stuff<SUP>&#174;</H1>
```

4 **Put your cursor just before the `</H1>` tag and add a `</SUP>` tag, as in the following code:**

```
<H1>Special HTML Stuff<SUP>&#174;</SUP></H1>
```

5 **Save and test your document.**

Not bad for three minutes work — you just put your registered trademark in superscript. Next you learn how to use a subscript tag.

6 **After the Acme Boats bit, type their slogan:** We run best in H2O.

```
<P>Copyright &#169; Acme Boats Inc. We run best in
    H2O.</P>
```

We didn't say it was a great slogan, but it's a slogan with a subscript.

7 **Now add `<SUB>...</SUB>` tags around the 2 in H2O.**

```
<P>Copyright &#169; Acme Boats Inc. We run best in
    H<SUB>2</SUB>O.</P>
```

8 **Save and test your document again.**

Your H2O should show up with the 2 in subscript, like this: H_2O.

Acme Boats is going to need to provide their address so you can buy their boats, based on the cool slogan. That's next on the agenda.

9 **Just under the Acme Boats copyright paragraph, add a set of `<ADDRESS>...</ADDRESS>` tags.**

The address tags do not go within a paragraph — actually, they are used instead of a paragraph. We put their address and contact information in here.

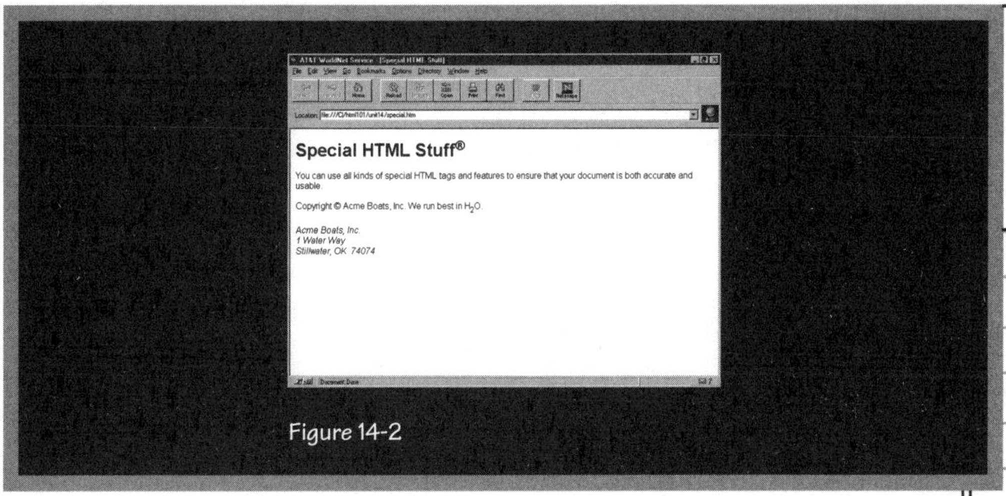

Figure 14-2: The
`<ADDRESS>`...
`</ADDRESS>` tag, in
combination with the
`<BR>` tag, works pretty
well, doesn't it?

10 **Put an address in between the** `<ADDRESS>`...`</ADDRESS>` **tags:**

```
<ADDRESS>
Acme Boats, Inc.
1 Water Way
Stillwater, OK 74074
</ADDRESS>
```

11 **Save and test your document.**

Notice that address ended up on one line. You need to use `<BR>` tags to put in the line breaks.

12 **Insert a** `<BR>` **at the end of each line in the address:**

```
<ADDRESS>
Acme Boats, Inc.<BR>
1 Water Way<BR>
Stillwater, OK 74074<BR>
</ADDRESS>
```

`<BR>` = line break

13 **Save and test your document.**

Now you've got each line of the address on a different line, but with less space than you'd have had with a paragraph tag, as shown in Figure 14-2.

Finally, you need to include a way to send e-mail to Acme Boats. Read on to find out how to include an e-mail link.

14 **Add another line to the address with the e-mail address**
info@acmeboats.com **and a** `<BR>` **at the end:**

```
<ADDRESS>
Acme Boats, Inc.<BR>
1 Water Way<BR>
Stillwater, OK 74074<BR>
info@acmeboats.com<BR>
</ADDRESS>
```

Figure 14-3: The
`mailto:` link looks
just like a regular link.

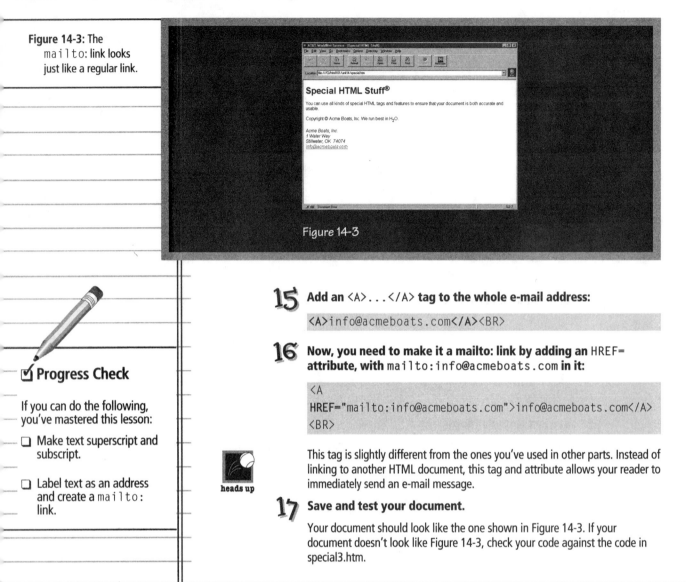

Figure 14-3

☑ Progress Check

If you can do the following,
you've mastered this lesson:

❏ Make text superscript and
subscript.

❏ Label text as an address
and create a `mailto:`
link.

heads up

15 **Add an `<A>...</A>` tag to the whole e-mail address:**

```
<A>info@acmeboats.com</A><BR>
```

16 **Now, you need to make it a mailto: link by adding an `HREF=`
attribute, with `mailto:info@acmeboats.com` in it:**

```
<A
HREF="mailto:info@acmeboats.com">info@acmeboats.com</A>
<BR>
```

This tag is slightly different from the ones you've used in other parts. Instead of
linking to another HTML document, this tag and attribute allows your reader to
immediately send an e-mail message.

17 **Save and test your document.**

Your document should look like the one shown in Figure 14-3. If your
document doesn't look like Figure 14-3, check your code against the code in
special3.htm.

Unit 14 Quiz

Circle the correct answer or answers for each question.

1. **A special character is**

   A. Someone who is nice, but otherwise kind of corny.

   B. Someone like your Aunt Flo, who is dearly loved but kind of odd.

   C. A character on your keyboard used to make symbols.

   D. Characters you can't make using single keys on your keyboard.

   E. Any alphabetic character on your keyboard.

2. **The symbols used to create special characters are**

   A. Funny looking little things.

   B. An &# plus a number, and then a ;

   C. Hard to remember.

   D. Not available as a regular key on a keyboard.

   E. All of the above

3. **<ADDRESS></ADDRESS> tags indicate**

   A. This text is an address.

   B. This text is in italics.

   C. This text should appear with automatic line breaks.

   D. This text makes a speech.

   E. None of the above

4. **Which one of the following statements is true?**

   A. HREF= is an attribute of the address tag.

   B. mailto: goes with HREF=.

   C. © HREF= address should go in every HTML document you create.

   D. A home page without <ADDRESS></ADDRESS> is like a fish without water.

   E. None of the above

5. ****

   A. Lets you subtract the formatting from the enclosed text.

   B. Indicates subscript.

   C. Substitutes the enclosed text for the address.

   D. Requires at least three attributes to be used properly.

   E. Is only used in documents that do not contain tables as a table substitute.

Unit 14 Exercise

1. Create a new document in WebEdit.

   You're going to just create a small part of an HTML document — your footer, to be precise. You want all of your documents to look consistent, complete with address, mailto: **link**, and a copyright statement. That's the bit you're creating now.

2. Feel free to add any other images or information that you feel should be available on all the HTML documents in your site. Important things you might want to add include:

   - company logo

   - other graphics

   - horizontal rule(s)

3. Save and test your document.

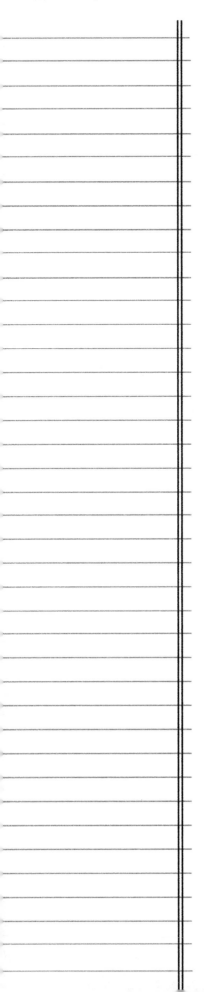

Part V Review

Unit 12 Summary

▶ **Background color:** You can add a color to the background to make your HTML document a bit snazzier. Keep in mind that background colors should enhance the document, not detract from it. The background color you choose should contrast with the text colors so that the document is easy to read.

▶ **RGB:** RGB stands for Red Green Blue and refers to a hexadecimal number you can use to indicate different colors. The six digits of an RGB number show the proportions of red, green, and blue used to create the color. To add a background color, add the BGCOLOR="#RRGGBB" attribute to the <BODY>...</BODY> tag. For example, #FF0000 is a hexidecimal number that represents red.

▶ **Text and link colors:** You can change the colors of text and links in your HTML documents by adding the TEXT="#RRGGBB" and LINK="#RRGGBB". Be sure that the text colors adequately contrast with any background colors you add.

▶ **Graphical backgrounds:** You can use a graphic for a background to enhance your HTML pages. You should be very careful about using graphics for backgrounds because they can make reading your text extremely difficult. You add background graphics by using the BACKGROUND="..." attribute with the <BODY>...</BODY> tag.

Unit 13 Summary

▶ **Special formatting effects:** You use special formatting effects when you need or want to present text in multiple columns, when you want to have side headings in your document, or when you want to control both horizontal and vertical alignment. Special formatting effects work only with newer browser software, so consider what browser your readers are using before adding these effects.

▶ **Sideheads:** You can use tables to create sideheads, which are headings that appear on the side rather than above text. To create sideheads, you use the same tags and attributes that you use to create tables, in addition to the VALIGN= attribute.

▶ **Alignment options:** You can use alignment options to align tables to the left, center, or right. To change alignment, simply add the ALIGN= or the VALIGN= attributes.

Unit 14 Summary

▶ **Special characters:** Characters are considered special if you can't type them using a single key or key combination on your keyboard. Examples include a copyright or trademark symbol. To create a special character, you enter a series of symbols and letters that browsers interpret as a specific character.

▶ **Special HTML tags:** Special HTML tags are ones such as the superscript, subscript, and address tags that allow you to create less-common HTML effects.

Part V Test

The questions on this test cover all the material from Part V, Units 12 through 14. Good luck!

True False

Each statement is either true or false.

T F 1. Special characters are ones that you cannot enter by using a single key or key combination on your keyboard.

T F 2. Background colors and graphics should not contrast with the text.

T F 3. Background colors change the base color that people see in their browsers from gray or white to whatever you specify.

T F 4. Just as you can change the alignment of tables, you also can align regular text either left, center, or right.

T F 5. The VALIGN= attribute changes vertical alignment.

T F 6. `<A HREF="...">...</A>` can only allow people to send e-mail.

T F 7. Most special effects tags and attributes are recognized only by newer browsers.

T F 8. RGB stands for Red Green Blue and refers to the way that monitors combine those three colors to make all other colors.

T F 9. Adding a dark background to a document with black text makes the document more readable.

T F 10. The `<BR>` tag is a paired tag.

T F 11. When you're inserting special characters, you must enter the number and the & sign, but the ; at the end is optional.

T F 12. After you pick a good background color, you must be sure to select a text color that provides very high contrast.

T F 13. Most commonly, sideheads appear in a narrow column on the left, and the text appears in a wider column on the right.

T F 14. The <A HREF=" ... "> ... </A> is used with the <ADDRESS> ... </ADDRESS> tag.

T F 15. If you've gone 60 mph for 1 hour, you've gone 60 miles, and the train that left Kansas City going eastbound has gone 1,240.

Part V Test

Multiple Choice

For each of the following questions, circle the correct answer or answers. Remember, you may find more than one answer for each question.

16. You need to be able to color text at the same time that you color the background because

A. If you only color the background, you restrict the choices you have for color combinations.

B. If you only color the background, the text won't show up at all.

C. If you only color the background, the text will always blend with the background.

D. None of the above

17. One reason you'd want to use tables for special formatting effects is to

A. Put information into a graphic format.

B. Put lines around a body of information.

C. Put information into multiple, thinner columns to help ease reading or to better present the information.

D. Put information into a single, fatter column.

18. Tiled means

A. That multiple copies will be placed side-by-side to fill all the available space.

B. That the floor contractor will come out and fix your bathroom floor.

C. That you're exhausted and can't lift a finger to finish this test.

D. That multiple copies will be placed on top of each other to fill all the depth of the monitor.

19. Special characters should be used

A. Infrequently.

B. Whenever necessary.

C. Only in combination with colored text.

D. To replace complex graphics.

20. Your creativity with tables is restricted by

A. Microsoft-approved TableUses.

B. The need to make sure that all readers with all browsers can easily read your material.

C. Nothing.

D. The SIDEHEAD and COLUMN attributes.

Part V Lab Assignment

Hey! You're getting close!

In this Lab Assignment, you continue creating your Web site. It should be coming along well at this point.

Step 1: Open documents

In WebEdit, open all the HTML documents you've developed so far for your Web site.

Step 2: Add backgrounds

In each of the HTML documents, add either a background color or background graphic.

Step 3: Color text and links

In each of the documents, color the document text and links. (You should have at least one link at this point, but add more if you'd like.)

Step 4: Add a table

In one of your HTML documents, create a table to present detailed information or to create a special effect, such as sideheads. You don't have to do both, but you can if you want.

Step 5: Save and test

You know the routine! How's it look?

In this part . . .

Throughout this book, you've learned about all kinds of different ingredients that can make up a good Web page or Web site. In this part, you assemble the ingredients, stir carefully, bake for exactly a little while, and then enjoy your Web site and a tall glass of milk.

In this last part, you learn how to take your HTML pages and turn them into a Web site. You learn how to organize your site, plan content and graphics, develop a theme, and establish links and navigation. You also learn the responsibilites of being a *Webmaster*, which is the new title you earn when you become an HTML-expert extraordinaire.

Planning and Organizing Your Web Site

Objectives for This Unit

✓ Figuring out the parts of your Web site

✓ Deciding on the Web site theme, content, and graphics

✓ Organizing and sketching your Web site

✓ Establishing navigational links

Prerequisites

▶ Understanding HTML basics (Part I)

▶ Understanding the basics of making links (Unit 6)

▶ Understanding the basics of including graphics (Part III)

on the CD

▶ step2.htm
▶ b-left.gif
▶ b-right.gif
▶ home.gif
▶ step1.htm
▶ step3.htm
▶ \html101\unit15\bbb\ (all files)

The last 14 units showed you the different things you can include in an HTML document and how to link your document to other documents and sites. As you completed the units, you became skilled at using tags and attributes to create various effects.

If you've been doing the Lab Assignments (you have been doing them, haven't you?), you've already started applying these skills to your own HTML documents — and you probably have quite a collection of them by now. But what you haven't done yet is develop your HTML documents into an effective Web site. (A *Web site* is an HTML document or set of documents that are published on a server.) You can't simply throw a bunch of stuff into HTML documents, link the documents together, and expect your creation to work well. You have to *make* the magic happen.

In this unit, you learn how to develop a Web site. Learning how to develop a Web site is not as concrete as learning various HTML tags and how to apply them, as you have been doing throughout this book. Instead, you learn to determine how to structure your Web site based on the information you want to present and your readers' information needs.

Web site is HTML
document or set
of documents
published on
a server

To make your HTML documents into an effective Web site, you need to do a few things (even if you haven't been following the Lab Assignments, you still need to complete these lessons):

- Determine Web site content, graphics, and theme.
- Determine Web site organization.
- Develop a home page.
- Establish navigational links.

The following lessons describe each step and show you how to apply them to your own Web site. We've used a fictitious company, Best Baby Blocks, as our example.

Lesson 15-1 — Determining Web Site Content, Graphics, and Theme

first consider
content, graphics,
theme

In this lesson, you focus on answering one big question: What's my Web site going to contain? When developing a Web site, the first thing you should consider is the content, graphics, and theme. If you already completed the Lab Assignments and are content with your HTML pages already, use the next few sections to see whether your pages are as complete as they should be.

Determining content

deciding content is
the most important
step in developing
site

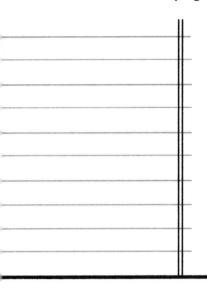

heads up

Determining your Web site content is probably the most important step in developing a Web site. Why, you ask? Well, most of the time, people visit your site because of the information (content) that you provide. (Some people, we suppose, visit sites to see nifty effects or cool graphics, or even to see how you created a certain effect, but that's not the main reason people use the Web.) Because most people are interested in information, you need to make certain that you're providing the information they need and providing it in a way that the readers can understand it.

reader profile tells
you who readers
are, information
they need, and how
to best set up your
site to fit their
needs

To do these two things, you need to develop a reader profile. Developing a reader profile is simply the process of determining who your readers are, what information they need, and how you can best present your Web site content to fit their needs. Developing a profile also will help you, the writer, determine what HTML tags to use, what kind of organization to use, and what kind of navigation to include.

The following exercise includes a number of questions that will help you make a reader profile. (We suggest that you get a piece of paper and a pencil and write down the answers to the following questions.) Following each question is a synopsis of the answers that we developed for the Best Baby Blocks Web site.

1 **Get a piece of paper and a pencil and answer the following questions.**

What information will your readers be looking for when they visit your site? Pricing lists? Product safety? Employee profiles? Product pictures? Instructions? Links to other information on the Web? Photos of your dog, Sparky? Other information?

Notes:

From your answers, you can determine what information to include in the Web site.

Readers of the Best Baby Blocks site will be looking for company information, product/safety information, and organizational/employee information. They won't care about links to other sites. They also will be interested in the contest to win toys.

2 **Write down the main categories and subcategories of information you plan to include, based on your answers in Step 1.**

We'll provide the following company information (as part of the Best Baby Blocks home page):

- Contest
- Product information
- Organizational/employee information

3 **Determine your readers' prior knowledge about the information you wrote down in Step 2.**

Are the readers laypersons? Are they experts? Are they technical people? Are they a combination?

The Best Baby Blocks readers don't know much about these topics, but it isn't exactly rocket science. Anything we want to provide will be fine. (See how easy this is when you can make up facts to suit whatever you want to do? Your answers will probably not be quite as simple, unfortunately.)

4 **Make a list of things you think the readers know and do not know about the information for your Web site.**

The Best Baby Block readers don't know specifics, although they understand the basic concepts (put block 1 on floor; put block 2 on block 1).

5 **Think about the browser software your readers will have.**

Will they be using newer software that can interpret the fancy HTML tags? Will they be using older browser software that might not interpret all the fancy stuff? Will they have a graphical or textual browser?

Answering these questions helps you determine how fancy your Web pages can be. For example, if your readers don't have newer browser software, including things like tables and forms won't be effective because their browsers can't interpret them anyway.

The Best Baby Block readers are likely to have fairly new browser software. We're targeting a high-tech, geeks-with-kids audience (like ourselves), and most (85-plus percent) of the browsers in use on the Internet can handle the HTML tags and attributes we want to use.

heads up

Reality check here: If you're establishing a Web site for your company, this answer is crucial. Looking at our decision another way, we've deliberately said that we don't care about the percentage, which is possibly up to 15 percent of our potential readers that cannot use our site as we designed it. Ask yourself if you can afford to ignore 15 percent of your potential customers. On the other hand, if the site isn't attractive and interesting, both visually and in terms of content, nothing else matters — nobody will spend much time at it.

6 **Make a list of the HTML effects you want to include in your Web pages, based on your answer in Step 5 (and based on what you know about using the effects well).**

Lists? Paragraphs? Graphics? Imagemaps? Tables? Forms? Colors? Background Colors or graphics? What else?

what kind of browser software are readers using?

Figure 15-1: The main graphic.

Notes:

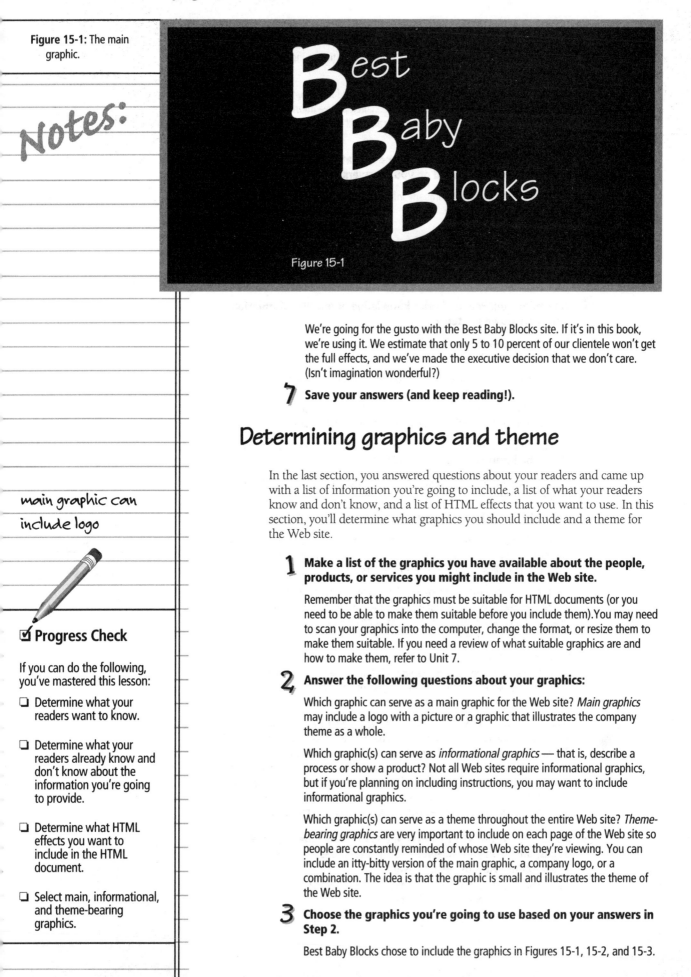

Figure 15-1

We're going for the gusto with the Best Baby Blocks site. If it's in this book, we're using it. We estimate that only 5 to 10 percent of our clientele won't get the full effects, and we've made the executive decision that we don't care. (Isn't imagination wonderful?)

7 Save your answers (and keep reading!).

Determining graphics and theme

In the last section, you answered questions about your readers and came up with a list of information you're going to include, a list of what your readers know and don't know, and a list of HTML effects that you want to use. In this section, you'll determine what graphics you should include and a theme for the Web site.

1 Make a list of the graphics you have available about the people, products, or services you might include in the Web site.

Remember that the graphics must be suitable for HTML documents (or you need to be able to make them suitable before you include them). You may need to scan your graphics into the computer, change the format, or resize them to make them suitable. If you need a review of what suitable graphics are and how to make them, refer to Unit 7.

2 Answer the following questions about your graphics:

Which graphic can serve as a main graphic for the Web site? *Main graphics* may include a logo with a picture or a graphic that illustrates the company theme as a whole.

Which graphic(s) can serve as *informational graphics* — that is, describe a process or show a product? Not all Web sites require informational graphics, but if you're planning on including instructions, you may want to include informational graphics.

Which graphic(s) can serve as a theme throughout the entire Web site? *Theme-bearing graphics* are very important to include on each page of the Web site so people are constantly reminded of whose Web site they're viewing. You can include an itty-bitty version of the main graphic, a company logo, or a combination. The idea is that the graphic is small and illustrates the theme of the Web site.

3 Choose the graphics you're going to use based on your answers in Step 2.

Best Baby Blocks chose to include the graphics in Figures 15-1, 15-2, and 15-3.

main graphic can include logo

✓ **Progress Check**

If you can do the following, you've mastered this lesson:

❑ Determine what your readers want to know.

❑ Determine what your readers already know and don't know about the information you're going to provide.

❑ Determine what HTML effects you want to include in the HTML document.

❑ Select main, informational, and theme-bearing graphics.

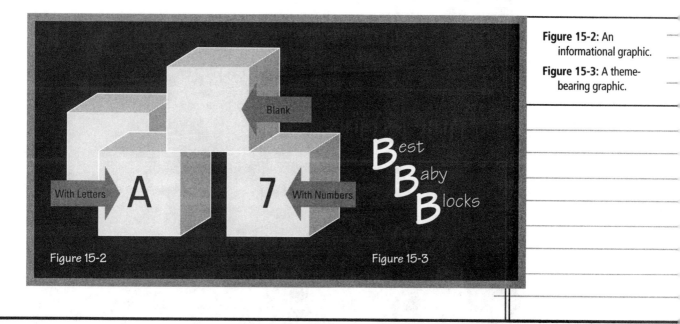

Figure 15-2

Figure 15-3

Determining Web Site Organization

Lesson 15-2

In the last lesson, you learned how to determine what information you're going to include and how to best include it in your Web site. Before you can run off and start linking a bunch of pages together, you need to determine the Web site organization. Yup. More planning stuff.

on the test

Determining your Web site organization before you start linking stuff together is extremely important. We can't stress this enough. Even if you have the greatest information and the coolest graphics in your Web site, they won't mean a thing if the readers can't effectively browse through your site. You have to get your readers to the information and graphics before they can use them.

So with that in mind — and we'll get off our soapbox now — this lesson will introduce you to three methods of organization that you can use in your Web site. You can choose to use one kind of organization, or you can combine them. The three methods of organization are the following:

- **Hierarchical organization:** This method is a great way to present topics of equal importance. For example, you might use hierarchical organization if you're putting your company's organizational chart online — you'd show the vice presidents at one level, the managers who work for each vice president at the next level lower, the people who work for each manager at the next lower level, and so on. Hierarchical organization offers readers the chance to skip right to the section of their choice, rather than wading through information. The structure of hierarchical organization looks something like Figure 15-4.

use hierarchical organization for topics of equal importance

Notes:

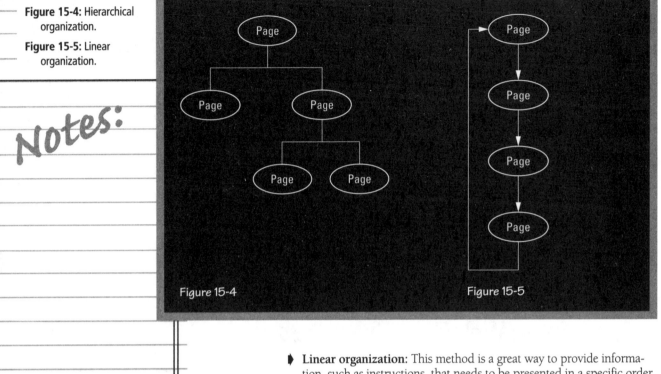

Figure 15-4   Figure 15-5

linear organization
is good for
instructions

when using webbed
organization, include
link to home page on
every page

♦ **Linear organization:** This method is a great way to provide information, such as instructions, that needs to be presented in a specific order. For example, if you're describing instructions on driving a car, you need to provide safety guidelines and instructions on turning on the car before you give the actual driving instructions. Linear organization looks something like Figure 15-5.

♦ **Webbed organization:** This method is a great way to present information that readers don't have to read in a specific order or information in which the level of importance doesn't matter. When you use webbed organization, keep in mind that readers can easily get lost in the information. If you choose this organization, be sure to include a link to the home page on every page. (A *home page* is the starting point for a group of related HTML documents.) Webbed organization looks something like Figure 15-6.

Okay. Now that you're familiar with the three methods of organization, use the following instructions to organize the information for your Web site.

1 **Find the lists you created in Lesson 15-1.**

You remember — the list of information your readers want to know, the list of what the readers do and don't know about the topics, and the list of HTML effects you want to include. Find them? Good.

2 **Using the list of information that the readers want to know, select the organization method (or methods) that best suits the topics.**

For Best Baby Blocks, we chose hierarchical organization for the organization information section, which is pretty much like an "org chart." The product information works best with webbed information because readers could easily get from any page to any other page. The contest needed to be linear so that readers would have to start at the beginning and could not skip steps.

3 **On a blank piece of paper, sketch out how you might organize the information.**

We use circles to sketch the pages. Start with a home page and work from there. Go get an eraser and try again, if necessary.

The Best Baby Blocks drawing is shown in Figure 15-7.

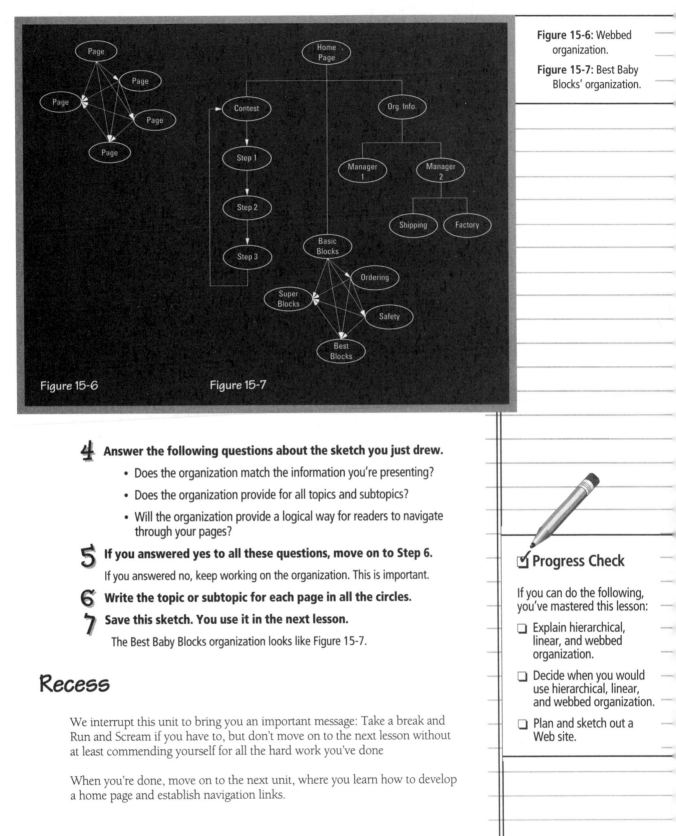

Figure 15-6

Figure 15-7

Figure 15-6: Webbed organization.

Figure 15-7: Best Baby Blocks' organization.

4 **Answer the following questions about the sketch you just drew.**

- Does the organization match the information you're presenting?
- Does the organization provide for all topics and subtopics?
- Will the organization provide a logical way for readers to navigate through your pages?

5 **If you answered yes to all these questions, move on to Step 6.**

If you answered no, keep working on the organization. This is important.

6 **Write the topic or subtopic for each page in all the circles.**

7 **Save this sketch. You use it in the next lesson.**

The Best Baby Blocks organization looks like Figure 15-7.

Recess

We interrupt this unit to bring you an important message: Take a break and Run and Scream if you have to, but don't move on to the next lesson without at least commending yourself for all the hard work you've done

When you're done, move on to the next unit, where you learn how to develop a home page and establish navigation links.

☑ **Progress Check**

If you can do the following, you've mastered this lesson:

❑ Explain hierarchical, linear, and webbed organization.

❑ Decide when you would use hierarchical, linear, and webbed organization.

❑ Plan and sketch out a Web site.

Lesson 15-3

Developing a Home Page

home page is
starting point for set
of HTML documents

In the last lesson, you sketched out the organization for your Web site. In this lesson, you create a home page for your Web site. A home page is simply the starting point for a set of HTML documents. The home page is the place where most people will enter your Web site and look for links to other pages within your site.

Home pages come in two varieties:

> ◆ **Home pages that link to other pages.** Most home pages link to other pages in the site. In this case, the home page serves as an index of what is in the site and generally describes what is included.

> ◆ **Home pages that stand alone.** Other home pages are stand-alone pages — that is, they don't link to anything else. In this case, the home page serves as a complete information source.

heads up

Keep in mind that your home page may be the only page your readers visit — so make the most of it!

Every home page should contain two essentials:

> ◆ **Contact information.** Contact information is important in case readers want to follow up on information they find in your site. If you don't include contact information, readers may not take the time to look you up at all. You can include a phone number, an address, an e-mail link, or a combination. Refer to Unit 14 and read up on the `<ADDRESS>...</ADDRESS>` tag and footers for the best way to provide contact information.

> ◆ **Last revision date.** The last revision date is important because it lets the reader know how current the information is. If you don't include the last revision date, readers won't know whether the information is useful to them.

Home pages also need to contain a few other elements:

> ◆ **A brief overview of what the site contains.** Home pages are often used as a guide to what the rest of the site contains. Even if readers don't want to browse your site on a particular visit, they will want to know what's in the site for future reference.

> ◆ **Links to each major topic.** Links to other topics are essential if your home page does, in fact, link to other stuff. Readers often like to see a list of links to other topics.

Home pages should also express your corporate or personal identity as well as the theme for the entire Web site. You can express identity and theme by including the following elements:

> ◆ **Main graphics.** Home pages should be flashy and inviting — an excellent opportunity to use a graphic or two. The home page is where you should put the main graphic or graphics you chose in Lesson 15-1.

> ◆ **Theme-bearing graphics.** Home pages may be a good place to put your theme-bearing graphics. If you do choose to put your theme-bearing graphic on the home page, put it in a place (such as a header — at the top of your pages — or footer) where you can continue to place it throughout the Web site.

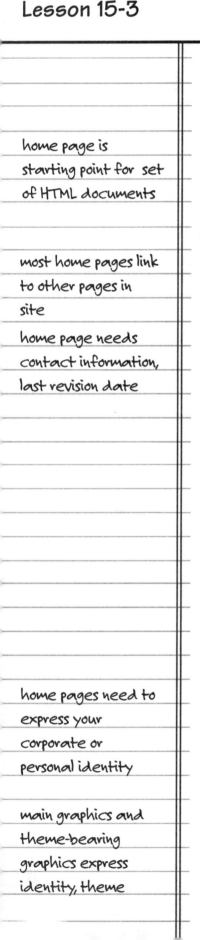

most home pages link
to other pages in
site

home page needs
contact information,
last revision date

home pages need to
express your
corporate or
personal identity

main graphics and
theme-bearing
graphics express
identity, theme

The following instructions walk you through the process of creating the home page for Best Baby Blocks. Following these steps is the Best Baby Blocks home page, which shows you how we incorporated these elements (your page will probably look different — be creative with the steps).

on the CD

1 In WebEdit, start a new HTML document, including the structure tags.

If you'd prefer to follow along with the same graphics or files, you're welcome to. You'll find the appropriate files in your \html101\unit15\bbb folder.

2 Add an appropriate `<TITLE>...</TITLE>` and `<H1>...</H1>` for your company.

Best Baby Blocks came up with the following code, which you can also see in \html101\unit15\bbbhome.htm:

```
<HEAD>
<TITLE>Best Baby Blocks</TITLE>
</HEAD>
<BODY>
<H1>Welcome to Best Baby Blocks!</H1>
```

3 Add a short introductory paragraph describing your company or information in your Web site.

The paragraph for Best Baby Blocks reads:

```
<P>Welcome to Best Baby Block Industries--dedi-
cated to producing the finest baby building
products now and in the future.</P>
```

4 Add an unordered list with the main links names you plan to use.

```
<UL>
<LI>Contest
<LI>Products and Safety Information
<LI>About the Staff and Company
<LI>
</UL>
```

5 Add the links to each of the three main categories.

Refer to your diagram from Lesson 15-2 for the names.

```
<UL>
<LI><A HREF="contest.htm">Contest</A>
<LI><A HREF="product.htm">Products and Safety
          Information</A>
<LI><A HREF="staff.htm">About the Staff and
          Company</A>
</UL>
```

6 Add the last revision date — try using italics.

Best Baby Blocks puts the revision date, along with a horizontal rule, at the bottom of the page.

```
<I>Revised: February 29, 1997</I>
<HR>
```

7 Include contact information somewhere at the bottom of the file.

Figure 15-8: The best Baby Blocks home page.

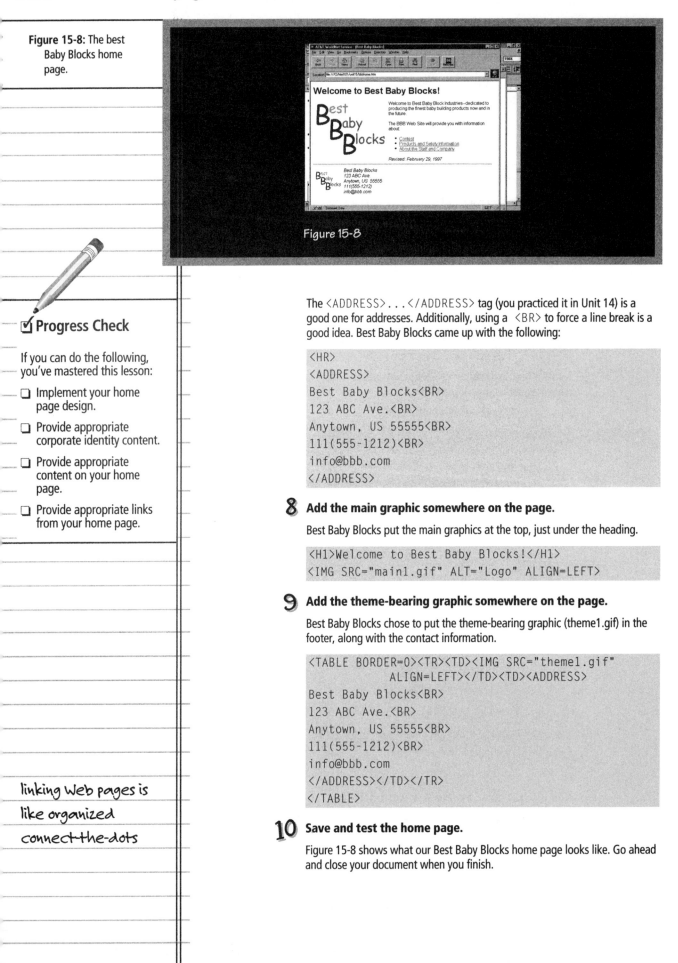

Figure 15-8

linking web pages is like organized connect-the-dots

The `<ADDRESS>...</ADDRESS>` tag (you practiced it in Unit 14) is a good one for addresses. Additionally, using a `<BR>` to force a line break is a good idea. Best Baby Blocks came up with the following:

```
<HR>
<ADDRESS>
Best Baby Blocks<BR>
123 ABC Ave.<BR>
Anytown, US 55555<BR>
111(555-1212)<BR>
info@bbb.com
</ADDRESS>
```

8 Add the main graphic somewhere on the page.

Best Baby Blocks put the main graphics at the top, just under the heading.

```
<H1>Welcome to Best Baby Blocks!</H1>
<IMG SRC="main1.gif" ALT="Logo" ALIGN=LEFT>
```

9 Add the theme-bearing graphic somewhere on the page.

Best Baby Blocks chose to put the theme-bearing graphic (theme1.gif) in the footer, along with the contact information.

```
<TABLE BORDER=0><TR><TD><IMG SRC="theme1.gif"
          ALIGN=LEFT></TD><TD><ADDRESS>
Best Baby Blocks<BR>
123 ABC Ave.<BR>
Anytown, US 55555<BR>
111(555-1212)<BR>
info@bbb.com
</ADDRESS></TD></TR>
</TABLE>
```

10 Save and test the home page.

Figure 15-8 shows what our Best Baby Blocks home page looks like. Go ahead and close your document when you finish.

Establishing Navigation Links   Lesson 15-4

You made it through the home page part. In this lesson, you learn how to link your pages together effectively. Linking Web pages is kind of like organized connect-the-dots. Learning how to provide effective navigation is important because the navigation you provide is what readers use to browse your site or to go directly to specific information.

In this section, we're not going to talk about regular links from, for example, your home page to each of your other main pages. We're assuming, at this point, that you have the unordered list and links down pat (if you need a quickie reminder, refer to Units 4 and 5). We're going to walk you through those fancy arrows and navigational aids.

on the test

To provide effective navigation, you need to do two things:

- Provide navigational links (either textual or graphical)
- Place navigation links strategically

Navigation links simply connect to other pages in your Web site. Navigation links are usually forward and back arrows, possibly with a link back to the home page or other related pages. Navigational links can either be text or a group of icons (navigation buttons). Neither type of menu is preferred; in fact, many sites combine the two.

Also, you have to place navigation links where your readers are most likely to need them. You can place links at the top of each page, at the bottom, or both. In most cases, placing menus at the top *and* bottom of pages is most effective because doing so gives readers a choice. If they're just skipping through pages, they may want to use links at the top. If they're reading your pages from top to bottom, they may want to use bottom navigation links (and not have to scroll up to the top again).

If your pages are really long (more than two screens), you also may want to provide navigation links in the middle of pages. Putting menus in the middle of a page is particularly handy, say, if the reader wants to skim through the pages, but doesn't want to read the whole thing.

To make a super-duper spiffy set of navigational links, try the following steps. Be warned: We're assuming you've got the basics nailed, so we're going to walk you through only one example.

on the CD

1 **Open step2.htm in WebEdit from your \html101\unit15 folder.**

2 **Toward the bottom of the page, just above the `<HR>`, insert the image called b-left.gif.**

These arrows were specially designed by the BBB Design Team — doing your own arrows and buttons can be a lot of fun.

```
<IMG SRC="b-left.gif" ALT="Previous">
```

3 **Now add images called home.gif and b-right.gif.**

```
<IMG SRC="b-left.gif" ALT="Previous">
<IMG SRC="home.gif" ALT="Home">
<IMG SRC="b-right.gif" ALT="Next">
```

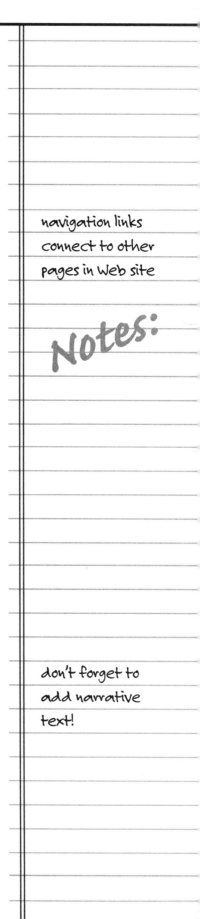

navigation links
connect to other
pages in Web site

Notes:

don't forget to
add narrative
text!

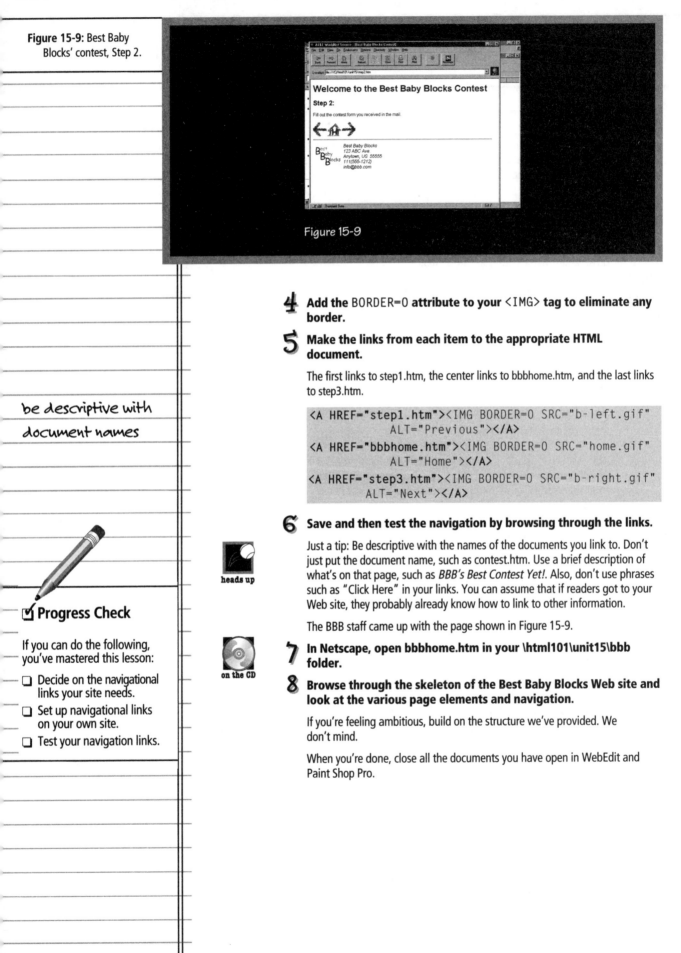

Figure 15-9: Best Baby Blocks' contest, Step 2.

Figure 15-9

4 Add the `BORDER=0` **attribute to your** `<IMG>` **tag to eliminate any border.**

5 **Make the links from each item to the appropriate HTML document.**

The first links to step1.htm, the center links to bbbhome.htm, and the last links to step3.htm.

```
<A HREF="step1.htm"><IMG BORDER=0 SRC="b-left.gif"
         ALT="Previous"></A>
<A HREF="bbbhome.htm"><IMG BORDER=0 SRC="home.gif"
         ALT="Home"></A>
<A HREF="step3.htm"><IMG BORDER=0 SRC="b-right.gif"
         ALT="Next"></A>
```

6 **Save and then test the navigation by browsing through the links.**

Just a tip: Be descriptive with the names of the documents you link to. Don't just put the document name, such as contest.htm. Use a brief description of what's on that page, such as *BBB's Best Contest Yet!*. Also, don't use phrases such as "Click Here" in your links. You can assume that if readers got to your Web site, they probably already know how to link to other information.

The BBB staff came up with the page shown in Figure 15-9.

7 **In Netscape, open bbbhome.htm in your \html101\unit15\bbb folder.**

8 **Browse through the skeleton of the Best Baby Blocks Web site and look at the various page elements and navigation.**

If you're feeling ambitious, build on the structure we've provided. We don't mind.

When you're done, close all the documents you have open in WebEdit and Paint Shop Pro.

be descriptive with document names

heads up

on the CD

☑ **Progress Check**

If you can do the following, you've mastered this lesson:

❏ Decide on the navigational links your site needs.

❏ Set up navigational links on your own site.

❏ Test your navigation links.

Unit 15 Quiz

This short quiz is designed to help you remember things you learned in Unit 15. For each of the following questions, circle the letter of the correct answer or answers.

1. **The main reason most people visit Web sites is to**

    A. Look at cool graphics.

    B. See how you created a certain effect.

    C. See the content you provide.

    D. Count the background tiles.

    E. Copy the content you provide into their own documents.

2. **A home page is**

    A. The only HTML document you put a graphic in.

    B. The starting point for a set of HTML documents.

    C. The starting point for linking all graphics.

    D. The first page of a book about building a house.

    E. Both B and C

3. **Things you should include on your home page are**

    A. Last revision date and contact information.

    B. A brief overview and links to other pages in the site.

    C. Main graphics and theme-bearing graphics.

    D. A, B, and C

    E. Only B and C

4. **Three types of organization you can use for a Web site include**

    A. Webbed, hierarchical, and line-drawn.

    B. Hierarchical, linear, and spidery.

    C. Linear, hierarchical, and moth-eaten.

    D. Hierarchical, linear, and webbed.

    E. Hierarchical, linear, and mouse-trapped.

5. **The difference between hierarchical and webbed organization is that**

    A. Webbed organization allows readers to follow a fairly specific path through the Web site.

    B. Hierarchical organization allows readers to follow a fairly specific path through the Web site.

    C. Webbed organization is linear; hierarchical is not.

    D. Webbed and hierarchical are the same.

    E. None of the above

Unit 15 Exercise

Organize the following information into topics and subtopics. Organize these topics into one (or more) organization methods. Sketch out the organization and describe (to your cat, if nobody else will listen) why you chose the method(s) you did.

Hint: There's no right or wrong answer — just have fun with it!

- Cats
- Dogs
- Mice
- Frisbees
- Tennis Balls
- Rodent Traps
- Dog Food
- Cat Food
- Training Tips
- Grooming Methods
  - Step 1: Get comb
  - Step 2: Find kitty
  - Step 3: Look under bed
  - Step 4: Hold kitty gently
  - Step 5: Comb kitty
- Walk dog
- Feeding tips
- Grooming tips

Doing Webmaster (That's You) Stuff

Objectives for This Unit

✓ Advertising your Web site

✓ Helping search engines find and index your site

✓ Planning site maintenance

Prerequisites

▶ Understanding HTML basics (Part I)

▶ Understanding how to organize and structure your Web site (Unit 15)

on the CD ▶ bbbhome.htm

In the last 15 units, you learned about developing HTML documents and graphics, creating various effects, and organizing and structuring your Web site. Now that you've mastered Web site construction, you're well on your way to earning the title of Webmaster.

heads up

Along with the title of Webmaster comes responsibilities, however. Specifically, you need to think about issues, including:

> ▶ Advertising your site

> ▶ Establishing keywords and helping search engines

> ▶ Maintaining your site

Before we get into these topics, you need to be familiar with some terminology. The different listings for Web sites on the Internet include two main categories: directories and search engines.

A *directory* is a list of Web sites, grouped by category. Yahoo! (`http://www.yahoo.com/`) is probably the best known directory. Just as you can go to a specific area in a library and then browse through related materials, directories on the Internet are particularly well suited for browsing.

A *search engine,* such as AltaVista or Webcrawler, sends out computer programs to roam the Internet and collect URLs. If you're looking for something in particular on the Internet, you would probably seek out a search service and simply enter the main terms related to what you're seeking.

think about advertising, keywords, search engines, site maintenance

directory lists Web sites, grouped by category

use search engines when you're looking for something in particular

You want to make sure that you list your site with a couple of the most highly trafficked directories (for example, Yahoo!) as well as with a couple of search services (for example, AltaVista).

Many popular directories and search engines now blur the lines by letting you search through directories or by providing categories within a search service. Don't worry about the specifics — all you need to think about is helping your prospective readers find your page.

If you're doing a personal page for your own satisfaction, you probably don't need to worry about advertising your page or making sure that people can search for and find it. Particularly if you are giving your URL to anyone who needs it, you don't need to make any special efforts to help people find your pages.

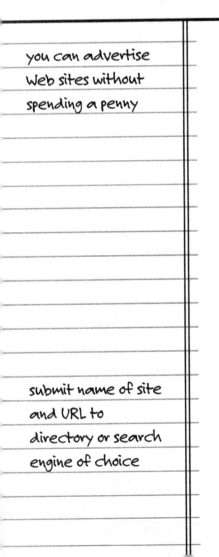

heads up

However, if you are working on a business or corporate site, or if you're trying to get visibility or promote a product through your Web site, you need to decide how to promote your site and need to add information to your documents to make finding your pages through the Internet easier. Don't worry, these promotional details are a snap compared to what you've been through in this book.

Lesson 16-1

Advertising Your Site

you can advertise Web sites without spending a penny

Advertising Web sites is much different from regular advertising. First, you can effectively advertise your site without paying a penny, so don't sweat the money. Second, if you do choose to pay others to help advertise your site, you should be paying someone for the effort in spreading your name, not for actual listings. Think of this option like paying someone to post notices about your company on bulletin boards. You provide the material — either a URL or a flyer — and someone else takes them around and tacks them up. You can do it yourself for free, but you don't have to.

heads up

You should consider advertising your site if you are trying to:

- Sell something
- Inform people about your company or services
- Provide useful information to a broad range of people

You can advertise your site either by placing announcements individually or by using services.

Advertising individually

submit name of site and URL to directory or search engine of choice

Advertising your site individually takes a little time, but doesn't cost anything. You simply submit the name of your site and URL (and sometimes a little more information) to each directory or search engine you'd like. Simply go to the directory or search engine of your choice (after your site is completely tested and ready for the big time) and look for a button that says Add URL or Add Link. Select that link, fill out the form, and you're set.

heads up

You don't need to hit all services. Pick a few of the top prospects and have fun. When you get tired of it, you're done. Links to a good site (like yours, we assume) tend to have a life of their own, so you don't need to be comprehensive.

For starters, try the following services:

Yahoo!   `http://www.yahoo.com/`

AltaVista   `http://www.altavista.digital.com/`

Webcrawler   `http://www.webcrawler.com/`

Lycos   `http://www.lycos.com/`

To submit your URL to individual sites, follow these steps:

1 Make sure that you are connected to the Internet.

You need to dial in if you're using a modem. If you're at the office on a full-time Internet connection, you're taken care of.

2 Make sure that you know the URL of *your* site.

Ask your Webmaster if you're not sure of the exact URL and then send it to a friend and ask them to check it out. Submitting your URL is the last place you want to accidentally mess up the address. Messing up your URL when submitting announcements for your site is like sending out incorrect change of address forms when you move.

3 Open Netscape.

4 Connect to one of the URLs listed before these steps, look for Add URL (or Add Site, or Submit URL), and have fun!

Repeat this step as often as you have patience to do so.

That's all there is to it. Not bad, huh?

Advertising by using services

heads up

Whatever you do, unless you're independently wealthy or have money burning a hole in your pocket, don't pay big bucks to have your Web site address submitted to dozens of search services. First, most people use one of the top ten or so services. Second, a number of sites exist solely to automatically submit your site to search engines at no cost to you.

You don't have to do much to advertise by using services available on the Internet. Simply find the free announcement services and follow their instructions to fill out the form and submit your site.

1 Make sure that you're still connected to the Internet and that Netscape is open.

2 Connect to one of the URLs listed earlier in this unit (Yahoo!, AltaVista, Lycos, and so on).

The welcome screen for the service and a place to enter search terms appear.

Notes:

don't pay to have your site listed with search services

3 Search for "free announcement service" sites.

4 Follow the links and have fun!

That's all you need to do. Depending on the backlog at the different services, you should see your site showing up at some places within 24 hours. Within two to three weeks, your site should show up everywhere. Not bad for five minutes of work.

---

commercial or
business-related
sites probably don't
want counters

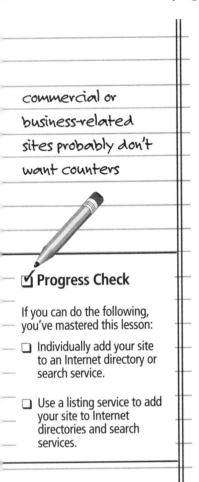

☑ **Progress Check**

If you can do the following, you've mastered this lesson:

❑ Individually add your site to an Internet directory or search service.

❑ Use a listing service to add your site to Internet directories and search services.

To count or not to count: That is the question!

Question: Shouldn't I have one of those dealies on my Web page that counts visitors (you know, like an odometer) so I can tell how many people visit my site?

Answer: If you're doing a personal Web site for your own satisfaction, go for a counter. Ask the people who run your server how to do it — it differs on different servers.

If you're doing any kind of commercial or business-related site, you probably don't want a counter. Think of it this way: Would you tell your competitors how many people come into your shop in a given day? Does a relationship between how many people come through the door and how many people buy something necessarily exist? Your Webmaster can help you find statistics on how many people visit your pages, but you probably don't want to advertise them to the world.

Lesson 16-2   Helping Search Engines

keep search engines
in mind as you
develop a Web site

In the last lesson, you learned to submit your site to directories and search engines so that people can find you. In this lesson, you will work on fine-tuning your pages so that everyone will be able to easily tell what they've found when they get to your site. After you've submitted your site to directories, you don't have to worry about them any more. However, you must keep search engines in mind as you develop your site.

on the test

Search engines send out programs to collect Web pages throughout the Internet. Search engines are kind of like a regular browser on autopilot. Eventually, they find your site (although submitting your URL is a more reliable way to be found at your convenience, not theirs). When search engines find you, they put your site into their indexes.

search engines find
relatively uncommon
words on your page

The index of most search engines contains all the relatively uncommon words from your page. For example, the first sentences of our Best Baby Blocks page are

```
Welcome to Better Baby Block Industries--dedicated to
  producing the finest baby building products now and in
  the future. The BBB Web Site will provide you with
  information about:
```

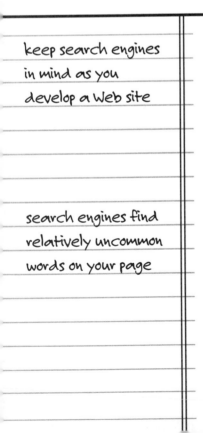

Most — but not all — search engines throw out common words or at least disregard them when you search. In this example, *Web site* would be discarded, as would all the common words like *and, the,* and *with*. Your job is to make sure that your documents contain the terms for which people will look.

on the test

Those terms that people will be looking for are called *keywords*. If you were surfing the Internet and wanted to look for baby blocks, you might search for `baby block` or you might search for something like `toys, baby toys, building blocks`, or even `safe traditional toys`.

You can make keywords by doing two things:

- Using `<META>` tags
- Using regular HTML tags

Using <META> tags

You can use `<META>` tags to load your Web page with extra keywords that help describe your site, even if you don't want to rewrite your page so that they appear in the text. Additionally, you can provide a description that will be presented along with your link by search engines. You can do all this by using `<META>` tags. Not all search engines recognize `<META>` tags, but many do, and the benefit you get from adding them is far greater than the trouble and time it takes. The `<META>` tags you use are

- `<META NAME="KEYWORD" CONTENT="...">`
- `<META NAME="DESCRIPTION" CONTENT="...">`

Adding `<META>` tags to help Internet search engines better categorize and find your site takes very little time. In this exercise, you add `<META>` tags to a version of the Best Baby Blocks home page.

on the CD

1 **Open bbbhome.htm from the Unit16 folder in WebEdit.**

2 **Position your cursor before the `</HEAD>` tag.**

The `<META>` tags must go in the document head, but where within the head doesn't matter.

3 **Enter a `<META>` tag.**

```
<META>
</HEAD>
```

4 **Add the `NAME="KEYWORDS"` attribute.**

```
<META NAME="KEYWORDS">
```

5 **Add the `CONTENT=` attribute.**

```
<META NAME="KEYWORDS" CONTENT="">
```

6 **Fill in the `CONTENT=` attribute with all the appropriate words you can think of, separated by commas.**

```
<META NAME="KEYWORDS" CONTENT="blocks, toys, safe,
          economical, cheap, colorful, cool">
```

(margin notes)

make sure that your documents contain terms people will be looking for

use <META> tags to load your Web page with extra keywords that describe your site

Notes:

don't forget the quotes

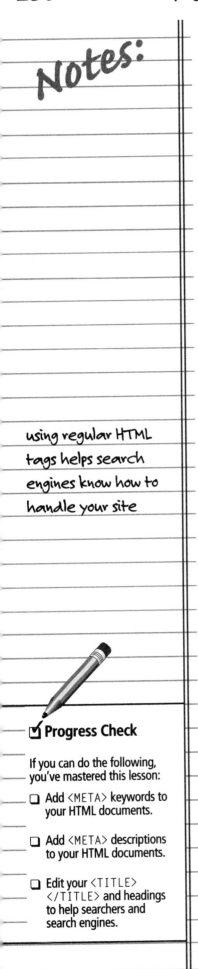

7 Add another `<META>` tag.

```
<META NAME="KEYWORDS" CONTENT="blocks, toys, safe,
            economical, cheap, colorful, cool">
<META>
```

8 Add a `NAME="DESCRIPTION"` attribute.

```
<META NAME="KEYWORDS" CONTENT="blocks, toys, safe,
            economical, cheap, colorful, cool">
<META NAME="DESCRIPTION">
```

9 Add a `CONTENT=` attribute with a clear, concise sentence, describing what people will find at your site. Here's what we wrote:

```
<META NAME="DESCRIPTION" CONTENT="Best Baby Blocks
provides product information, notes about our
staff, and a monthly Contest!">
```

There you go! Providing that sort of information in every page doesn't hurt, but at the very least, put it in the main page.

Using regular HTML tags

Using regular HTML tags carefully also can help search engines (and searchers) have a better idea what to do with your site. Try to provide the most helpful, descriptive titles and headings you can think of. These titles (and headings, to a lesser extent) help your readers and prove helpful when your site is added to directories and indexes.

The tags of particular importance are `<TITLE>...</TITLE>` and the headings.

To edit a title so it will be more useful to searchers, do the following:

on the CD

1 Open bbbhome.htm from the Unit16 folder in WebEdit.

2 Edit the `<TITLE>...</TITLE>` of the document to be more descriptive and useful to searchers.

As it stands now, "Best Baby Blocks" is accurate, but doesn't provide any additional information to help people decide whether they should visit your site. Changing title to something like "Welcome to the Best Baby Blocks Site: Suppliers of Toys to the Information Generation" may be a more appropriate description.

3 Edit the headings to help searchers.

You should try to provide full synopses of content in the headings, rather than just simple words. Although individual words are great in context, when they come up through an Internet search engine, they aren't quite as helpful. You may want something like this:

```
<H1>Best Baby Blocks Welcomes You to the BBB Home
        Page</H1>
```

using regular HTML tags helps search engines know how to handle your site

✓ **Progress Check**

If you can do the following, you've mastered this lesson:

❑ Add `<META>` keywords to your HTML documents.

❑ Add `<META>` descriptions to your HTML documents.

❑ Edit your `<TITLE>` `</TITLE>` and headings to help searchers and search engines.

4 **Add additional headings to help identify key information.**

You might add a `<H2>`...`</H2>` above the unordered list with something like this:

```
<H2>Best Baby Blocks Site Content</H2>
```

Now, all you have to do is to remember all this stuff when you're working on getting the site.

When you're done, go ahead and close the file.

Maintaining Your Site

Lesson 16-3

One last thing (finally!) you have to do as a Webmaster is to maintain your site. Maintaining your site is easier than it sounds, so don't panic.

As you developed your Web site, you included two different types of information in the pages:

- **Static information:** Includes general information that won't often change, such as contact information or copyright information.

- **Dynamic information:** Includes variable information that you should update frequently. This information is the meat of your pages.

Figure 16-1 gives an example of both static and dynamic information.

As a Webmaster, you need to update the dynamic information frequently so that readers have reason to revisit your site. (Why would they visit a site that always has the same ol' information in it, right?)

heads up

Be sure to update your site frequently so that you provide readers with current, fresh information.

To make sure that you keep your site updated, follow these steps:

1 **Get out your personal calendar. (No, not your boss's calendar....)**

2 **Mark your calendar, say, every two to three weeks for updating your Web site.**

3 **Go have a beer.**

Congratulations! You are officially a Webmaster Extraordinaire. Good luck with your HTML development!

☑ Progress Check

If you can do the following, you've mastered this lesson:

- ❏ Describe and give examples of static and dynamic information.

Figure 16-1: Static and dynamic information.

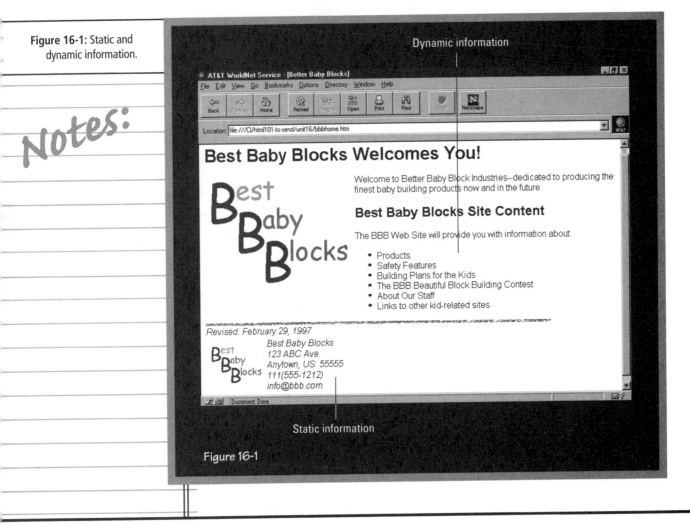

Notes:

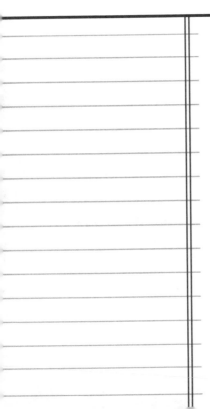

Unit 16 Quiz

This short quiz is designed to help you remember things you learned in Unit 16. For each of the following questions, circle the letter of the correct answer or answers.

1. **An Internet directory is**

   A. A big book.

   B. A categorized collection of links to Web sites.

   C. A browsable collection of links to Web sites.

   D. Expensive to add a link to.

   E. A complete collection of searchable links to all Web pages everywhere.

2. **A search engine is**

   A. Expensive to add a link to.

   B. Easier to browse through than an Internet directory.

   C. Rarely used by people without Web pages.

   D. A searchable collection of links to Web pages.

   E. All of the above

3. **You can**

   A. Add your Web site to directories and search engines for free.

   B. Have a service automatically add your site to lots of directories and search engines at once for free.

   C. Pay big bucks to add your Web site to directories and search engines.

   D. Send presents to the authors of this book for saving you cash.

   E. A, B, and D

4. **META tags must be used within**

   A. `<HEAD>`...`</HEAD>`.

   B. `<BODY>`...`</BODY>`.

   C. `<TITLE>`...`<TITLE>`.

   D. Any tags.

   E. `<META>` tags do not go within any other tags.

5. **Internet search engines generally look at these items in which order?**

   A. `<META>`, `<TITLE>`...`</TITLE>`, headings, content

   B. Content, headings, `<META>`, `<TITLE>`...`</TITLE>`

   C. `<BODY>`...`</BODY>`, `<TITLE>`...`</TITLE>`, `<H1>`...`</H1>`

   D. Search engines don't look at any particular part of the document.

   E. Only the `<META>` tag

Unit 16 Exercise

1. Use your Web browser to search one or more of the Internet search services to find a free announcement service.

2. Use the same search service to look for potential competitors for your company. Did they do what they should have done to make sure that they were found? Should you send them a copy of this book?

3. Evaluate whether users can successfully find your competitors in and take the time to look at the source code of their documents to see whether they have tried these tips.

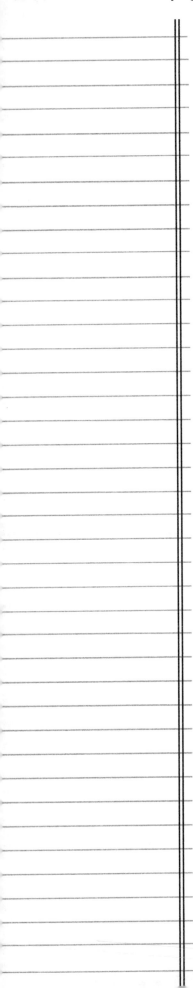

Part VI Review

Unit 15 Summary

- **Web site:** A Web site is an HTML document or set of documents for a particular organization, topic, or person.

- **Home page:** A home page is the starting point for a set of HTML documents. Home pages should be flashy and inviting and should contain contact information, last revision date, a short description of the site, links to information in the site, and graphics.

- **Web site organization:** Three types of Web site organization exist. Use hierarchical organization when you have more than one major topic. Use linear organization when you are describing instructions or a process. Use webbed organization when you want readers to cross-reference information easily.

- **Reader profile:** A reader profile determines who your reader is, what information they need, and how you can best present your Web site content to fit their information needs. Developing a profile also will help you, the writer, determine what HTML tags you should and should not use, what kind of organization to use, and what kind of navigation to include.

- **Graphics:** Graphics have three uses in Web sites. Main graphics usually contain a logo and/or illustrates the company theme. Informational graphics describe a process or show a product. Theme-bearing graphics are small and should be placed on all pages in the Web site.

- **Navigation links:** These links connect to other pages in your Web site. They are usually forward and back arrows and possibly have a link back to the home page or other related pages. They can either be text, a group of icons (navigation buttons), or a combination of the two.

Unit 16 Summary

- **Site advertising:** Site advertising means to put announcements about the site on Internet directories and search engines. You do not have to pay to advertise.

- **Search engine:** A specialized Web site, a search engine maintains an index of many Web sites on the Internet. You can use the search engine to try to find sites with specific content.

- **Directory:** A specialized Web site, a directory keeps a categorized listing of numerous Web sites. You can browse or search through these listings to find sites based on category.

- **Announcement services:** You can use announcement services, either free or at a charge, to advertise your listing on search engines and directories.

- **Keywords:** Keywords are used within the `<META>` tag to add additional terms that describe the content of the page. You use `<META NAME="KEYWORDS" CONTENT="keywords go here">` within the `<HEAD>...</HEAD>` of the document.

- **Description:** Descriptions are used in the `<META>` tag to add a sentence or phrase that describes the content of the page. You use `<META NAME="DESCRIPTION" CONTENT="phrase goes here">` within the `<HEAD>...</HEAD>` of the document.

Part VI Test

The questions on this test cover all the material from Units 15 and 16. This test is the last one in the book. Hurrah!

True   False

Each statement is either true or false.

T   F   1. Theme-bearing graphics are usually large and appear only a few times throughout the Web site.

T   F   2. You can place navigation links at the top, middle, or bottom of Web pages, or even combine locations.

T   F   3. Putting a navigation menu in the middle of a page is particularly useful when the reader wants to skim through the pages, but doesn't want to read the whole thing.

T   F   4. When making navigation links, you should use the file name and insert the words "click here."

T   F   5. A home page must link to other pages in the site or on the Web.

T   F   6. Determining your Web site organization before you start linking stuff together is important because getting readers to the information and graphics is more important than the information and graphics themselves.

T   F   7. Search engines allow you to browse by category.

T   F   8. Submit your site to directories if it's business-related and search engines if it's personal.

T   F   9. When it comes to announcement services, you get what you pay for.

T   F   10. The <META> tag goes within the <HEAD> . . . </HEAD> tags.

Multiple Choice

For each of the following questions, circle the correct answer or answers. Remember, you may find more than one answer for each question.

11. **The <META> tag**

   A. Allows you to provide additional information to help search engines categorize and find your document.

   B. Requires directories to choose which three categories your site will appear in.

   C. Accommodates people with nongraphical browsers.

   D. Causes browsers to highlight certain terms in all <BODY> text.

12. **Because people visit your site to find information you provide, you need to make certain that you're**

   A. Providing the information they need.

   B. Providing only enough information to fill a tile, till a file, or file a pile, depending on the circumstances.

   C. Providing the information in a way that the readers can understand it.

   D. Providing information mainly on the home page.

13. **Questions you might ask when developing a reader profile include**

   A. What information will your readers be looking for when they visit your site?

   B. What do the readers already know (and not know) about the information in the Web site?

   C. Will the readers be using newer or older browser software?

   D. What HTML effects do I want to include in the Web site?

Part VI Test

14. **Three types of graphics you can use in Web sites include**

    A. Webbed, informational, and theme-bearing.

    B. Main, informational, and theme-bearing.

    C. Hierarchical, linear, and webbed.

    D. Suitable, non-suitable, and scanned.

15. **The difference between a directory and a search engine is**

    A. A directory is published like a phone book; a search engine chugs along like a train.

    B. A directory is a list of Web sites grouped by category; a search engine is a program that roams the Internet and collects URLs.

    C. A directory is like an information booth; a search engine looks for lost URLs.

    D. A directory searches for specific information on the Web; a search engine searches for URLs.

16. **You should advertise your Web site if**

    A. You are trying to sell something.

    B. You are trying to inform people about your company or services.

    C. You are trying to provide useful information to a broad range of people.

    D. You are trying to gather information from your readers.

17. **Keywords are**

    A. Words that people search for in Web site documents.

    B. Words that start with certain letters.

    C. Words that open certain directories so that you can access additional information.

    D. Words, such as "Open Sesame," that can open mysterious HTML documents.

18. **To provide effective navigation, you need to**

    A. Provide a relief map of the site on the home page.

    B. Provide navigational links (either textual or graphical).

    C. Place navigation links strategically.

    D. Place navigation links only at the top of pages.

19. **When using an advertising service**

    A. You should call Darrin Stevens from *Bewitched*.

    B. You should be sure to spend megabucks.

    C. You should not spend any money at all.

    D. You should hire an accountant to help do the financing.

20. **The <META> tag is used**

    A. To load your Web page with Majorly Exciting Tag Attributes.

    B. To load your Web page with information that sounds cool but doesn't mean anything.

    C. To load your Web page with extra links that point to other sites on the Web.

    D. To load your Web page with extra information that helps describe your site.

Part VI Lab Assignment

Finalize your Web site!

Step 1: Check the information

Verify that the information you provide meets your readers' information needs.

Step 2: Organize

Organize your HTML pages using one (or more) of the organization choices you learned about in this part of the book.

Step 3: Create a home page

Make sure that your page includes all the essential elements covered in this part of the book (and a few optional ones, too, just for fun!).

Step 4: Add graphics

You should add an informational graphic as well as a logo or something similar to the home page.

Step 5: Add navigation links

Make sure that your readers can link from your home page to all of your other pages and back from those pages to your home page.

Step 6: Test your Web site

Be sure that *all* the links work and that everything looks good. If you've got some time and access to another computer or Web browser, try your site in another browser as well.

Step 7: Publish!

Contact your Web administrator and put your Web site on a Web server.

Step 8: Submit your Web site information

Submit your Web site information to directories and search services. (After about a week or so, you should try using the directories and services to find your Web site.)

Congratulations! You are now the proud owner of a new Web site. Enjoy!

Answers

Unit 1 Quiz Answers

Question	Answer	If You Missed It, Try This	Question	Answer	If You Missed It, Try This
1.	C	1-1	4.	C	1-2
2.	E	1-2	5.	E	1-1
3.	C	1-1			

Unit 2 Quiz Answers

Question	Answer	If You Missed It, Try This	Question	Answer	If You Missed It, Try This
1.	C	2-3	4.	D	2-5
2.	A	2-3	5.	A	2-2
3.	True	2-1			

Part I Test Answers

Question	Answer	If You Missed It, Try This	Question	Answer	If You Missed It, Try This
1.	False	1-1	11.	C	1-1
2.	False	1-2	12.	A	1-1
3.	True	1-2	13.	A	1-2
4.	False	2-1	14.	A and B	2-1
5.	False	2-5	15.	B	2-2
6.	True	2-4	16.	C	2-2
7.	False	2-5	17.	D	2-5
8.	False	3-2	18.	C	2-7
9.	True	3-3	19.	A and B	3-1
10.	False	3-2	20.	A	3-3

Unit 3 Quiz Answers

Question	Answer	If You Missed It, Try This	Question	Answer	If You Missed It, Try This
1.	A	3-3	4.	D	3-1
2.	C	3-3	5.	C	3-2
3.	B	3-3			

Unit 4 Quiz Answers

Question	Answer	If You Missed It, Try This	Question	Answer	If You Missed It, Try This
1.	A and B	4-3	5.	A	4-3
2.	C	4-1	6.	D	4-4
3.	D	4-4	7.	E	4-1
4.	C	4-4 and 4-5			

Unit 5 Quiz Answers

Question	Answer	If You Missed It, Try This	Question	Answer	If You Missed It, Try This
1.	C	5-1	5.	A and B	5-2
2.	D	5-1	6.	A	5-4
3.	D	5-1	7.	D	5-4
4.	C	5-1			

Part II Test Answers

Question	Answer	If You Missed It, Try This	Question	Answer	If You Missed It, Try This
1.	False	3-2	9.	False	3-2
2.	False	3-3	10.	True	3-3
3.	True	3-2	11.	B	5-1
4.	False	5-1	12.	A and B	5-1
5.	False	5-1	13.	D	4-4
6.	True	5-1	14.	C	4-1
7.	True	4-4 and 4-5	15.	B	
8.	False	4-4	16.	D	Unit 5 Recess

Question	Answer	If You Missed It, Try This	Question	Answer	If You Missed It, Try This
17.	D	5-1	20.	A-10, B-11, C-6, D-4, E-12, F-7, G-2, H-13, I-3, J-8	Part 5 and Part 6
18.	A	3-1			
19.	C	4-3			

Unit 6 Quiz Answers

Question	Answer	If You Missed It, Try This	Question	Answer	If You Missed It, Try This
1.	A and B	6-4	4.	B	6-3
2.	D	6-3	5.	D	6-1
3.	B	6-4			

Unit 7 Quiz Answers

Question	Answer	If You Missed It, Try This	Question	Answer	If You Missed It, Try This
1.	E	Intro to Unit 7	4.	A	7-1
2.	C	7-4	5.	C	7-4
3.	E	7-3			

Unit 8 Quiz Answers

Question	Answer	If You Missed It, Try This	Question	Answer	If You Missed It, Try This
1.	C	8-2	4.	E	8-2
2.	C	8-5	5.	A and C	8-3
3.	E	8-1			

Unit 9 Quiz Answers

Question	Answer	If You Missed It, Try This	Question	Answer	If You Missed It, Try This
1.	A, B, and C	9-2	4.	C	9-1
2.	C	9-3	5.	A, B, and D	9-1
3.	A and C	9-3			

Part III Test Answers

Question	Answer	If You Missed It, Try This	Question	Answer	If You Missed It, Try This
1.	True	6-3	11.	A, C, and D	9-1
2.	False	7-4	12.	A	7-3
3.	True	8-2	13.	D	6-3
4.	False	8-5	14.	A	6-3
5.	False	6-4	15.	B and C	7-1
6.	False	6-3	16.	D	Unit 8 Recess
7.	False	6-4	17.	A	9-1
8.	True	9-1	18.	B	9-1
9.	True	Intro to Unit 7	19.	D	8-3
10.	False	9-1	20.	A	7-4

Unit 10 Quiz Answers

Question	Answer	If You Missed It, Try This	Question	Answer	If You Missed It, Try This
1.	A, B and E	10-2	4.	C	10-3
2.	A	10-2	5.	A	10-4
3.	A and B	10-3			

Unit 11 Quiz Answers

Question	Answer	If You Missed It, Try This	Question	Answer	If You Missed It, Try This
1.	A and E	11-2	4.	E	11-7
2.	A	11-4	5.	B and E	11-6
3.	A and C	11-3			

Part IV Test Answers

Question	Answer	If You Missed It, Try This	Question	Answer	If You Missed It, Try This
1.	False	10-1	6.	False	10-2
2.	True	10-1	7.	True	11-1
3.	True	10-1	8.	True	11-1
4.	False	11-4	9.	True	10-1
5.	True	11-3	10.	True	All lessons in Unit 11

Question	Answer	If You Missed It, Try This	Question	Answer	If You Missed It, Try This
11.	A	10-2	17.	A, B, and D	11-6
12.	A	11-1	18.	D	11-7
13.	B	10-2	19.	A-3, B-5, C-1, D-4, E-2	10-2
14.	B	10-3			
15.	A	11-2	20.	A-3, B-4, C-1, D-2	11-1
16.	C	11-5			

Unit 12 Quiz Answers

Question	Answer	If You Missed It, Try This	Question	Answer	If You Missed It, Try This
1.	A	Intro to Unit 12	4.	D	12-1
2.	C	12-1	5.	C	12-1
3.	B	12-3			

Unit 13 Quiz Answers

Question	Answer	If You Missed It, Try This	Question	Answer	If You Missed It, Try This
1.	E	Intro to Unit 13	4.	E	13-4
2.	C and D	Intro to Unit 13	5.	A	13-2
3.	B	13-4			

Unit 14 Quiz Answers

Question	Answer	If You Missed It, Try This	Question	Answer	If You Missed It, Try This
1.	D	14-1	4.	B	14-2
2.	B and D	14-1	5.	B	14-2
3.	A	14-2			

Part V Test Answers

Question	Answer	If You Missed It, Try This	Question	Answer	If You Missed It, Try This
1.	True	14-1	4.	True	13-4
2.	False	12-1	5.	True	13-4
3.	True	12-1	6.	False	14-2

Question	Answer	If You Missed It, Try This	Question	Answer	If You Missed It, Try This
7.	True	12-1	14.	False	14-2
8.	True	12-1	15.	True	:>)
9.	False	12-2	16.	A	12-2
10.	False	14-2	17.	B and C	13-1
11.	False	14-1	18.	A	12-3
12.	True	12-2	19.	B	14-1
13.	True	13-2	20.	B	Intro to Unit 13

Unit 15 Quiz Answers

Question	Answer	If You Missed It, Try This	Question	Answer	If You Missed It, Try This
1.	C	15-1	4.	D	15-2
2.	B	15-3	5.	B	15-2
3.	D	15-3			

Unit 16 Quiz Answers

Question	Answer	If You Missed It, Try This	Question	Answer	If You Missed It, Try This
1.	C	Intro to Unit 16	4.	A	16-2
2.	D	Intro to Unit 16	5.	A	16-2
3.	E	16-1			

Part VI Test Answers

Question	Answer	If You Missed It, Try This	Question	Answer	If You Missed It, Try This
1.	False	15-1	12.	A and C	15-2
2.	True	15-4	13.	A, B, and C	15-1
3.	True	15-4	14.	B	15-1
4.	False	15-4	15.	B	Intro to Unit 16
5.	False	15-3	16.	A, B, C, and D	16-1
6.	True	15-2			
7.	False	Intro to Unit 16	17.	A	16-2
8.	False	16-1	18.	B and C	15-4
9.	False	16-1	19.	C	16-1
10.	True	16-2	20.	D	16-2
11.	A	16-2			

About the CD

The *Dummies 101: HTML* companion CD-ROM contains programs and exercise files that you use while you're following along with the lessons in the book. We guide you through using the programs and the samples in the appropriate lessons. You'll find the stuff on the CD extremely useful in mastering HTML!

Before you can use the exercise files or programs contained on the CD, you need to install them on your computer. Because the extra programs were created by different companies, they have their own separate installation procedures. No problem, though! Each installation process is easy and quick, thanks to the *Dummies 101: HTML* Launching Pad.

After you install the *Dummies 101* files and programs by following the instructions given in this appendix, you're ready to begin the lessons in the book. We suggest waiting to open the files until you are working on the lesson that tells you to do so. If for some reason you need a fresh copy of a missing or damaged file, you can reinstall that file from the CD by using the Custom Installation procedure described in this appendix.

System Requirements

Before installing the CD, check out the following system requirements. If your computer doesn't meet the minimum requirements, you may have trouble using the CD.

- Microsoft Windows 95 or Windows 3.1*x* installed on your computer

- At least 8MB of RAM installed on your computer

- At least 2MB of free hard-disk space available if you want to install just the exercise files; at least 17MB to install all the programs

- Internet connection, or a modem and a credit card

If you need more information on PC or Windows 95 basics, check out *PCs For Dummies,* 4th Edition, by Dan Gookin; *Windows 3.11 For Dummies* for *Dummies 101: Windows 95* by Andy Rathbone, and *Modems For Dummies,* 2nd Edition, by Tina Rathbone (published by IDG Books Worldwide, Inc.).

Putting the CD Files on Your Hard Drive

The CD contains both exercise files and programs. The exercise files are sample HTML documents and graphics files that you use while following along with the lessons in the book. *You need to put these files on your hard drive.* After you're done with the book, you can remove these files by using the simple uninstall process described later in this appendix.

The programs are integrated with the lessons in the book and are necessary to get the full benefit of working through the exercises. If you have an Internet service provider, and Netscape Navigator or another Web browser on your computer, however, you may choose to work with your current version rather than installing and registering for AT&T WorldNet Service.

Installing the Launching Pad

The Launching Pad is a window that allows you to begin installation of all the programs and exercise files with a click of your mouse button. To install the Launching Pad, follow these steps:

1 Insert the *Dummies 101* CD-ROM (label side up) into your computer's CD-ROM drive.

Be careful to touch only the edges of the CD-ROM. (The CD-ROM drive is the one that pops out with a recessed circle in the drawer.)

In Windows 95, the Launching Pad should appear automatically if your computer's AutoPlay feature is working. Close the Launching Pad for now by clicking the Close button in the upper right corner of the window.

2 Windows 95 users: Click the Start button and choose Run.

Windows 3.1x users: Click File⇨Run in the Windows Program Manager.

3 Type d:\setup in the text box of the Run dialog box; then click OK or press Enter.

Note: If your CD-ROM drive is not drive D on your computer, substitute the appropriate letter before the colon.

If you are working in Windows 95, you see a message that confirms that an item named Dummies 101 was created in the Programs menu on the Start button; if you are working in Windows 3.1x, you see a message that confirms that a program group named Dummies 101 was created in the Program Manager. Inside that group is an icon named Dummies 101- HTML Launching Pad.

4 Click the Yes button to start the Launching Pad.

The Dummies 101 - HTML Launching Pad appears on-screen.

In the future, Windows 3.1x users can start the Launching Pad by opening the Dummies 101 program group and double-clicking the Dummies 101 - HTML Launching Pad icon; Windows 95 users can start the Launching Pad by clicking the Start button and then choosing Programs⇨Dummies 101⇨Dummies 101 - HTML Launching Pad.

Installing the exercise files

To install the exercise files you need for the lessons in the book, follow these steps:

1 Close all other programs that are running in Windows, including any programs running in the background, such as antivirus programs.

2 Make sure that the Launching Pad window is open.

In Windows 3.1x, open the Dummies 101 program group and double-click the Dummies 101- HTML Launching Pad icon; in Windows 95, click the start button and then choose Programs⇨Dummies101⇨Dummies 101 - HTML Launching Pad.

3 Click the Install Exercise Files button and follow the prompts on-screen.

When you have choices in the installation process, accept the suggestion the installation program makes. The lessons in this book assume that you accepted the default installation options.

4 Click No when asked if you want to view the folder so that you return directly to the Installer.

The readme.txt file opens.

5 After you read the readme.txt file, close the window.

Remember: The files accompany the book's lessons. If you make changes to a file before you work on the lesson that uses it, you may need to reinstall the exercise files for that unit in order to complete the lesson. Simply place the CD in your drive, start the Launching Pad, and click the Install Exercise Files button. In the Choose an Installation Option window, choose Custom Installation. You will be able to reinstall all the files for any unit.

Installing AT&T WorldNet™ Service

AT&T WorldNet Service is a world-class Internet service with outstanding customer support. When you sign up for AT&T WorldNet Service, you get a special version of Netscape Navigator, the world's most popular Web browser, at no charge. (Note that this version of Netscape Navigator is licensed exclusively for use with AT&T WorldNet Service.)

heads up

The CD contains an exportable version of AT&T WorldNet Service and Netscape Navigator. However, AT&T WorldNet Service is currently supported only in the United States. Future AT&T international access is subject to regional variations.

heads up

Warning: If you already have an Internet Service Provider, do not install the AT&T WorldNet Service software.

Before you install the software and register for AT&T WorldNet Service, have your credit card ready to provide account billing information.

To install the software, follow these steps:

1 **Close all other programs that are running in Windows, including programs running in the background, such as antivirus programs.**

2 **Make sure that the Launching Pad window is open.**

3 **Make sure that your modem is switched on and ready.**

4 **Windows 3.1x users: Click the Install AT&T WorldNet Service (16-bit) button.**

Windows 95 users: Click the Install AT&T WorldNet Service (32-bit) button.

Accept the installation defaults whenever you're prompted to provide information.

5 **If you are asked whether you want to read the Troubleshooting Guide, click the No button.**

You may notice that new items have been added to your Start menu (Windows 95) or the Program Manager (Windows 3.1x).

6 **Windows 3.1x users: In the Program Manager, open the AT&T WorldNet Service program group.**

Windows 95 users: Double-click the folder on your desktop named *AT&T WorldNet Service*.

7 **To begin setup of your AT&T WorldNet Service account, double-click the Double-click to Set Up Account icon.**

Follow the instructions to register your account. Use the following registration codes: L5SQIM631 if you are an AT&T long-distance residential customer, and L5SQIM632 if you use another long-distance phone company. After registration is complete, you are asked to restart your computer.

That's it! The software is installed and ready to go! Double-click the AT&T WorldNet Service icon to explore the Internet. If you have problems, call AT&T WorldNet Service Customer Care at 1-800- • 400-1447.

AT&T WorldNet Service software is stored in C:\Program Files\WorldNet (Windows 95) or C:\WORLDNET (Windows 3.1x).

Installing WebEdit 2.0

WebEdit is an HTML editing program you use to create World Wide Web pages. It allows you to easily create and edit HTML documents. By using WebEdit in combination with Web browsers such as Netscape or Mosaic, you'll be making Web pages like a pro in no time. *Note:* This is a 30-day trial version of WebEdit 2.0.

To install the software, follow these steps:

1 **Close all other programs that are running in Windows, including programs running in the background, such as antivirus programs.**

2 **Make sure that the Launching Pad window is open.**

3 **Windows 3.1 users: Click the Install WebEdit 2.0 for Windows 3.1 button.**

Windows 95 users: Click the Install WebEdit 2.0 for Windows 95 button.

Accept the installation defaults whenever you're prompted to provide information.

The WebEdit software is installed in the folder C:\Program Files\WebEdit (Windows 95) or C:\WEBEDIT (Windows 3.1).

Installing Paint Shop Pro

Paint Shop Pro is a popular shareware image editor. You can use this program to create and edit graphics for your Web pages. *Note:* This is a 30-day trial version of Paint Shop Pro.

To install the software, follow these steps:

1 **Close all other programs that are running in Windows, including programs running in the background, such as antivirus programs.**

2 **Make sure that the Launching Pad window is open.**

3 **Windows 3.1 users: Click the Install Paint Shop Pro (16-bit) button.**

Windows 95 users: Click the Install Paint Shop Pro (32-bit) button.

Accept the installation defaults whenever you're prompted to provide information. Answer Yes when asked whether you want to add icons to the Program Manager and No when asked whether you'd like to run Paint Shop Pro now.

The Paint Shop Pro software is stored in the directory C:\PSP in both versions of Windows.

If you have problems with the installation process, call the IDG Books Worldwide, Inc. Customer Support number: 800-762-2974 (outside the U.S.: 317-596-5261).

heads up

Removing the exercise files

After you have been through the book and no longer need the exercise files, you can uninstall them by following these steps:

1 **Windows 95 users: Click on the Start button on the taskbar.**

Windows 3.1x users: From the Program Manager, open the Dummies 101 group.

2 **Windows 95 users: Click on Programs⇨Dummies 101⇨Uninstall Dummies 101 - HTML Files.**

Windows 3.1x users: Double-click the Uninstall Dummies 101 - HTML Files icon.

To remove all files, click on the Automatic button in the Uninstall window. If you feel comfortable doing a custom uninstall, click the Custom button.

heads up

As soon as you click on the Automatic button, your files are as good as gone. You can get the original files back by going through the original installation process again, but any files you created or changed are gone forever. If you want to keep any of the files that were installed, move them to a different folder before you begin the uninstall process. You should be absolutely certain that you want to delete all the files before you click on Automatic.

Removing the program files under Windows 95

If you choose to remove the program files after you've finished the book, you can simply use the Add/Remove Programs control panel to uninstall the software. (This process works for most programs in Windows 95.)

Note: WebEdit and Paint Shop Pro are shareware programs. If you do not choose to register them, you must remove them from your system.

1 **Click the Start button and then choose Settings⇨Control Panel.**

2 **Double-click the Add/Remove Programs control panel.**

3 **To remove the software you no longer need, click the program's name in the list of programs in the Install/Uninstall list.**

4 **Click the Add/Remove button.**

Respond <u>Y</u>es when asked whether you want to remove the selected item and its contents.

There you go — they're gone!

Removing the program files under Windows 3.1x

You can remove Paint Shop Pro pretty easily, although removing the other programs requires a few additional steps.

Note: WebEdit and Paint Shop Pro are shareware programs. If you do not choose to register them, you must remove them from your system.

To uninstall Paint Shop Pro, follow these steps:

1 **Open the Paint Shop Pro program group from the Program Manager.**

2 **Double-click on the Uninstall Paint Shop Pro icon.**

3 **Follow the instructions on-screen to complete removal of the software.**

Properly removing WebEdit and AT&T WorldNet Service requires a more detailed uninstallation process than merely deleting the folders. Many popular uninstaller programs are available on the market, such as CleanSweep 95 by Quarterdeck. You can find uninstaller programs such as CleanSweep in just about any major software store. Take a look at programs like this one and others to uninstall software in the future.

If you're pressed for disk space, you can uninstall the AT&T WorldNet Service and WebEdit software by deleting the \PSP and \WORLDNET directories from your hard drive. Deleting these folders will not get rid of a few files scattered in your Windows directory, but it will do.

Before you uninstall the AT&T WorldNet Service software, be sure to cancel your account with AT&T.

Index

Introducing
AT&T WorldNet^{SM} Service

A World of Possibilities...

With AT&T WorldNet^{SM} Service, a world of possibilities awaits you. Discover new ways to stay in touch with the people, ideas, and information that are important to you at home and at work.

Make travel reservations at any time of the day or night. Access the facts you need to make key decisions. Pursue business opportunities on the AT&T Business Network. Explore new investment options. Play games. Research academic subjects. Stay abreast of current events. Participate in online newsgroups. Purchase merchandise from leading retailers. Send e-Mail.

All you need is a computer with a mouse, a modem, a phone line, and the software enclosed with this mailing. We've taken care of the rest.

If You Can Point and Click, You're There.

Finding the information you want on the Internet with AT&T WorldNet Service is easier than you ever imagined it could be. That's because AT&T WorldNet Service integrates a specially customized version of the popular Netscape Navigator™ software with advanced Internet directories and search engines. The result is an Internet service that sets a new standard for ease of use — virtually everywhere you want to go is a point and click away.

We're With You Every Step of the Way.
24 Hours a Day, 7 Days a Week.

Nothing is more important to us than making sure that your Internet experience is a truly enriching and satisfying one. That's why our highly trained customer service representatives are available to answer your questions and offer assistance whenever you need it — 24 hours a day, 7 days a week. To reach AT&T WorldNet Customer Care, call **1 800 400-1447**.

Safeguard Your Online Purchases

By registering and continuing to charge your AT&T WorldNet Service to your AT&T Universal Card, you'll enjoy peace of mind whenever you shop the Internet. Should your account number be compromised on the Net, you won't be liable for any online transactions charged to your AT&T Universal Card by a person who is not an authorized user.*

*Today cardmembers may be liable for the first $50 of charges made by a person who is not an authorized user, which will not be imposed under this program as long as the cardmember notifies AT&T Universal Card of the loss within 24 hours and otherwise complies with the Cardmember Agreement. Refer to Cardmember Agreement for definition of authorized user.

Minimum System Requirements

To run AT&T WorldNet Service, you need:

- An IBM-compatible personal computer with a 386 processor or better
- Microsoft Windows 3.1x or Windows 95
- 8MB RAM (16MB or more recommended)
- 11MB of free hard disk space
- 14.4 Kbps (or faster) modem (28.8 Kbps is recommended)
- A standard phone line

Installation Tips and Instructions

- If you have other Web browsers or online software, please consider uninstalling them according to vendor's instructions.

- At the end of installation, you may be asked to restart Windows. Don't attempt the registration process until you have done so.

- If you are experiencing modem problems trying to dial out, try different modem selections, such as Hayes Compatible. If you still have problems, please call Customer Care at **1 800 400-1447**.

- If you are installing AT&T WorldNet Service on a PC with Local Area Networking, please contact your LAN administrator for set-up instructions.

- Follow the initial start-up instructions given to you by the vendor product you purchased. (See Appendix B of *Dummies 101: HTML.*) These instructions will tell you how to start the installation of the AT&T WorldNet Service Software.

- Follow the on-screen instructions to install AT&T WorldNet Service Software on your computer.

When you have finished installing the software you may be prompted to restart your computer. Do so when prompted.

Setting Up Your WorldNet Account

The AT&T WorldNet Service Program group/folder will appear on your Windows desktop.

- Double click on the WorldNet Registration icon.
- Follow the on-screen instructions and complete all the stages of registration.

After all the stages have been completed, you'll be prompted to dial into the network to complete the registration process. Make sure your modem and phone line are not in use.

Registering With AT&T WorldNet Service

Once you have connected with AT&T WorldNet online registration service, you will be presented with a series of screens that will confirm billing information and prompt you for additional account set-up data.

The following is a list of registration tips and comments that will help you during the registration process.

I.   Use the following registration codes, which can also be found in Appendix B of *Dummies 101: HTML:* L5SQIM361 if you are an AT&T long-distance residential customer, and L5SQIM632 if you use another long-distance phone company.

II. We advise that you use all lowercase letters when assigning an e-Mail ID and security code, since they are easier to remember.

III. Choose a special "security code" that you will use to verify who you are when you call Customer Care

IV. If you make a mistake and exit the registration process prematurely, all you need to do is click on "Create New Account". Do not click on "Edit Existing Account".

V.   When choosing your local access telephone number, you will be given several options. Please choose the one nearest to you. Please note that calling a number within your area does not guarantee that the call is free.

Connecting to AT&T WorldNet Service

When you have finished registering with AT&T WorldNet Service you are ready to make online connections.

- Make sure your modem and phone line are available.
- Double click on the AT&T WorldNet Service icon.

Follow these steps whenever you wish to connect to AT&T WorldNet Service.

Choose the Plan That's Right for You.

If you're an AT&T Long Distance residential customer signing up in 1996, you can experience this exciting new service for 5 free hours a month for one full year. Beyond your 5 free hours, you'll be charged only $2.50 for each additional hour. Just use the service for a minimum of one hour per month. If you intend to use AT&T WorldNet Service for more than 5 hours a month, consider choosing the plan with unlimited hours for $19.95 per month.*

If you're not an AT&T Long Distance residential customer, you can still benefit from AT&T quality and reliability by starting with the plan that offers 3 hours each month and a low monthly fee of $4.95. Under this plan you'll be charged $2.50 for each additional hour, or AT&T WorldNet Service can provide you with unlimited online access for $24.95 per month. It's entirely up to you.

Explore our AT&T WorldNet Service Web site at:
http://www.att.com/worldnet

Over 200 local access telephone numbers throughout the U.S.

IDG BOOKS WORLDWIDE, INC.
END-USER LICENSE AGREEMENT

<u>Read This</u>. **You should carefully read these terms and conditions before opening the software packet(s) included with this book ("Book"). This is a license agreement ("Agreement") between you and IDG Books Worldwide, Inc. ("IDGB"). By opening the accompanying software packet(s), you acknowledge that you have read and accept the following terms and conditions. If you do not agree and do not want to be bound by such terms and conditions, promptly return the Book and the unopened software packet(s) to the place you obtained them for a full refund.**

1. <u>License Grant</u>. IDGB grants to you (either an individual or entity) a nonexclusive license to use one copy of the enclosed software program(s) (collectively, the "Software") solely for your own personal or business purposes on a single computer (whether a standard computer or a workstation component of a multiuser network). The Software is in use on a computer when it is loaded into temporary memory (i.e., RAM) or installed into permanent memory (e.g., hard disk, CD-ROM, or other storage device). IDGB reserves all rights not expressly granted herein.

2. <u>Ownership</u>. IDGB is the owner of all right, title, and interest, including copyright, in and to the compilation of the Software recorded on the disk(s)/CD-ROM. Copyright to the individual programs on the disk(s)/CD-ROM is owned by the author or other authorized copyright owner of each program. Ownership of the Software and all proprietary rights relating thereto remain with IDGB and its licensors.

3. <u>Restrictions on Use and Transfer</u>.

    (a) You may only (i) make one copy of the Software for backup or archival purposes, or (ii) transfer the Software to a single hard disk, provided that you keep the original for backup or archival purposes. You may not (i) rent or lease the Software, (ii) copy or reproduce the Software through a LAN or other network system or through any computer subscriber system or bulletin-board system, or (iii) modify, adapt, or create derivative works based on the Software.

    (b) You may not reverse engineer, decompile, or disassemble the Software. You may transfer the Software and user documentation on a permanent basis, provided that the transferee agrees to accept the terms and conditions of this Agreement and you retain no copies. If the Software is an update or has been updated, any transfer must include the most recent update and all prior versions.

4. <u>Restrictions on Use of Individual Programs</u>. You must follow the individual requirements and restrictions detailed for each individual program in Appendix B of this Book. These limitations are contained in the individual license agreements recorded on the disk(s)/CD-ROM. These restrictions may include a requirement that after using the program for the period of time specified in its text, the user must pay a registration fee or discontinue use. By opening the Software packet(s), you will be agreeing to abide by the licenses and restrictions for these individual programs. None of the material on this disk(s) or listed in this Book may ever be distributed, in original or modified form, for commercial purposes.

5. <u>Limited Warranty</u>.

    (a) IDGB warrants that the Software and disk(s)/CD-ROM are free from defects in materials and workmanship under normal use for a period of sixty (60) days from the date of purchase of this Book. If IDGB receives notification within the warranty period of defects in materials or workmanship, IDGB will replace the defective disk(s)/CD-ROM.

    (b) **IDGB AND THE AUTHORS OF THE BOOK DISCLAIM ALL OTHER WARRANTIES, EXPRESS OR IMPLIED, INCLUDING WITHOUT LIMITATION IMPLIED WARRANTIES OF MERCHANTABILITY AND FITNESS FOR A PARTICULAR PURPOSE, WITH RESPECT TO THE SOFTWARE, THE PROGRAMS, THE SOURCE CODE CONTAINED THEREIN, AND/OR THE TECHNIQUES DESCRIBED IN THIS BOOK. IDGB DOES NOT WARRANT THAT THE FUNCTIONS CONTAINED IN THE SOFTWARE WILL MEET YOUR REQUIREMENTS OR THAT THE OPERATION OF THE SOFTWARE WILL BE ERROR FREE.**

    (c) This limited warranty gives you specific legal rights, and you may have other rights, which vary from jurisdiction to jurisdiction.

6. <u>Remedies</u>.

    (a) IDGB's entire liability and your exclusive remedy for defects in materials and workmanship shall be limited to replacement of the Software, which may be returned to IDGB with a copy of your receipt at the following address: Disk Fulfillment Department, Attn: Dummies 101: The Internet For Windows 95, IDG Books Worldwide, Inc., 7260 Shadeland Station, Ste. 100, Indianapolis, IN 46256, or call 1-800-762-2974. Please allow 3-4 weeks for delivery. This Limited Warranty is void if failure of the Software has resulted from accident, abuse, or misapplication. Any replacement Software will be warranted for the remainder of the original warranty period or thirty (30) days, whichever is longer.

    (b) In no event shall IDGB or the authors be liable for any damages whatsoever (including without limitation damages for loss of business profits, business interruption, loss of business information, or any other pecuniary loss) arising from the use of or inability to use the Book or the Software, even if IDGB has been advised of the possibility of such damages.

    (c) Because some jurisdictions do not allow the exclusion or limitation of liability for consequential or incidental damages, the above limitation or exclusion may not apply to you.

7. <u>U.S. Government Restricted Rights</u>. Use, duplication, or disclosure of the Software by the U.S. Government is subject to restrictions stated in paragraph (c) (1) (ii) of the Rights in Technical Data and Computer Software clause of DFARS 252.227-7013, and in subparagraphs (a) through (d) of the Commercial Computer — Restricted Rights clause at FAR 52.227-19, and in similar clauses in the NASA FAR supplement, when applicable.

8. <u>General</u>. This Agreement constitutes the entire understanding of the parties and revokes and supersedes all prior agreements, oral or written, between them and may not be modified or amended except in a writing signed by both parties hereto which specifically refers to this Agreement. This Agreement shall take precedence over any other documents that may be in conflict herewith. If any one or more provisions contained in this Agreement are held by any court or tribunal to be invalid, illegal, or otherwise unenforceable, each and every other provision shall remain in full force and effect.

IDG BOOKS WORLDWIDE REGISTRATION CARD

Visit our Web site at http://www.idgbooks.com

ISBN Number: 0-7645-0032-5

Title of this book: Dummies 101®: HTML

My overall rating of this book: ❑ Very good [1] ❑ Good [2] ❑ Satisfactory [3] ❑ Fair [4] ❑ Poor [5]

How I first heard about this book:

❑ Found in bookstore; name: [6]   ❑ Book review: [7]

❑ Advertisement: [8]   ❑ Catalog: [9]

❑ Word of mouth; heard about book from friend, co-worker, etc.: [10]   ❑ Other: [11]

What I liked most about this book:

What I would change, add, delete, etc., in future editions of this book:

Other comments:

Number of computer books I purchase in a year: ❑ 1 [12] ❑ 2-5 [13] ❑ 6-10 [14] ❑ More than 10 [15]

I would characterize my computer skills as: ❑ Beginner [16] ❑ Intermediate [17] ❑ Advanced [18] ❑ Professional [19]

I use ❑ DOS [20] ❑ Windows [21] ❑ OS/2 [22] ❑ Unix [23] ❑ Macintosh [24] ❑ Other: [25] _____
(please specify)

I would be interested in new books on the following subjects:
(please check all that apply, and use the spaces provided to identify specific software)

❑ Word processing: [26]   ❑ Spreadsheets: [27]

❑ Data bases: [28]   ❑ Desktop publishing: [29]

❑ File Utilities: [30]   ❑ Money management: [31]

❑ Networking: [32]   ❑ Programming languages: [33]

❑ Other: [34]

I use a PC at (please check all that apply): ❑ home [35] ❑ work [36] ❑ school [37] ❑ other: [38] _____

The disks I prefer to use are ❑ 5.25 [39] ❑ 3.5 [40] ❑ other: [41] _____

I have a CD ROM: ❑ yes [42] ❑ no [43]

I plan to buy or upgrade computer hardware this year: ❑ yes [44] ❑ no [45]

I plan to buy or upgrade computer software this year: ❑ yes [46] ❑ no [47]

Name: _____ Business title: [48] _____ Type of Business: [49] _____

Address (❑ home [50] ❑ work [51]/Company name: _____)

Street/Suite# _____

City [52]/State [53]/Zip code [54]: _____ Country [55] _____

❑ **I liked this book!** You may quote me by name in future
IDG Books Worldwide promotional materials.

My daytime phone number is _____

IDG BOOKS WORLDWIDE ™

THE WORLD OF
COMPUTER
KNOWLEDGE®

❑ YES!
Please keep me informed about IDG Books Worldwide's World of Computer Knowledge. Send me your latest catalog.

BESTSELLING
BOOK SERIES
FROM IDG